Assessment Workbook for Medical Practices
Fifth Edition

Carolyn Pickles, MBA, FACMPE

Alys Novak, MBA

Medical Group Management Association
104 Inverness Terrace East
Englewood, CO 80112-5306
877.275.6462
mgma.com

Medical Group Management Association® (MGMA®) publications are intended to provide current and accurate information and are designed to assist readers in becoming more familiar with the subject matter covered. Such publications are distributed with the understanding that MGMA does not render any legal, accounting, or other professional advice that may be construed as specifically applicable to individual situations. No representations or warranties are made concerning the application of legal or other principles discussed by the authors to any specific factual situation, nor is any prediction made concerning how any particular judge, government official, or other person will interpret or apply such principles. Specific factual situations should be discussed with professional advisers.

Production Credits
Publisher/Senior Content Manager: Marilee E. Aust
Editorial/Production Manager: Anne Serrano, MA
Editorial and Production: Glacier Publishing Services, Inc.
Cover Design: Ian Serff, Serff Creative Group, Inc.

Library of Congress Cataloging in Publication Data

Pickles, Carolyn.
   Assessment workbook for medical practices. -- 5th ed. / Carolyn Pickles, Alys Novak.
       p. ; cm.
   Rev. ed. of: An assessment manual for medical groups / Darrell L. Schryver. c2002.
   Includes bibliographical references.
   Summary: "This workbook, based on the ACMPE Body of Knowledge, helps you assess and develop expertise in medical practice management. Whether your medical practice is academic, private, large multispecialty, or part of an IDS care organization, the insights to be gained through the use of this easy-to-use resource are enormous"-- Provided by publisher.
   ISBN 978-1-56829-381-3
   1. Group medical practice--Management. 2. Group medical practice--Finance.
   3. Medicine--Practice--Management. 4. Medical care--Marketing. 5. Medical offices--Management. 6. Physicians--Finance, Personal. 7. Cash management. I. Novak, Alys. II. Schryver, Darrell L. Assessment manual for medical groups. III. Medical Group Management Association. IV. Title.
   [DNLM: 1. Practice Management, Medical--economics. 2. Group Practice--economics. W 80]
   R729.5.G6A876 2011
   610.6'5--dc22

                        2010043136

Item 8259
ISBN: 978-1-56829-381-3

Printed in the United States of America
10 9 8 7 6 5 4 3 2 1

Contents

Preface to the Fifth Edition

With change in healthcare a constant, both in the delivery of services and the structure and management of organizations providing those services, the need for a comprehensive medical group practice assessment tool is stronger today than ever. The *Assessment Workbook for Medical Practices*, 5th Edition, is just such a tool.

The workbook is based on the American College of Medical Practice Executives® (ACMPE®) *Body of Knowledge for Medical Practice Management* (Body of Knowledge). The ACMPE is the standard-setting and certification body of the Medical Group Management Association. The Body of Knowledge was created more than 10 years ago and has recently undergone a thorough review and validation by members of the medical practice profession. Today, its domains and tasks serve as the skeletal structure of the *Assessment Workbook for Medical Practices*, 5th Edition, and as "the authoritative guide to managing a successful medical practice."

Eight domains form the basis of the workbook: Business Operations, Financial Management, Human Resource Management, Information Management, Organizational Governance, Patient Care Systems, Quality Management, and Risk Management. Within each domain's chapter are specific tasks and detailed areas for consideration. Whether the practice is academic, private, large multispecialty, or part of an integrated delivery system or accountable care organization, the insights to be gained through the use of this workbook are enormous. The corporate context or legal structure may vary, but the fundamentals in the effective and efficient delivery of healthcare coupled with the successful management of the medical practice are consistent throughout.

In more than 10 years of practice management and nearly 7 years in consulting, the previous editions of the assessment manual have proved invaluable as a guide for personal professional development as well as group improvement. I've employed them as a guide for mentoring of practice administrators as well as an educational tool for physician leadership. The manuals provided the guide for evaluation of every aspect of the practice's operations as well as every skill required of management.

Since 1979, when the first edition of the *Medical Group Practice Assessment Manual* by Cindy Walters Henderson and Stephen J. Williams was published by the Center for Research in Ambulatory Healthcare Administration (now the MGMA Center for Research), countless individuals have contributed to its growth including MGMA members at large as well as members of the MGMA Healthcare Consulting Group. The current edition represents the work of two stalwart members of the MGMA family, Carolyn Pickles and Alys Novak.

This is a book to be used. It should sit on the desk of every practice administrator and be well known by physician leaders. The page corners should be dog-eared and the pages made brilliant with yellow highlighters. Middle managers should employ its content for performance assessment and professional growth. The manual, in this new edition more rightly called a workbook, will light your way. It will show you the questions to ask, the areas to explore. Employed with an understanding of its intent, the *Assessment Workbook* can assist you and your leadership in making informed decisions.

Healthcare is changing, and the rate appears to be accelerating daily. The *Assessment Workbook for Medical Practices*, 5th Edition, is a must-have tool that will assist you and your practice in meeting the challenges of the future.

Kenneth T. Hertz, FACMPE
Consultant

Acknowledgments

The authors deeply appreciate the assistance of the following content experts who reviewed this workbook to ensure it reflects the latest best-practice information and is presented in an appropriate way for today's medical practice administrators. Special thanks goes to our subject matter experts, who took the time to review and provide feedback on the workbook.

Cynthia Peters Arnold, MBA, CMPE
Medical Practice Consultant
JHD Group
Dallas and New York

Genie Blough, MBA, FACMPE
Medical Practice Consultant
Principal, Blough Associates, LLC
Mobile, Ala.

Owen J. Dahl, MBA, FACHE, CHBC
Principal
Owen Dahl Consulting
The Woodlands, Texas

Tom Ealey, MA, CPA
Associate Professor
Alma College
Alma, Mich.

Edward Gulko, MBA, FACMPE, FACHE
Administrator
Englewood Orthopedic Associates
Englewood, N.J.

Anne Huben-Kearney, RN, CPHQ, CPHRM
Vice President, Risk Management
ProMutual Group
Boston, Mass.

Kathryn Mahaffey, MPA
COO, SIU HealthCare
Southern Illinois University School of Medicine
Springfield, Ill.

Rosemarie Nelson, MS
Principal
MGMA Healthcare Consulting Group
Syracuse, N.Y.

Additional thanks goes to the following for sharing ACMPE resources and talents. This workbook would not have been possible without their guidance and assistance:

Heather McHugh, MBA
ACMPE Certification Manager
American College of Medical Practice Executives
Englewood, Colo.

Marilee E. Aust
Publisher/Senior Content Manager
Medical Group Management Association
Englewood, Colo.

Anne Serrano, MA
Editorial/Production Manager
Medical Group Management Association
Englewood, Colo.

We extend special thanks to Kenneth T. Hertz, FACMPE, who took the time out of his busy schedule to set the scene for the *Assessment Workbook for Medical Practices*, 5th Edition. As a consultant, he well knows the value of evaluating the practice – and the practice administrator.

Introduction

Why an assessment workbook? As experienced healthcare administrators ourselves, as well as being consultants, we well understand how challenging it can be to assess how you are doing in terms of managing your medical practice. More likely, you spend most, if not all, of your time dealing with daily matters or immediate crises. It is very difficult to find enough time to do a thorough practice evaluation, and to involve your team in that effort.

We hope this workbook will provide the motivation you need to see how close you come to best practices. It is quick and easy to use. The process involved in completing the workbook is interactive and hands-on. You can do a section at a time and take the time you need. You learn how close to the mark your medical practice is currently. Most importantly, you get ideas about how to improve the practice in the future.

Another motivator: If you are seeking certification, the workbook is an excellent way to make sure you are up to speed on each domain identified in the ACMPE *Body of Knowledge for Medical Practice Management* – tasks and knowledge/skill matters. Even if you are not going for an American College of Medical Practice Executives (ACMPE) certification, wouldn't you like to know "how am I doing"?

Designed to move you to action, the workbook clearly points out what could be better. We hope you take the challenge!

How Are You Doing?

It's human nature to want to do a good job. But how do you know if you are doing a poor, fair, adequate, or excellent job of administering your medical practice? Practice managers need a means by which to assess their efforts and the effectiveness of the practices they manage. This workbook provides that means.

The workbook is based on the Body of Knowledge, developed as a resource for individuals to assess and develop expertise in medical practice management. The Body of Knowledge contains eight domains, each of which includes a series of tasks, followed by knowledge/skill statements. The eight domains are

- Business Operations
- Financial Management
- Human Resource Management
- Information Management
- Organizational Governance
- Patient Care Systems
- Quality Management
- Risk Management

Because the Body of Knowledge provides the content framework for the ACMPE board certification program, the workbook, in addition to being a uniquely useful self-assessment method, is also a very effective review tool to prepare for the certification examination process. If you are not familiar with the Body of Knowledge, refer to the next section of the workbook for a detailed view.

What Is the Body of Knowledge?

Every profession possesses a body of knowledge representing the entirety of information about that profession. Every book that is written, every article published, every change in legislation – they all contribute to the body of knowledge. A formal, documented body of knowledge undergoes a continuous, rigorous review and validation by members of that profession. It is one way that professionals establish their claim to an expertise that deserves recognition.

The Body of Knowledge for Medical Practice Management represents just such an achievement. It defines and legitimizes the unique knowledge and skill set for the medical practice management profession. It helps set the standards that preserve the profession's integrity and promote its growth. *The Body of Knowledge for Medical Practice Management* is the most comprehensive, authoritative resource for those who seek to assess and develop their skills and knowledge in this profession. Its contents are based on extensive studies by ACMPE, which engaged hundreds of group practice management professionals to identify and validate the role of the medical practice executive and the knowledge and skills required for competent performance. Change to the Body of Knowledge indicates the profession's vibrancy. It is a living, continuing education platform that changes as the profession evolves.

The role of a medical practice management professional is decidedly dynamic. Changes in the healthcare industry, healthcare legislation, technological leaps in information management, and many other factors contribute to the evolution of the profession. To download a free copy of *The Body of Knowledge for Medical Practice Management*, 2nd Edition brochure, go to www.mgma.com/bok/.

What Do You Know and Show?

The workbook enables you to ascertain that you possess practice-management-specific knowledge and have translated it into skills – actions achieving best practices. There is an important distinction to make between knowledge and skill. Knowledge means having an intellectual understanding of a concept that occurs as a result of acquiring education and information. MGMA offers many education, book, website, and other resources to members that will help you expand your knowledge about actions you decide to take. Visit www.mgma.com for more information.

Ongoing education is one way to continue to gain knowledge (reading, seminars, webinars, audio conferences, and so on). Discussion with peers, physicians, advisers, and others is another way. Skill, on the other hand, means demonstrating the understanding of a concept through actions and behavior.

Which Practices Will Benefit, What Timing Is Best?

Medical practices of all sizes benefit from practice assessment, thus the workbook is designed to meet the needs of small, medium, and large practices of different types from private, academic, hospital-affiliated, nonprofit, and more. Accordingly, it reflects broad, general position titles that may or may not exist in your practice. When answering questions that include position titles, you may need to consider who in your practice is involved with the tasks noted and answer the questions accordingly.

The assessment can be completed as a single project or in stages. While most sections are distinct and separate, there is periodic overlap to enhance coverage of a topic and flow of material. Users are encouraged to, over time, complete all of the workbook and accompanying worksheets.

Who Should Be Involved?

There are several ways to approach completing the workbook. In a smaller practice, likely the practice manager will complete the entire workbook independently. In medium- to large-sized practices with management staff, sections may be assigned to different individuals. For instance, a human resource manager (or person handling that function) might complete the human resources domain chapter, and a clinical manager might address patient care systems. Alternatively, sections can be assigned based on the task level.

There are distinct benefits to having multiple individuals involved in completing the workbook, with the primary gains being the power of the collective mind, team building, and shared learning. The practice might also consider engaging outside assistance with the workbook. There are qualified consultants throughout the country to provide such assistance.

What Is the Package?

Note that the workbook comes with a CD to enable sharing, copying, and so on. Completion of the workbook involves information gathering, analyzing, evaluating, and the like. Take the time necessary to take full advantage of all of these aspects of the assessment process.

The text is divided into chapters (one for each domain). There are questions, checklists, forms for notes and action items, and worksheets. Two predominant question and checklist formats are used throughout the workbook, as follows:

Questions to consider	YES	NO If no, why not?	NOT APPLICABLE (note reason)

and

Check all that apply	Method	Circle one	Describe action needed

Questions focus on what represents best practice for most practices, and those are represented by a "YES" answer. Your practice, however, may be an exception, indicating a "NO" answer, because it is, for instance, very small, academic, hospital-affiliated, nonprofit, or in a particular type of geographic setting or community. In other words, you may have unique best practices. Certain situations may represent concepts that do not apply to your practice, thus "NOT APPLICABLE" is also noted as an answer choice.

Note that "NO" is shown as "If no, why not?," encouraging the user of the workbook to define the reason for the exception. We recommend that the reason also be defined when the answer is "NOT APPLICABLE." Reasons can be recorded in either the NOT APPLICABLE column or on the Supplemental Notes worksheet provided in each chapter of the workbook. This activity is especially helpful for triggering team discussion.

Checklists are structured with answers in a list format, with space to note whether each is effective or not as well as necessary action. We recommend you analyze each answer in terms of whether it works – or not – then note steps to bring about required change.

Checklists throughout the workbook include an "Other" option. While we attempted to document common best-practice scenarios, the lists are not all-encompassing. Use the "Other" section liberally and be certain to document what defines "Other."

How to Move to Action

Record challenges, issues, and other pertinent information on the Supplemental Notes worksheets. Before recording "NO" or "NOT APPLICABLE," however, take a moment to ask yourself if it is time to move to the industry best practice and if so, what action you need to take. Action needed to move to the best practice might include information gathering, analysis, decision making, and procedural or other changes – followed by implementation. Take a "why, who, what, when, where, how" approach when considering action.

Actions require results. Maybe a new policy needs to be developed. Maybe an adviser relationship isn't effective and a new adviser needs to be found. Whatever the required action, note it and use the Action Items worksheets as guides to determine implementation steps. Be sure to fill in the prioritization column to help you determine which tasks to address first.

What Now?

We firmly believe that medical practices benefit from regular and ongoing assessment. What is industry standard today may not be next year. Laws, ownership, and employees change. Operationally, routines change. Assessment is not a one-time event. We encourage you to use this important tool at least annually. Develop yourself as a professional; improve your medical practice!

Carolyn Pickles, MBA, FACMPE
Practice Management Consultant

Alys Novak, MBA
Business Consultant, Writer/Editor

Stop!

Before you start the assessment process, first complete the Practice Profile form on the next page. This will help you focus on the characteristics of your medical practice as you go through the checklists.

Note that at the bottom of the page you are asked to estimate how well your medical practice will do on an evaluation scale of 1–5 (low to high). There is no assessment score so this is just a best-guess estimate of how close you think the group is to industry best practices. In this pre-assessment exercise, you are also asked to specify what you would like to learn from the assessment process.

Please return to the Practice Profile page when you have completed the assessment to see how close you came to your estimate – and note what you actually learned.

Practice Profile

Complete this form before beginning the Assessment Workbook *to help focus on "who you are."*
(copy as needed)

Name of practice _____ Year founded _____

Type of practice (private, academic, etc.) _____

Setting (rural, urban, suburban, etc.) _____

Affiliations (hospital, university, etc.) _____

Major payers _____

Total number of providers _____   Total number of staff _____
           Mid-levels _____   Number of sites _____
           Physicians _____

_____ Single specialty   _____ Multispecialty

Specialties (indicate number of providers by specialty)

_____ _____

_____ _____

_____ _____

_____ _____

Major strengths _____

Major challenges _____

Annual charges _____ Annual revenue _____

Other pertinent practice information _____

_____

_____

_____

_____

_____

Name(s) and title(s) of individual(s) completing the workbook

_____   _____

_____   _____

_____   _____

_____   _____

Complete this section of the form to "best guess" the results of the assessment.

Does your practice meet best-practice standards?   Y   N

How do you expect to rate?   1   2   3   4   5   (low to high)

What do you *hope* to learn from this process? _____

_____

_____

_____

_____

Complete this section of the form after finishing the assessment.

Did you meet the pre-assessment rating (that is, did you meet your expectations)?   Y   N

Were the results better or worse?   Better   Worse

What is your post-assessment rating?   1   2   3   4   5   (low to high)

What *did* you learn from this process? _____

_____

_____

_____

_____

CHAPTER 1

Business Operations

How do you develop and implement an effective business plan? A marketing plan? How do you ensure the effective management of day-to-day operations? Why should you do these things? Often medical practices get so intense about their clinical operations that they forget they are businesses – and must be run like businesses. The primary responsibility goes to you, the administrator, who must answer multiple questions. What does your business operations plan cover? Chances are you'll find that you become involved with everything from increasing revenue to project management as you seek to achieve plan goals. How about the purchase of materials and equipment? You need to know not only what equipment is needed, but also how to establish procedures for ordering and monitoring supplies. How about facilities planning? You are responsible for keeping tabs on both current and future building needs as well as considering utility requirements. How and when do you work with outsourced resources and business partners? You determine critical qualifications and monitor performance. You are it!

TASK 01: DEVELOP, IMPLEMENT, AND MONITOR BUSINESS OPERATION PLANS

Operating a business is a complex undertaking. Success is dependent, in part, on the development of a sound business plan to guide the organization. The business plan needs to support the organization's vision, mission, and strategic plan. There are different types of business plans. Each has a distinct use and value. They include operational, financial, feasibility, and financing plans. Are each of these in place and used in your practice? Are they aligned with the vision, mission, and strategic plan?

The first step in developing a plan is to identify the practice's goals and needs. Leaders can each have different views, so it's important to develop a consensus. Have you defined the goals and needs of your practice? Was there buy-in and was consensus achieved? A business plan is just a plan unless it is implemented. In other words, an action (or project) plan is necessary to operationalize the plan. Who will complete what tasks and by when? Is your plan just another piece of paper, or is it a real tool used to run the practice? How does a practice evaluate its success? One way is to measure the results of the plan and operations. Are you monitoring your plan and operations? Project management is an integral part of business planning. What's your level of understanding of project management techniques? With shrinking reimbursements, practices commonly include enhancing revenue in their business plans. There are a myriad of ways to increase revenues and improve the revenue cycle. How familiar are you with the various options? Complete the following section to find out.

01.A Business Plan Alignment

Questions to consider	YES	NO If no, why not?	NOT APPLICABLE (note reason)
Do you have a business plan?			
Is the business plan reviewed and updated on a periodic basis?			
Is the business plan aligned with the practice's values, mission, and strategic plan?			
Does the budget reflect priorities contained in the business plan?			
Is the business plan approved by the practice leadership?			

01.B Types of Business Plans

Which of the following types of business plans do you use?

Check all that apply	Plan	Circle one	Describe action needed
	Feasibility plan (to acquire a practice, new office, equipment, service, etc.)	Effective Not Effective	
	Financial plan (ongoing)	Effective Not Effective	
	Operational plan	Effective Not Effective	
	Financing plan (bank, lease, etc.)	Effective Not Effective	
	Other:	Effective Not Effective	

Does the feasibility plan include the following components? (Note that different components pertain to different projects.)

Check all that apply	Component	Circle one	Describe action needed
	Executive summary	Effective Not Effective	
	Concept	Effective Not Effective	
	Strengths and weaknesses	Effective Not Effective	
	Opportunities and threats	Effective Not Effective	
	Market and competition	Effective Not Effective	
	Legal and regulatory considerations	Effective Not Effective	
	Referral issues	Effective Not Effective	
	Payer issues	Effective Not Effective	
	Alternatives	Effective Not Effective	

Check all that apply	Component	Circle one	Describe action needed
	Marketing	Effective Not Effective	
	Financial analysis (outlay, revenue, expense, budget, source, break even, cash flow, return on investment, risk, etc.)	Effective Not Effective	
	Resource needs (space, equipment, staffing, etc.)	Effective Not Effective	
	Third-party involvement (joint venture or other)	Effective Not Effective	
	Overview of practice, with and without project	Effective Not Effective	
	Practice financial data, with and without project	Effective Not Effective	
	Management	Effective Not Effective	
	Summary	Effective Not Effective	
	Other:	Effective Not Effective	

Questions to consider	YES	NO If no, why not?	NOT APPLICABLE (note reason)
Have you taken a realistic approach to feasibility studies (for example, no excessive overstating or understating)?			

Does the financial plan include the following components?

Check all that apply	Component	Circle one	Describe action needed
	Accounting methods	Effective Not Effective	
	Balance sheet (current and historical)	Effective Not Effective	
	Income statement (current and historical)	Effective Not Effective	
	Budget	Effective Not Effective	
	Statement of cash flow	Effective Not Effective	
	Break-even analysis	Effective Not Effective	

Check all that apply	Component	Circle one	Describe action needed
	Noncash items (leases, capital expenditures, etc.)	Effective Not Effective	
	Summary of risk	Effective Not Effective	
	Operational plan, financing plan, and/ or feasibility plan (as required, and as attachments)	Effective Not Effective	
	Other:	Effective Not Effective	

Does the operational plan include the following components?

Check all that apply	Component	Circle one	Describe action needed
	Executive summary	Effective Not Effective	
	Overview of practice and services provided	Effective Not Effective	
	Market analysis	Effective Not Effective	
	Financial analysis	Effective Not Effective	
	Management section	Effective Not Effective	
	Summary	Effective Not Effective	
	Other:	Effective Not Effective	

Does the financing plan include the following components?

Check all that apply	Component	Circle one	Describe action needed
	Income statement (current and historical)	Effective Not Effective	
	Balance sheet (current and historical)	Effective Not Effective	
	Statement of cash flow (current and historical)	Effective Not Effective	
	Accounts receivable (A/R) report	Effective Not Effective	
	Details regarding other collateral	Effective Not Effective	
	Feasibility plan (as attachment)	Effective Not Effective	
	Operational and financial plans (as required, and as attachments)	Effective Not Effective	
	Other:	Effective Not Effective	

01.C Organizational Goals and Needs

Questions to consider	YES	NO If no, why not?	NOT APPLICABLE (note reason)
Do you focus on the practice's culture?			
Do you focus on organizational change and growth?			
Is there a structure in place to periodically identify organizational goals and needs?			
Are the organizational goals and needs in alignment with the practice's values, mission, and strategic plan?			

Do the goals and needs include the following components?

Check all that apply	Component	Circle one	Describe action needed
	Problems or issues of concern	Effective Not Effective	
	Anticipated resolutions (goals, etc.)	Effective Not Effective	
	Required resources	Effective Not Effective	
	Time lines	Effective Not Effective	
	Affected stakeholders	Effective Not Effective	
	Other:	Effective Not Effective	

01.D Planning for the Future

Questions to consider	YES	NO If no, why not?	NOT APPLICABLE (note reason)
Is there a governance and management structure in place to implement the operational plan?			
Are action items identified?			
Are responsibilities assigned?			
Are time lines identified?			
Are goals determined?			
Is follow-up completed as required?			

01.E Review of Business Plan and Operations

Questions to consider	YES	NO If no, why not?	NOT APPLICABLE (note reason)
Does periodic review and monitoring of the business plan and operations occur?			
Are issues addressed with the board (or administration, practice owners, etc.), as required?			
Do you focus on building consensus and buy-in with stakeholders?			
Are the business plan and operations adjusted as necessary?			

01.F Project Management

Do you use the following project management techniques? Mark all in use.

Check all that apply	Technique	Circle one	Describe action needed
	Documentation of project and project goals	Effective Not Effective	
	Work plan and task details	Effective Not Effective	
	Names, roles, and contact information for responsible parties	Effective Not Effective	
	Time lines and project milestones are identified	Effective Not Effective	
	Regular and ongoing communication about project and issues between project manager and project team	Effective Not Effective	
	Revisions to plan, time lines, and responsible parties are documented and communicated within the team as required	Effective Not Effective	
	Regular reporting to stakeholders	Effective Not Effective	

Check all that apply	Technique	Circle one	Describe action needed
	Post-implementation analysis of project	Effective Not Effective	
	Other:	Effective Not Effective	

01.G Opportunities to Increase Revenue

Questions to consider	YES	NO If no, why not?	NOT APPLICABLE (note reason)
Do you maintain awareness regarding ways to increase revenue (professional peer network, associations, educational meetings, journals, social networking, consultants, etc.)?			
Have you established an ongoing focus on ways to increase revenue?			

Have you given consideration to the following revenue opportunities?

Check all that apply	Opportunity	Circle one	Describe action needed
	Extension of services (new procedures, etc.)	Effective Not Effective	
	Ancillary services (lab, X-ray, etc.)	Effective Not Effective	
	Products	Effective Not Effective	
	Midlevel providers	Effective Not Effective	
	Employed physicians	Effective Not Effective	
	Renegotiate payer reimbursements	Effective Not Effective	
	Increase hours	Effective Not Effective	
	Rent or sub-rent unused space	Effective Not Effective	
	Other:	Effective Not Effective	

Questions to consider	YES	NO If no, why not?	NOT APPLICABLE (note reason)
Do you develop a detailed analysis of top ideas (for example, via a feasibility plan)?			
Do you present to and obtain buy-in from the board (or administration, practice owners, etc.)?			

TASK 02: DEVELOP, IMPLEMENT, AND OVERSEE SYSTEMS FOR THE PURCHASE OF MATERIALS AND EQUIPMENT

Goods and services are required to provide medical care in the practice setting. EKG machines, gauze, paper and pens, cleaning services – the list is endless as to what is needed. It's helpful to have a master list of routinely ordered items, as well as records about assets. What tools do you use to organize the materials needed in your practice? Inventory and ordering systems help avoid the event in which an employee looks in the supply area only to find, for instance, that there are no syringes left. What's your system? Supplies can be a costly part of expenses. It's important to plan what will be purchased and the related costs. The bid process is essential, as is centralization of the purchasing function to obtain volume discounts. What methods are used in your practice for procurement? Inventory control procedures are necessary to avoid loss. What systems do you have in place to manage inventory? Biohazardous waste disposal is commonly an outsourced service in the medical practice setting. Regulations govern how waste is stored, handled, and disposed of. Is your practice compliant? Options exist for the purchase of capital equipment, each with pros and cons. They include outright purchase, lease, and more. Are you familiar with the various choices? Do you understand the key differences between each? Vendor relationships are key in procurement. It's important to develop and maintain positive, mutually satisfactory working relationships with vendors, while at the same time staying abreast of market forces and periodically obtaining competitive pricing. How satisfactory are your vendor relationships? Proceed to find out.

02.A Types of Supplies and Equipment

Questions to consider	YES	NO If no, why not?	NOT APPLICABLE (note reason)
Do you maintain a list of all supplies (billable and nonbillable) used including manufacturer, brand, size, model, color, and so on?			
Are clinical leaders engaged in helping to standardize supplies purchased?			
Do you maintain a list of all equipment used including manufacturer, brand, model, serial number, and so on?			
Are fixed assets tagged as property of the practice?			
Do you maintain fixed asset records for accounting purposes (a fixed asset book with a copy of the invoice, asset number, location, date placed in service, and so on)?			

02.B Ordering, Use, and Monitoring of Supplies and Equipment

Questions to consider	YES	NO If no, why not?	NOT APPLICABLE (note reason)
Are procedures documented for ordering supplies and equipment?			
Are procedures documented for use and monitoring of supplies and equipment?			
Are supplies kept in central approved locations and distributed or charged out as needed?			
Is equipment inspected informally periodically and annually with formal documentation of findings?			
Are equipment maintenance records maintained for the life of the asset?			

02.C Purchasing Procurement

Questions to consider	YES	NO If no, why not?	NOT APPLICABLE (note reason)
Is there control over types of items ordered as a means to maintain quality and control price (brand, type, model, color, etc.)?			
Are purchase orders (POs) used?			
Do POs each have a unique pre-assigned number?			
Is purchasing authority delegated and documented, including dollar limits?			
Are POs available only to individuals with purchasing authority?			
Is there a PO approval process for cyclical purchases?			
Is there a PO approval process for noncyclical purchases?			
Do POs reflect items, quantity, cost, and terms?			

Questions to consider	YES	NO If no, why not?	NOT APPLICABLE (note reason)
Is there a limited number of individuals who receive goods?			
Are the received goods inspected for damage?			
Is damage addressed promptly?			
Are received goods matched to the packing slip and PO to confirm item, quantity, and so on?			
Are POs noted with date of receipt, initials of receiver, and necessary notations regarding variances?			
Are POs and packing slips matched up and forwarded to accounts payable (A/P)?			
Does the A/P staff match vendor invoices to POs and packing slips; verify each invoiced item, quantity, price, mathematical calculation, and due date; and file all for easy retrieval?			
Are bid and request for proposal processes used to ensure optimal pricing and selection?			

Questions to consider	YES	NO If no, why not?	NOT APPLICABLE (note reason)
Are terms negotiated?			
Is there control over samples to avoid inappropriate relationships between individuals having purchasing authority and vendors?			
Are group purchasing organization(s) used when appropriate?			

02.D Inventory Control Plan

Questions to consider	YES	NO If no, why not?	NOT APPLICABLE (note reason)
Is an inventory system used for supplies and equipment?			
Is the inventory system adequate (general procedures, efficiency, avoidance of overstocking/ understocking, outages, asset control, etc.)?			
Is a physical inventory taken on a regular and routine basis?			
Are inventory discrepancies addressed?			
Are inventory order points established for each supply item?			
Are appropriate levels of quantities ordered in a timely manner?			
Is the quantity on hand used prior to expiration?			

02.E Disposal of Biohazardous Waste

Does the practice create biohazardous waste?

Check all that apply	Waste
	Blood
	Body fluids
	Pathology
	Sharps
	Microbiology
	Other:

Questions to consider	YES	NO If no, why not?	NOT APPLICABLE (note reason)
Are required containers, labels, bags, boxes, and so on used for biohazardous waste in areas where waste is created?			
Are transport boxes for biohazard bags and wall-mounted sharps containers kept in a secure area?			
Does a biohazardous waste service complete pick-ups on a regularly scheduled basis?			
Are manifests signed by an authorized practice representative and maintained as required?			
Are final manifests received and maintained as required?			

02.F Equipment Purchase vs. Lease

Do you clearly understand the issues associated with purchasing vs. leasing? Check off areas of knowledge and note where additional education is needed.

Check all that apply	Topic	Circle one	Describe action needed
	Fixed asset	Effective Not Effective	
	Depreciation expense	Effective Not Effective	
	Cash flow	Effective Not Effective	
	Salvage value	Effective Not Effective	
	Tax credit	Effective Not Effective	
	Interest	Effective Not Effective	
	Capital	Effective Not Effective	

Check all that apply	Topic	Circle one	Describe action needed
	Useful life	Effective Not Effective	
	Lease to own	Effective Not Effective	
	Other:	Effective Not Effective	

Questions to consider	YES	NO If no, why not?	NOT APPLICABLE (note reason)
When purchasing equipment, is a cash flow analysis completed to analyze financial options, including determination of present value?			

02.G Vendor Relationships

Questions to consider	YES	NO If no, why not?	NOT APPLICABLE (note reason)
Are your relationships with vendors respectful and mutually satisfactory?			
Are vendors not intrusive?			
Are vendor relationships evaluated periodically in terms of satisfaction, service, cost, and so on?			
Do vendors provide value (information about existing and alternate products and services, in-services about use of equipment, etc.)?			
Are vendors replaced as necessary to obtain better pricing, better service, group purchasing opportunity, and so on?			
Are satisfactory references obtained on new vendors?			

TASK 03: MANAGE FACILITIES PLANNING AND MAINTENANCE ACTIVITIES TO MEET THE ORGANIZATION'S CURRENT AND FUTURE NEEDS

An inefficient layout can cost precious time for busy providers. Maximizing patient flow and exam room configuration makes for better use of the biggest resource in a practice – provider time. Does your workflow help or hinder practice efficiency? A dingy, dirty office is a turnoff for patients. The message: If this is what the office is like, what's the care like? Everything counts, from the dirt on the rug to the date and condition of magazines to the trash in the parking lot. Effective facility management is required. What's your skill level? This section also addresses information about effective utility management and compliance with Occupational Safety and Health Administration (OSHA) and Americans with Disabilities Act (ADA) requirements. Answer the following to find out how you rate in facility matters.

03.A Facility Planning

Questions to consider	YES	NO If no, why not?	NOT APPLICABLE (note reason)
Do you have a clear understanding of facility needs (medical space, patient flow, operations, etc.)?			
Does the current space meet the needs of the practice, both clinical and nonclinical?			
Is the layout conducive to efficiency and work flow?			
Is the layout conducive to efficient patient flow and safety?			
Is there sufficient storage?			

Questions to consider	YES	NO If no, why not?	NOT APPLICABLE (note reason)
Is the appearance of the facility clean and neat, not worn?			
Is the space decorated appropriately?			
Is it easy for patients to find their way around?			
Is there adequate parking?			
Is the exterior well lit?			
Are future needs periodically analyzed?			
Are facility expansion projects undertaken with the help of recommended experts (architect, builder, etc.)?			

03.B Facility Management

Questions to consider	YES	NO If no, why not?	NOT APPLICABLE (note reason)
Do you make regular rounds of the practice space to identify maintenance and repair issues?			
Do you make regular rounds of leased space to identify maintenance and repair issues?			
Are the grounds routinely inspected for landscaping issues?			
Do you routinely tour the practice space to observe housekeeping issues?			
Are the maintenance, landscaping, and housekeeping staffs adequate and attentive to duties?			
Are the maintenance, landscaping (including snow removal), and housekeeping staffs service oriented and cost effective?			
Is there a vendor file for occasional repair firms (HVAC, roof, carpet cleaning, tile and carpet, paint and wallpaper, etc.)?			
Are facility vendors periodically evaluated in terms of cost and service?			

Questions to consider	YES	NO If no, why not?	NOT APPLICABLE (note reason)
Are fire extinguishers routinely inspected as required?			
Do fire safety personnel teach PASS (Pull, Aim, Squeeze, Sweep) to all employees on a regular and routine basis?			
Is there an emergency evacuation plan in place and tested on a periodic basis?			
Is there periodic inspection and maintenance of practice systems (alarm, locks, voice, data, pest control, etc.)?			

03.C Mechanical, Electrical, and Plumbing

Questions to consider	YES	NO If no, why not?	NOT APPLICABLE (note reason)
Do you regularly monitor utility usage?			
Is the pricing cost effective?			
Is the service timely?			
Is there periodic inspection and maintenance of building systems (HVAC, electrical, plumbing, and so on)?			

03.D Regulatory Compliance, Including Occupational Safety and Health Administration (OSHA) and Americans with Disabilities Act (ADA)

Questions to consider	YES	NO If no, why not?	NOT APPLICABLE (note reason)
Is the practice compliant with ADA with regard to physical access by the disabled?			
Is "reasonable accommodation" made on an as-needed basis?			
Is consideration for ADA given when renovating or building new construction?			
Is there adequate handicapped parking?			
Are safety hazards such as tripping hazards, boxes in hallways, faulty electrical cords, blocked exits, boxes in electrical room, and so on addressed?			
Are accident and injury records maintained?			
Is the practice compliant with other OSHA requirements specific to the specialty or type of service (chemotherapy drug mixing, laboratory, etc.)?			
Are the OSHA "Right to Know" laws posted, and are the material safety data sheets accessible as required?			

TASK 04: MANAGE DISCERNMENT PROCESS FOR IDENTIFICATION AND UTILIZATION OF OUTSOURCED EXPERTISE AND BUSINESS PARTNERS

Practices typically outsource certain functions. Common examples are cleaning and laundry; other possibilities include billing and transcription. There are a number of considerations when deciding whether to outsource. Do you know what they are? Another outside relationship is that of the business partner. It may make sense to consider aligning with an organization such as an independent practice association (IPA) or physician–hospital organization (PHO). For potential success, an in-depth analysis should occur. What's the purpose of the relationship? How compatible are the organizations? In some instances a practice may want to consider a partnership or merger. One common reason is to expand services. Cultures, business practices, leadership, and more need to be examined and reestablished if the relationship goes forward. When contemplating joining forces with another practice, do you know what to consider and how to proceed? Practice administrators are commonly generalists. It's important to have relationships with advisers such as accountants and lawyers and to know when outside advice is needed. Do you have the necessary relationships and do you know when to seek advice? All external relationships require management and monitoring. Answer the following questions on outsourced expertise and business partners to find where you stand in this area.

04.A Outsourced Expertise

Questions to consider	YES	NO If no, why not?	NOT APPLICABLE (note reason)
Are noncare functions assessed periodically for possible outsourcing (billing, transcription, payroll, bookkeeping, cleaning, laundry, shredding, etc.)?			
Are cost, time savings, quality, efficiency, expertise, control, potential loss of jobs, increased availability of resources, oversight requirements, and so on assessed?			
Are business associate agreements implemented when appropriate?			
Are outsourcing relationships assessed periodically for cost, service, etc.?			

04.B Selection of Business Partners

Questions to consider	YES	NO If no, why not?	NOT APPLICABLE (note reason)
Have the practice's reasons for pursuing business partners (for example, goals and objectives, resources, expertise) been identified?			
Have the strengths and weaknesses of respective organizations been considered?			
Have the compatibility (for example, cultures, values, missions, and strategic plans) and fit been assessed?			
Have the organizational readiness and willingness to partner been assessed?			
Has the optimal structure/model (single-specialty practice, multispecialty practice, IPA, PHO, management services organization, etc.) been considered?			
Have you consulted with counsel as a part of the process?			

04.C Pursue and Establish Partnerships and Strategic Alliances

Questions to consider	YES	NO If no, why not?	NOT APPLICABLE (note reason)
Is due diligence followed when pursuing and establishing partnerships and strategic alliances?			
Have routines in other areas of practice (recruiting, compensation, benefits, service contracts, insurance payer contracts, other contracts, technology, staffing roles and responsibilities, financial strength, assets, liabilities, etc.) been examined?			
Have roles and responsibilities with shared oversight been determined and assigned?			
Are the most qualified individuals placed in leadership roles?			
Is there a focus on building new relationships based on trust?			
Is key information documented in partnership agreements?			
Has a new vision, mission, and strategic plan been created?			

Questions to consider	YES	NO If no, why not?	NOT APPLICABLE (note reason)
Has new governance been created?			
Has a new operating plan been created?			
Have goals and objectives been identified?			
Are results measured?			
Is there regular and ongoing communication among leadership?			
Is consultation with counsel a part of the process?			
Are partnerships and alliances periodically reviewed?			
Are partnerships and alliances continued or ended as appropriate?			
Are positive working relationships maintained if ended?			

04.D Knowledge and Skills of Financial Advisers, Accountants, Attorneys, Architects, and Others

Do you clearly understand the expertise and specialized knowledge that outside advisers offer?

Check all that apply	Adviser	Circle one	Describe action needed
	Financial advisers (retirement planning, investing, etc.)	Effective Not Effective	
	Accountants (financial reporting, taxation, etc.)	Effective Not Effective	
	Attorneys (corporate law, human resources law, etc.)	Effective Not Effective	
	Architects (facility design, ADA compliance, building codes, etc.)	Effective Not Effective	
	Insurance brokers/agents (health, life, disability, etc.)	Effective Not Effective	
	Banker (banking, loans, credit card processing, etc.)	Effective Not Effective	
	Consultants (practice management, human resources, safety, quality, etc.)	Effective Not Effective	
	Real estate brokers (purchase and sale of real estate, etc.)	Effective Not Effective	

Check all that apply	Adviser	Circle one	Describe action needed
	Auditors (annual audit services, etc.)	Effective Not Effective	
	Other:	Effective Not Effective	

04.E Manage and Monitor Partnerships and Alliances

Questions to consider	YES	NO If no, why not?	NOT APPLICABLE (note reason)
Have you established time lines, outcomes, reporting, contacts, and costs with vendors?			
Is the board (or administration, practice owners, etc.) kept apprised of projects, including final reporting?			
Are post-project assessments completed?			

TASK 05: DEVELOP AND IMPLEMENT A MARKETING AND COMMUNICATION PLAN

Ensuring the focus on customers is never-ending, and it cannot be lost in the heat of daily clinical operations. Patients (present and future), payers, vendors, business and community partners, and employees all have their own expectations of the medical practice, and their satisfaction is critical to the success of the group. How do you build a plan that is focused on customer profiles and needs? Outside consultants can help you get the data needed. Are you on top of social, technological, economic, and political trends? You, the physicians, and the staff can all be trend-watchers who anticipate impacts and opportunities. How do you manage market research, branding, advertising, and promotion? Again, outsiders have the expertise to smooth the process. Finally, how tied are you to the local community? The more the practice becomes part of the community, the more you will gain and retain patients.

05.A Customer Focus

Check ways that are used to focus on diverse customers.

Check all that apply	Method	Circle one	Describe action needed
	Leaders are educated on a range of customers – not just patients.	Effective Not Effective	
	Market segments are identified and profiled for clinical and nonclinical staff.	Effective Not Effective	
	Employees are recognized as a major customer group as well as patients and consumers.	Effective Not Effective	
	Key relationships are also identified as referrers, payers, vendors, and community.	Effective Not Effective	
	Customer motivation is defined as physiological, psychological, or environmental.	Effective Not Effective	
	Patient marketing strategies are based on customer experience with service.	Effective Not Effective	
	Outcomes meet or exceed expectations of targeted individuals and institutions.	Effective Not Effective	
	Customer satisfaction is geared to matching expectations with performance.	Effective Not Effective	

Check all that apply	Method	Circle one	Describe action needed
	Marketing is defined as creating, communicating, and delivering value to customers.	Effective Not Effective	
	Offering benefits to stakeholders and organizations is key to managing relationships.	Effective Not Effective	
	Other:	Effective Not Effective	

0.5B Marketing/Communication Plans

Note vital components in the marketing plan.

Check all that apply	Component	Circle one	Describe action needed
	The marketing plan is based on a strategic plan in terms of goals.	Effective Not Effective	
	The major components are specified as practice structure, financial resources, goals, situational analysis, market/patient analysis, competitive analysis, service range, marketing mix (product, price, place, promotion, and positioning), promotional plan, and tactics.	Effective Not Effective	
	The market profit potential is measured based on market segment/industry analysis.	Effective Not Effective	

Check all that apply	Component	Circle one	Describe action needed
	Situational analysis is used to check social, technological, economic, and political trends.	Effective Not Effective	
	Competitive analysis is used to profile key competitor strengths and weaknesses.	Effective Not Effective	
	Consumer analysis is used to identify demographics, needs, and buying decisions.	Effective Not Effective	
	The uniqueness of the practice or a strategic edge is identified (for example, unmatched service mix).	Effective Not Effective	
	Proof of patient satisfaction, credentials, and awards provides evidence of satisfactory results.	Effective Not Effective	
	The marketing message is clearly stated in terms of distinctive edge and proof.	Effective Not Effective	
	Other:	Effective Not Effective	

0.5C Local Market

Check ways you keep tabs on local market conditions.

Check all that apply	Method	Circle one	Describe action needed
	Leaders are educated on the importance of keeping tabs on community indicators.	Effective Not Effective	
	Local economics are observed to reduce surprises related to industries and population.	Effective Not Effective	
	Layoffs, closures, area recession, or new growth are recognized as affecting the group.	Effective Not Effective	
	Business conditions and economic activity are tracked over time.	Effective Not Effective	
	Demographic shifts are seen as potentially affecting the patient population mix.	Effective Not Effective	
	Local as well as regional conditions are monitored to track external market changes.	Effective Not Effective	
	Leader participation in the community is encouraged to get a sense of shifts and trends.	Effective Not Effective	
	Other:	Effective Not Effective	

0.5D Market Research, Market Strategy, and Advertising

Note methods used to research the market and strategy, and advertise.

Check all that apply	Method	Circle one	Describe action needed
	Research emphasis is on maximizing government and industry data to start.	Effective Not Effective	
	Outside marketing experts are used to research, report, and strategize.	Effective Not Effective	
	Many methods are used including observation, focus groups, interviewing, and surveys.	Effective Not Effective	
	Market strategies considered are service mix, target markets, competition, and goals.	Effective Not Effective	
	Leaders strategize on the impact of marketing changes on budget, staff, and message.	Effective Not Effective	
	The pros and cons of advertising the medical practice are considered, including the effectiveness for the group.	Effective Not Effective	
	Leaders are educated on advertising as any form of paid promotion via mass media.	Effective Not Effective	
	Media is defined as print (publication) or electronic (TV, radio, Internet).	Effective Not Effective	

Check all that apply	Method	Circle one	Describe action needed
	The marketing team analyzes each medium for audience, price and cost, and reporting.		
	Advertising recommendations are made to leaders, and realistic benefits are noted.		
	Advertising in different media is tested over time for effectiveness with targets.		
	Other:		

0.5E Public and Media Relations

Check how you make use of public relations (PR).

Check all that apply	Method	Circle one	Describe action needed
	Leaders are educated on PR as unpaid promotion with third-party legitimacy.	Effective Not Effective	
	Leaders are informed about the need to maintain positive relations with media.	Effective Not Effective	
	A media/PR liaison is designated to communicate regularly.	Effective Not Effective	
	Someone is designated to handle negative publicity and crisis/disaster communication (this may be an internal source or a combination of internal with external professional assistance).	Effective Not Effective	
	Physicians are encouraged to speak at conferences that offer related publicity.	Effective Not Effective	
	Other avenues are explored such as appearing on TV or radio as a credible source on health.	Effective Not Effective	
	Print items (flyers, handouts, articles, and brochures) are used as targeted promotion.	Effective Not Effective	
	Focus is placed on clinical and nonclinical staff as vital PR vehicles to get messages out.	Effective Not Effective	

Check all that apply	Method	Circle one	Describe action needed
	The Internet and a website are key PR tools for recruiting employees and patients, as well as for communicating information to patients about local flu clinics, educational sessions, and so on.	Effective Not Effective	
	An electronic health-related newsletter is made available to local residents.	Effective Not Effective	
	Outside advisers with healthcare experience are used to help plan and evaluate.	Effective Not Effective	
	Other:	Effective Not Effective	

0.5F Corporate Image/Brand

Note ways used to develop and maintain a desired brand or image.

Check all that apply	Method	Circle one	Describe action needed
	An outside consultant is hired to help guide branding and imaging efforts.	Effective Not Effective	
	Differences related to branding on practice founding and on rebranding over time are noted.	Effective Not Effective	
	The company brand history, competitive brands, and brand trends are analyzed by an adviser.	Effective Not Effective	
	Leaders are educated on brand items including name, logo, and colors used on communications.	Effective Not Effective	
	Meeting the service expectations of patients and referrers is recognized as an image goal.	Effective Not Effective	
	Successful patient interactions with the practice are encompassed in the brand and image (such as e-mails to physicians quickly answered).	Effective Not Effective	
	The brand is expected to convey strength, competencies, and competitive advantages.	Effective Not Effective	

Check all that apply	Method	Circle one	Describe action needed
	Brand decision making is focused on factors differentiating the group from others.	Effective Not Effective	
	Brand criteria are recognized as being identifiable, consistent, and memorable.	Effective Not Effective	
	Other:	Effective Not Effective	

0.5G Community Outreach and Collaboration

Check the ways in which you promote community involvement in marketing.

Check all that apply	Method	Circle one	Describe action needed
	Education is provided to everyone on how community service bolsters the practice.	Effective Not Effective	
	Exposure is key to attracting new patients and strengthening the current patient bond.	Effective Not Effective	
	A community ambassador pool is developed based on staff skills and interests.	Effective Not Effective	

Check all that apply	Method	Circle one	Describe action needed
	Public speaking, local media releases, and open houses are used to build credibility.	Effective Not Effective	
	Leaders, physicians, and staff are educated on community needs.	Effective Not Effective	
	Clinical and nonclinical staff are encouraged to get involved in community health issues.	Effective Not Effective	
	Physicians and administrators are encouraged to sit on local boards and committees.	Effective Not Effective	
	Partnerships with local hospitals and other healthcare providers are sought.	Effective Not Effective	
	Collaborations with local businesses are promoted, matching expertise and resources.	Effective Not Effective	
	Other:	Effective Not Effective	

BOTTOM LINE—BUSINESS OPERATIONS

"Business operations" encompasses so many elements - operational planning, purchasing, facilities management, external advisers and partners, and marketing and communications - that it is hard to know where to start. But start you must each day. As the clinicians concentrate their focus on patient care, you, as the administrator of a medical practice, must ensure their work is facilitated by an effective business model that leads to ongoing success.

Business Operations
Supplemental Notes
(copy as needed)

Task	Notes

Business Operations
Action Items
(copy as needed)

Task	Action	Responsible Party	Due Date	Priority

Financial Management

Developing and implementing a budget, establishing internal controls and processes for external audits, managing the revenue cycle, monitoring performance and reporting it to stakeholders, overseeing payroll, and establishing financial adviser and payer relationships are all key to success in managing your practice's finances. How would you be able to measure results without financial principles? How would practices compare their results to the results of similar organizations without generally accepted accounting principles (GAAP)? Knowledge and understanding of financial principles is necessary to maintain a profitable practice. Sound financial management begins with development of a budget and concludes with reporting, analysis, and corrective action. It's a responsibility and task that you need to address on a daily basis. What are the ways in which you ensure sound financial management of your practice and how do you assess its performance? Complete this section to determine your effectiveness.

TASK 01: DEVELOP AND IMPLEMENT THE ORGANIZATION'S BUDGET TO ACHIEVE ORGANIZATIONAL OBJECTIVES

Practices need accounting systems to record a wide variety of financial information. To help make accounting data more useful, GAAP serve as standards by which to record and interpret data. There are different methods of accounting in GAAP. What system does your organization use? Does your practice use a budget? Budgeting, along with solid accounts payable (A/P) and accounts receivable (A/R) systems, helps plan for the future financially, allowing for revenue growth, control of expenses, and minimization of loss. When it's time to analyze your practice's financial data, does the chart of accounts help or hinder?

Depreciation methods can affect profitability and tax obligations. Are your depreciation methods appropriate? When practices have unanticipated equipment needs, a line of credit enables them to quickly purchase what is needed. The accounting system, along with the various applications that feed automatically or manually into it, is the means by which practices record all of their financial transactions. Complete the following to determine how your financial systems measure up.

01.A Types of Accounting Used

Check off types of accounting used (financial, tax, managerial, cost, etc.) and note applications.

Check all that apply	Type	Applications
	Financial	
	Tax	
	Managerial	
	Cost	
	Other:	

Questions to consider	YES	NO If no, why not?	NOT APPLICABLE (note reason)
Do the accounting types optimize accurate recording, interpretation, analysis, reporting (internally and externally), and the ability to make financial decisions?			
For practices that use cost accounting, is a standard cost accounting system used (standard, activity-based, etc.)?			

Note cost accounting system design and applications.

System	Applications

Questions to consider	YES	NO If no, why not?	NOT APPLICABLE (note reason)
Are fixed and variable costs identified?			
Are direct and indirect costs identified?			
Are overhead allocations logical and calculated consistently?			
Do key parties (department managers, board) agree with assumptions in the system?			

01.B Financial Accounting Principles (GAAP)

Questions to consider	YES	NO If no, why not?	NOT APPLICABLE (note reason)
Is GAAP used for financial statements?			
Is a cash basis allowed and used for tax returns?			
Are depreciation methods consistent with GAAP?			
Is accelerated depreciation used for tax purposes?			

01.C Methods of Accounting

Check off the method of accounting used in the organization.

Cash	Accrual	Other

Questions to consider	YES	NO If no, why not?	NOT APPLICABLE (note reason)
Is this method appropriate for the practice?			
Does this method optimize accurate recording, interpretation, analysis, reporting (internally and externally), and the ability to make financial decisions?			

01.D Budgeting

Is budgeting done formally or informally?

If Formal:

Questions to consider	YES	NO If no, why not?	NOT APPLICABLE (note reason)
Is it completed on at least an annual basis?			
Is it documented?			
Is it integrated with the organization's business plan?			
Is it integrated with statistical projections?			
Does it include agreed-upon and realistic specific financial goals and objectives?			
Is the time line appropriate for organizational needs?			

Questions to consider	YES	NO If no, why not?	NOT APPLICABLE (note reason)
Does it include internal and external evaluation of key factors (for example, healthcare environment, economic environment, insurance trends, service demand, physician recruitment, space needs, reimbursement trends and changes, staffing needs, service offerings, capital needs)?			
Does it incorporate analysis of each physician's future plans (retirement, hours, practice patterns, staffing, reimbursement, etc.)?			
Does it include statistical projections by provider?			
Does it include related financial analysis involving key data (revenue effect, expense effect, anticipated income, cash flow requirements, etc.)?			
Does it include optimistic, probable, and pessimistic levels of encounters and surgeries?			
Is the plan approved by the board?			

If Informal:

Describe how it works:

Questions to consider	YES	NO If no, why not?	NOT APPLICABLE (note reason)
Is the approach effective for the organization?			
Is an annual budget developed?			
Note basis (prior-year, zero-based, other).			

Check off types of budgets and note application(s).

Check all that apply	Type	Circle one	Describe action needed
	Revenue Application:	Effective Not Effective	
	Capital Application:	Effective Not Effective	
	Expense Application:	Effective Not Effective	
	Provider Compensation Application:	Effective Not Effective	
	Cash Application:	Effective Not Effective	
	Departmental (as-needed basis) Application:	Effective Not Effective	
	Statistics Application:	Effective Not Effective	
	Operating Application:	Effective Not Effective	
	Other: Application:	Effective Not Effective	

Questions to consider	YES	NO If no, why not?	NOT APPLICABLE (note reason)
Are budgets developed in conjunction with operational planning and statistical projections (for example, goals and objectives)?			
Do department managers prepare budgets for their areas of responsibility?			
Are budgets approved by the board?			
Are budgets updated as changes occur?			
Are budget changes prepared by department managers?			
Are budget changes approved by the board?			
Is budget data reflected on financial statements in monthly and year-to-date amounts?			
Do statements include comparisons to same month prior year and year-to-date prior year?			

Questions to consider	YES	NO If no, why not?	NOT APPLICABLE (note reason)
Is the budget performance monitored?			
Is responsibility for budget variances assigned to department managers?			
Does the board monitor budget performance?			
Are budgets used to set goals, assign responsibility, and assess performance?			
Are budgets used to control departmental practice activities?			
Are budgets used to control practice activities?			
Do department managers receive monthly financial statements reflecting actual vs. budget?			
Are department managers accountable only for aspects of the budget they control?			

01.E Accounts Payable and Accounts Receivable

Accounts Payable

Questions to consider	YES	NO If no, why not?	NOT APPLICABLE (note reason)
Are pre-numbered checks used?			
Is documentation required for all checks before they are signed?			
Note method by which checks are signed (hand, signature stamp, electronic, etc.).			
Are there appropriate controls over access to signature stamp(s) and electronic signature(s)?			
Are employees who handle A/P bonded?			
Are bills paid in a timely manner?			
Is there sufficient cash flow to take available prompt payment discounts?			
Are all available discounts taken?			
Are invoices with prompt payment discounts paid at the end of the discount period?			

Accounts Receivable

Questions to consider	YES	NO If no, why not?	NOT APPLICABLE (note reason)
Are you aware of key payers?			

If not, try completing Worksheet FM-1: Payer Analysis. Here's how. Record the names of payers with whom the practice has a contractual relationship. If there are multiple product lines for a single payer, list by payer and plan. Note the volume of patients/visits/Current Procedural Terminology (CPT) codes or other indicator (check off which), charges, payments, adjustments, and A/R aging for each. Total each column; for A/R aging total, enter practice level totals. Calculate percentage of unit volume to identify the largest payer for units rendered. Calculate percentage of charges, payments, and adjustments by payer to identify the largest sources of service, revenue, and adjustments. Calculate the aging percentages by payer. For A/R aging percentages totals, enter practice level data. Analyze the data. Which payer produces the highest volume? Which payer represents the greatest source of revenue? Which payer is associated with the highest amount of adjustments? Which payers pay on a less timely basis? What other payer information do you notice? Be creative with the worksheet and perform other calculations that seem of interest. Note payer-specific strategic issues on the Supplemental Notes worksheet.

Questions to consider	YES	NO If no, why not?	NOT APPLICABLE (note reason)
Are payer administrative hassles periodically assessed?			

If not, refer to Worksheet FM-2: Administrative Complexity Worksheet – Individual. Add any additional elements of concern. Distribute it to providers and staff to obtain administrative complexity rankings and issues by payer. Compile responses onto Worksheet FM-3: Administrative Complexity Worksheet – Practice. Note payers that present the greatest difficulty, payer contracts to renegotiate, and payer relationships to terminate. Think about the impact of dropping any payers and possible strategies to replace lost revenue (new payer contracts, new services, or additional providers).

01.F Chart of Accounts

Questions to consider	YES	NO If no, why not?	NOT APPLICABLE (note reason)
Is a chart of accounts used?			
Is the chart of accounts adequate for the practice's financial record-keeping and analysis?			

Does the chart of accounts contain the following ranges of sequential numbers and descriptors?

Check all that apply	Area	Circle one	Describe action needed
	Assets	Effective Not Effective	
	Liabilities	Effective Not Effective	
	Owners' equity	Effective Not Effective	
	Revenue	Effective Not Effective	
	Adjustments to revenue	Effective Not Effective	
	Operating expenses	Effective Not Effective	

Check all that apply	Area	Circle one	Describe action needed
	Services and general expenses	Effective Not Effective	
	Provider-related expenses	Effective Not Effective	
	Taxes and other expenses	Effective Not Effective	
	Other:	Effective Not Effective	

Questions to consider	YES	NO If no, why not?	NOT APPLICABLE (note reason)
Does the chart of accounts contain sequential subcategories and descriptors (location or physician or other level)?			
Does the chart of accounts break down data to maximize analysis and reporting for financial, tax, other reporting, and decision making?			
Are all financial activities (assets, liabilities, revenue, expenses, etc.) classified accurately?			
Is the chart of accounts compatible with the practice's computer system as well as the Certified Public Accountant's (CPA's) system?			

01.G Depreciation

Questions to consider	YES	NO If no, why not?	NOT APPLICABLE (note reason)
Is there a system for tracking assets and leasehold improvements?			
Does the system include description, purchase date, purchase amount, chart of accounts code, location of use, and retirement date?			
Is there a system for recording depreciation and updating net book value?			
Is depreciation recorded at least monthly based on prior-year records, and additional entries recorded each month (or quarter) based on prior-month (or quarter) fixed asset purchases and leasehold improvements?			

Check off the type(s) of depreciation used and note applications.

Check all that apply	Type	Circle one	Describe action needed
	Straight Line Application:	Effective Not Effective	
	Accelerated Application:	Effective Not Effective	
	Section 179 Application:	Effective Not Effective	
	Other: Application:	Effective Not Effective	

01.H Flow of Financial Information

With regard to the ways data is entered into the accounting system, note the method of entry (manual accounting entry, interface, etc.).

Type of Data	Method of Entry
Revenue	
Payroll	
A/P	
Other:	
Other:	
Other:	

01.I Accounting Systems and Software

Questions to consider	YES	NO If no, why not?	NOT APPLICABLE (note reason)
Is accounting software used?			
Does the software meet the practice's needs?			
If accounting applications are outsourced, are they periodically assessed, including for cost-effectiveness?			
Are the accounting software service and support satisfactory?			
Are updates received?			
Are the reports adequate?			
Do applications interface?			

01.J Capital Financing

Questions to consider	YES	NO If no, why not?	NOT APPLICABLE (note reason)
Is a pro forma prepared prior to making capital purchases?			
Are capital purchases approved by the board?			
Are there established sources for capital financing?			
Is a capital line of credit in place?			
Are the terms competitive?			
Is the line sufficient?			
Is a general line of credit in place?			
Are the terms competitive?			
Is the line sufficient?			
Is the practice not overextended with regard to loan payments?			

TASK 02: ESTABLISH INTERNAL CONTROLS FOR CASH MANAGEMENT

Avoiding loss – through accounting flaws, errors, omissions, theft, and embezzlement – is a primary concern in the area of financial management. Do you have procedures in place to determine the weaknesses in your systems? What about bank reconciliation? Are your bank accounts reconciled on a timely and regular basis? Are there processes in place to periodically monitor your practice's financial controls to make certain they are working and you have identified and addressed any gaps? Are revenue and expenses monitored against the budget and prior period? Best practice involves separation of duties. To the extent possible based on the size of your organization, does, for instance, the person who pays the bills differ from the person who reconciles the checking account? Reconciliation of the revenue posted in your practice management system to that posted in your accounting system is another way to avoid loss. Is that process completed in your practice on a regular basis? What about check signing and other types of authorizations? Do you have processes in place to oversee those tasks? Work through this section to determine the effectiveness of the cash management controls in your practice.

02.A Risk and Potential Loss

Questions to consider	YES	NO If no, why not?	NOT APPLICABLE (note reason)
Are charges entered on the date of service?			
Is there a system in place for identifying and tracking down missing encounter forms?			
Are encounter totals balanced to computer-generated reports of charges entered?			

Check off payment sources.

Check all that apply	Source	Circle one	Describe action needed
	Mail (patient)	Effective Not Effective	
	Mail (insurance)	Effective Not Effective	
	Locked box	Effective Not Effective	
	In person (time of service and walk-in)	Effective Not Effective	
	Electronic (insurance, via electronic funds transfer)	Effective Not Effective	
	Electronic (patient, via patient portal, third-party service company, etc.)	Effective Not Effective	
	Credit card (in person, mail, and telephone)	Effective Not Effective	
	Debit card (in person, mail, and telephone)	Effective Not Effective	
	Gift certificate	Effective Not Effective	
	Other:	Effective Not Effective	

Questions to consider	YES	NO If no, why not?	NOT APPLICABLE (note reason)
Are time-of-service payments kept in a secure location during the day?			
Are receipts given for all types of in-person payments?			
Are mailed payment totals and locked-box payment reports reconciled against deposit totals?			
Are in-person payments reconciled to receipt totals?			
Are electronic insurance payments posted electronically?			
Are electronic insurance payment amounts reconciled to the explanation of benefits?			
Are electronic patient payment amounts reconciled to related report totals (processing vendor reports, bank statements, etc.)?			
Is the credit/debit card machine batched out daily and totals compared to the credit/debit card slip total?			
Are all types of revenue entered in the practice management system on a same- or next-day basis?			

Questions to consider	YES	NO If no, why not?	NOT APPLICABLE (note reason)
Are deposits made on a daily basis?			
Is remote deposit capture used?			
Is there daily balancing of payments received, deposited, and posted in the practice management system?			
Is petty cash used?			
Is petty cash kept in a secure location during the day and overnight?			
Is petty cash reviewed daily for sufficiency (bills, coins, and total)?			
Is the customary balance of petty cash adequate?			
Is the disbursement documentation for petty cash appropriate?			
Are over/under situations monitored and addressed?			

Questions to consider	YES	NO If no, why not?	NOT APPLICABLE (note reason)
Is petty cash reconciled and replenished at least monthly?			
Are payments of all types, explanations of benefits, and unposted encounter forms placed in a fireproof safe on an overnight basis?			
Is work not in process (payments of all types, explanations of benefits, and unposted encounter forms) kept in the safe during the day?			
Are other documents of value (insurance policies, stock certificates, etc.) stored in the safe?			
Is the safe kept locked when not in use?			
Is access to the safe limited to two or three key individuals?			

02.B Bank Reconciliation Procedures

Questions to consider	YES	NO If no, why not?	NOT APPLICABLE (note reason)
Does the practice use electronic banking?			
Are all types of deposits reconciled to the bank statement?			
Are all types of automatic debits (payroll, payroll taxes, other) reconciled to the bank statement?			
Are checks reconciled and outstanding checks addressed?			
Are bank accounts reconciled at least monthly?			
Are credit and debit card statements reconciled each month?			
Are other monthly reconciliations completed as required?			
As required by state law, are unclaimed check processes followed?			
Are cash balances reviewed daily?			

02.C Monitor and Evaluate Internal Financial Controls

Questions to consider	YES	NO If no, why not?	NOT APPLICABLE (note reason)
Are financial controls evaluated on a periodic basis (as needed, at least annually)?			
Is the review of processes completed by the board?			
Are steps taken to analyze and correct any areas of exposure?			

02.D Monitor Revenue and Expenses to Budget and Prior Period Amounts

Questions to consider	YES	NO If no, why not?	NOT APPLICABLE (note reason)
Are revenue and expenses analyzed each month?			
Are revenue and expenses compared to the budget?			
Are they compared to a prior period as well as the same period last year?			
Are year-to-date amounts compared to last year, year to date?			
Is a year-end analysis to budget and prior year also completed?			
Are variances analyzed and documented?			
Are results presented to the board?			
Do the debits always equal the credits?			

Questions to consider	YES	NO If no, why not?	NOT APPLICABLE (note reason)
Are accounts with abnormal balances (for example, an asset or expense account with a credit balance; a liability, equity, or income account with a debit balance) reviewed on a monthly basis and adjusted as necessary?			
Are account balances reviewed for accuracy and adjusted as necessary?			
Are payroll-related accounts reconciled to the payroll system?			
Are adjusting entries from the accountant posted and balanced to the accountant's statements?			
Are income statement accounts at zero for each new fiscal year?			
Are profits or losses posted to retained earnings and all income statement accounts zeroed out?			
Are amounts in the balance sheet accounts at year end entered as the beginning balances for the new fiscal year?			

02.E Procedures for and Separation of Accounting Functions

Is responsibility assigned to separate individuals for the following functions?

Check all that apply	Function	Circle one	Describe action needed
	Purchasing	Effective Not Effective	
	Receiving	Effective Not Effective	
	Opening the mail	Effective Not Effective	
	Payment and adjustment posting	Effective Not Effective	
	Charge entry	Effective Not Effective	
	Preparation of deposit	Effective Not Effective	
	Take deposit to bank	Effective Not Effective	
	A/P	Effective Not Effective	
	Check signing	Effective Not Effective	

Check all that apply	Function	Circle one	Describe action needed
	Bank account reconciliation and credit/debit card statement reconciliation	Effective Not Effective	
	Approval of hours worked	Effective Not Effective	
	Preparation of payroll	Effective Not Effective	
	Distribution of paychecks	Effective Not Effective	
	General ledger	Effective Not Effective	
	Daily and monthly charges, payments, etc.	Effective Not Effective	
	Other:	Effective Not Effective	

02.F Reconciliation of Billing and Accounting Systems

Are the following practice management system reports printed and reconciled at month end, with levels at total, payer, provider, procedure, and so on?

Check all that apply	Report	Circle one	Describe action needed
	Charges	Effective Not Effective	
	Revenue	Effective Not Effective	
	Adjustments	Effective Not Effective	
	A/R aging	Effective Not Effective	
	Productivity (units, relative value units [RVUs], etc.)	Effective Not Effective	
	Other:	Effective Not Effective	

Questions to consider	YES	NO If no, why not?	NOT APPLICABLE (note reason)
Are revenue totals reconciled to the accounting system daily, monthly, and at year end?			
Are variances resolved?			

02.G Policies for Approvals, Authorizations, Verifications, Check Signing, Invoices, Etc.

Questions to consider	YES	NO If no, why not?	NOT APPLICABLE (note reason)
Are signatures on credit/debit card receipts verified against signatures on cards?			
Are expiration dates on credit/debit cards verified?			
Are cards swiped at the time of service?			
For credit/debit payments received by mail or telephone, is transaction data entered into swipe device on the date received?			
Are self-pay checks reviewed for completeness?			
Are checks returned when incomplete per bank requirements?			

TASK 03: IMPLEMENT AND MAINTAIN A PROCESS FOR EXTERNAL FINANCIAL AUDITS

External financial audits provide a means to confirm that your practice's financial procedures and protocols are appropriate and accurate. There are different levels of service provided by external auditors. Are you familiar with them? Do you know what services are right for your organization? You are likely familiar with GAAP. Are you equally familiar with GAAS (generally accepted auditing standards)? Are your experiences with the practice accountant and auditor satisfactory? Are they educational and informative in terms of what you need to do from the accounting and bookkeeping perspectives? Answer the following questions to determine the effectiveness of your practice audits.

03.A External Audits, Review, or Compilation of Financial Statements

Questions to consider	YES	NO If no, why not?	NOT APPLICABLE (note reason)
Is there an annual outside audit or review or compilation of financial statements?			

03.B Types of Audits and Audit Reports

Questions to consider	YES	NO If no, why not?	NOT APPLICABLE (note reason)
Is there an appropriate level of service for the practice (audit, review, or compilation)?			
Is the opinion unqualified or qualified? _____			
If not unqualified, are identified issues corrected in a timely manner?			

03.C Generally Accepted Auditing Standards (GAAS)

Questions to consider	YES	NO If no, why not?	NOT APPLICABLE (note reason)
Is there assurance from the auditor that he or she follows GAAS?			

03.D Relationships with Accountants and Auditors

Questions to consider	YES	NO If no, why not?	NOT APPLICABLE (note reason)
Does the practice use a CPA?			
Is the relationship mutually satisfactory?			
Is the CPA responsive to needs?			
Does the CPA provide tax compilation services and tax planning advice throughout the year and at year end?			

Questions to consider	YES	NO If no, why not?	NOT APPLICABLE (note reason)
Does the CPA render other financially related advice on a regular and as-needed basis?			
Does the CPA complete physician–owner individual tax returns and corporate tax return?			
Does the CPA meet annually with the board to discuss the review of the financial statements?			
Is there a current engagement letter?			
Are appropriate practice representatives assigned to work with the accountants and auditors?			
Is requested information provided to the accountants and auditors in a timely manner?			
Is service provided by the accountants and auditors in a timely manner?			

TASK 04: DEVELOP AND IMPLEMENT REVENUE CYCLE MANAGEMENT AND ACCOUNTS RECEIVABLE MANAGEMENT

Optimizing cash flow is a result of effective revenue cycle management, which starts with front-end procedures such as insurance verifications, authorizations, and copay collections. It ends with A/R follow-up, and in between are coding, encounter processing, charge entry, medical records documentation, claims submission, and billing. The results of the entire cycle are monitored by calculating and reviewing various trends such as days in A/R, A/R aging, and revenue. Due to the interconnectedness of these processes, an error in one stage can affect another stage. (For instance, a data entry error in entering a patient's insurance information during the registration process can lead to a rejected claim.) Note your answers to the following questions to determine the effectiveness of your practice's revenue cycle management.

04.A Front-End Operations

Questions to consider	YES	NO If no, why not?	NOT APPLICABLE (note reason)
Does the practice use practice management software?			
Is there an electronic health record (EHR) system?			
Are appointments computerized?			
Are patients asked to verify their identity during telephone calls (by stating their date of birth, for example)?			
Is a mini-registration completed (name, date of birth, address, home/work/cell numbers, e-mail address, insurance payer and plan, copay, and so on) when making new patient appointments?			

Questions to consider	YES	NO If no, why not?	NOT APPLICABLE (note reason)
Is key registration data (date of birth, address, home/work/ cell numbers, e-mail address, insurance payer and plan, copay, balance due, and so on) verified when making established patient appointments?			
Are checklists of specific items to cover during each call used for appointments made via the telephone?			
Are appointment cards used for appointments made in person?			
Are appointments confirmed two days prior?			
Is an automated system used to confirm appointments?			
Are no-shows recorded?			
Are confirmations, cancellations (including reasons), reschedules, and so on recorded?			
Are confirmations, cancellations, and reschedules analyzed for trending patterns?			

Questions to consider	YES	NO If no, why not?	NOT APPLICABLE (note reason)
Is insurance coverage verified prior to appointments?			
Is an electronic system used to verify coverage?			
Is coverage verified with ALL payers?			
Is verification of coverage recorded?			
Is receipt of a valid referral verified prior to an appointment?			
Is the date of referral and referral number recorded in the practice management system?			
Is a reminder given to the patient when the referral is expired and/ or used up?			
Is pre-authorization obtained for procedures as required by payers?			
Are pre-authorizations verified prior to appointments?			

Questions to consider	YES	NO If no, why not?	NOT APPLICABLE (note reason)
Are pre-authorizations recorded in the computer system?			
As necessary, are dates finalized with insurance companies?			
Are payers notified if there are changes?			
Is new patient paperwork posted on the practice website for downloading and completing prior to an appointment?			
Are patients without web access instructed to arrive 15 minutes early to complete new patient paperwork?			
If using paper charts, are chart contents compiled prior to new patient appointments?			
Is registration paperwork completed and entered for nonoffice-based care?			
Is registration information updated on a regular and periodic basis?			
Is patient identification confirmed at every visit?			

Questions to consider	YES	NO If no, why not?	NOT APPLICABLE (note reason)
Are insurance cards scanned into the practice management system for every new patient?			
Are patients' insurance cards examined at every visit, compared to previous cards, and if changed, scanned into the practice management system?			
Is contact information (address, home/work/cell telephone numbers, e-mail address, and so on) reviewed at each visit?			
Are kiosks used?			
Are electronic patient signatures used to sign registration paperwork (assignment of benefits, waiver, financial policy, privacy notice acknowledgment, for example)?			
Are patients registered promptly and in a timely manner?			
If using a sign-in sheet, is patient privacy protected?			
Is patient arrival time recorded?			

Questions to consider	YES	NO If no, why not?	NOT APPLICABLE (note reason)
Are overdue balances collected at check-in?			
Are copays collected at check-in (if it is known at check-in that a copay is due)?			
If not, are copays collected during the check-out process?			
For patients not covered by a managed care plan with a copay, are patient balances collected at the time of service (self-pay, high-deductible plan, etc.)?			
Are time-of-service and walk-in patient payments entered in the practice management system on a same-day basis?			

04.B Medical Record Documentation, Encounter Form, and Coding

Questions to consider	YES	NO If no, why not?	NOT APPLICABLE (note reason)
Is medical record documentation created for ALL patient encounters?			
If entries are handwritten, are the notes legible?			
Are all notes reviewed by the provider, signed, and dated?			
Are all test results signed and dated upon review?			
Is documentation filed in charts in an efficient and timely manner?			
Is communication of test results to patients documented with date and signature?			
Do visit notes include documentation according to the Centers for Medicare & Medicaid Services (CMS) 1995 or 1997 *Documentation Guidelines for Evaluation and Management Services*?			
Does documentation support diagnosis code(s)?			

Questions to consider	YES	NO If no, why not?	NOT APPLICABLE (note reason)
Does documentation support evaluation and management codes?			
Does the date of service in the chart agree with the date entered in the practice management system?			
Are patient histories up to date?			
Are medication and allergy lists up to date?			
Do medication lists include all medications, dosages, and directions, including over the counter, samples, herbal supplements, and vitamins?			
Are charts clearly marked "allergy" or the "absence of allergy" (NKA)?			
Are chart contents easy to retrieve?			
Is paperless electronic encounter form processing used?			

Questions to consider	YES	NO If no, why not?	NOT APPLICABLE (note reason)
If not, does the encounter form reflect all common CPT and International Classification of Diseases (ICD) codes?			
Does it have space to write in unlisted services?			
Does it reflect patient demographic information?			
Is it completed clearly and completely by providers?			
When multiple services are provided for different diagnoses, are codes linked clearly by the provider?			
Are modifiers specified as appropriate?			
Are encounter forms completed during the visit and taken to check-out by patients?			
If using an electronic medical record (EMR), does the software recommend (not assign) CPT codes?			
Do providers code encounters?			

Questions to consider	YES	NO If no, why not?	NOT APPLICABLE (note reason)
If providers do not code encounters, do certified procedural coders (CPCs)?			
Is the appropriate number of CPCs on staff?			
Does the CPC staff provide ongoing coding education for providers?			
Does the CPC staff periodically and regularly conduct prospective audits of chart documentation against CPT and ICD codes?			
Are providers notified as to results?			
Are necessary coding modifications made prior to claims submissions?			
Does the CPC staff make recommendations regarding quality of chart entries?			
On an annual basis, does the CPC staff examine the encounter form for updates to CPT and ICD coding changes?			
Are current-year CPT and ICD books used?			

04.C Charge Audit, Charge Entry, and Fees

Questions to consider	YES	NO If no, why not?	NOT APPLICABLE (note reason)
Is an encounter form completed for all services rendered – regardless of location?			
Are encounter forms entered on a same-day basis?			
Is encounter form tracking used?			
Are missing encounter forms found and entered?			
Is automation (EHR or scanning technology, for example) used to enter charges?			
Are encounters batched by charge total on a daily basis?			
Is a computer-generated batch report of charge totals produced daily?			
Are encounter batches and batch reports reconciled and discrepancies addressed?			

Questions to consider	YES	NO If no, why not?	NOT APPLICABLE (note reason)
Is balancing verified by another individual (member of the bookkeeping staff, supervisor, or manager, for example)?			
Is batch integrity maintained when paper documents are filed?			
Are paper batch documents (encounters, batch forms, or computer-generated batch reports, for example) filed for easy retrieval?			
Are fees reviewed on an annual basis?			
For at least the top 90 percent of CPT codes by revenue, are allowables for all payers and all product lines obtained annually?			
Is there a method in place to analyze and compare fees to payer allowables?			
Is there a method in place to analyze cost as compared to fee and allowable?			

If no methods are in place, try this simple approach: Run a report on your practice management system that shows revenue by CPT code. Calculate which codes represent the top 90 percent of revenue. On Worksheet FM-4: Fee Analysis Worksheet, enter the codes and associated practice fees. If available, list the cost per CPT code. List the payers with whom your practice has a contractual relationship. If the payer has multiple product lines and the allowables differ by product, enter the payer/product. Contact each payer to obtain the allowables for the codes listed and the effective date of the allowables. (Remember to request the data at the product line level if the allowables differ by product.) Enter the allowable amounts and effective dates in the space provided.

Questions to consider	YES	NO If no, why not?	NOT APPLICABLE (note reason)
Are all practice fees above cost?			
Are all practice fees above payer allowable amounts?			
For at least the top 90 percent of CPT codes by revenue, are allowables entered into the practice management system?			
Is there follow-up with the payer to renegotiate when reimbursement is below the allowable?			

04.D Claims Submission and Patient Billing

Questions to consider	YES	NO If no, why not?	NOT APPLICABLE (note reason)
Are claims submitted daily?			
Are claims submitted electronically?			
Are as many claims submitted electronically as possible?			
Is claim-scrubbing software used?			
Are claims submitted in a clean fashion?			
Is training provided for reception staff when patterns emerge indicating registration problems that lead to submission issues?			
Are submission reports retained as proof of timely filing?			
Are patient statements produced at least weekly?			

Questions to consider	YES	NO If no, why not?	NOT APPLICABLE (note reason)
Are statements based on date of service, not last name or other?			
Does the practice have a minimum balance?			
Are statements clear and easy to interpret?			
Do statements include a means to pay by credit card on the return stub?			
Do statements provide detail rather than a balance forward format?			
Are pre-addressed return envelopes provided?			
Are statements produced within no more than a 30-day cycle?			

04.E Accounts Receivable Follow-Up

Questions to consider	YES	NO If no, why not?	NOT APPLICABLE (note reason)
Is a collection module used?			
Do A/R staff work 90- and 120-plus-day buckets on a regular basis?			
Is a tight collection time frame maintained, not to exceed 120 days in total?			
Are all collection-related activities documented?			
Is initial and subsequent follow-up with payers timely?			
Is interest paid by payers for claims not paid within time frames specified by law?			
For patient balances, is a combination of statements, telephone calls, and letters used in a consistent and regimented manner?			
Are laws regarding collection telephone calls (for example, the Fair Debt Collection Practices Act) adhered to?			

Questions to consider	YES	NO If no, why not?	NOT APPLICABLE (note reason)
Is a collection agency used?			
Is the collection agency a reputable firm with competitive rates?			
Are results evaluated at least annually?			
Is provider approval obtained before turning accounts over?			
Is there a collection agency minimum?			
Are uncollectible unpaid patient balances below the collection agency minimum written off?			
Is payment required if/when these patients return to the practice?			
Are systems in place to track these patients and amounts?			
Is the practice's bad debt rate in line with industry standards?			

Questions to consider	YES	NO If no, why not?	NOT APPLICABLE (note reason)
Are financial hardship and charity care policies in place?			
Are these policies compliant with related laws?			
Are payment plans offered?			
Is there follow-up with patients who don't adhere to payment plans?			
Are bankruptcy protocols in place?			
Is the practice compliant with bankruptcy laws?			
Is denied claim information analyzed for payer error?			
Is there follow-up (resubmit, appeal, etc.) with payers as appropriate?			
Are denials posted and tracked by type?			

Questions to consider	YES	NO If no, why not?	NOT APPLICABLE (note reason)
Are necessary system modifications made to reduce denials?			
Are patients billed as allowed and required by payers?			
Are waiver forms used as required by payers?			
Are all write-offs tracked by type, including withholds?			
Are write-offs analyzed for trending patterns?			
Are write-off authority protocols in place?			

04.F Billing Trends (Net Charges, Cash Collections, Days in Accounts Receivable, Percent of Accounts Receivable Over 90 Days)

Questions to consider	YES	NO If no, why not?	NOT APPLICABLE (note reason)
Are charge totals monitored monthly?			
Are charge totals benchmarked to industry standards?			
Are variances analyzed and addressed?			
Are adjustments monitored monthly?			
Are trends analyzed and addressed?			
Are collections monitored daily?			
Are collections monitored monthly?			
Are collections benchmarked to industry standards?			

Questions to consider	YES	NO If no, why not?	NOT APPLICABLE (note reason)
Are variances analyzed and addressed?			
Are days in A/R monitored monthly?			
Are days in A/R benchmarked to industry standards?			
Are variances analyzed and addressed?			
Are aging percentages monitored monthly?			
Are aging percentages benchmarked to industry standards?			
Are variances analyzed and addressed?			
Are other indicators such as RVUs monitored monthly?			
Note what they are:			

Questions to consider	YES	NO If no, why not?	NOT APPLICABLE (note reason)
Are other indicators benchmarked to industry standards?			
Are variances of other indicators analyzed and addressed?			
Do accounts continue to age (in other words, not re-age) when secondary payers are billed?			
Are accounts aged by service date?			

TASK 05: ANALYZE AND MONITOR FINANCIAL PERFORMANCE AND REPORT FINANCIAL RESULTS TO STAKEHOLDERS

What steps do you take to retrospectively review monthly, quarterly, and yearly performance in your practice, and how do you report information about results to the board? It's important that you understand and produce the necessary reports – and complete an internal analysis – to determine how the practice is performing from a financial perspective. What is the income year-to-date as compared to last year? What are the reasons for the increase or decrease? How do the A/R aging percentages compare to last month? How do they compare to the same period last year? Benchmarking your statistics against industry statistics is another way to analyze performance. Key financial information about your practice needs to be summarized and presented to the board, too. Complete the following section to determine how your approach to monitoring financial performance and reporting it to the necessary parties measures up.

05.A Financial Statements

Questions to consider	YES	NO If no, why not?	NOT APPLICABLE (note reason)
Are financial statements generated within one to three days after the end of the period?			

Are the following minimum financial statements generated on a monthly and fiscal year-end basis?

Check all that apply	Statement	Circle one	Describe action needed
	Balance Sheet	Effective Not Effective	
	Income Statement	Effective Not Effective	
	Other:	Effective Not Effective	

Questions to consider	YES	NO If no, why not?	NOT APPLICABLE (note reason)
Are statements accurate and complete?			
Are all users able to understand and interpret reports?			

Do the board and managers understand the following terms?

Term	Yes	No	Describe action needed
Assets			
Liabilities			
Equity			
Investments			
Distributions			
Revenue			
Expenses			
Gains			
Losses			
Net income			
Other:			

05.B Financial Analysis

Questions to consider	YES	NO If no, why not?	NOT APPLICABLE (note reason)
Is the financial health of the organization periodically and regularly analyzed on an overall basis as well as at other levels (physician, department, or location, for example)?			

Are the following items analyzed and compared to the prior period, budget, forecast, or other prospective internal data on a monthly and fiscal year-end basis?

Check all that apply	Item	Circle one	Describe action needed
	Revenue	Effective Not Effective	
	Expenses	Effective Not Effective	
	Income	Effective Not Effective	
	A/R	Effective Not Effective	
	Collections	Effective Not Effective	
	Payer mix	Effective Not Effective	

Check all that apply	Item	Circle one	Describe action needed
	Collections by payer	Effective Not Effective	
	Charges	Effective Not Effective	
	Payments	Effective Not Effective	
	Adjustments	Effective Not Effective	
	RVUs	Effective Not Effective	
	Other:	Effective Not Effective	

Are measures of profitability and profitability ratios calculated and analyzed at least annually and compared to the prior period?

Check all that apply	Measure	Circle one	Describe action needed
	Total medical revenue after operating costs	Effective Not Effective	
	Total medical revenue after operating costs per full-time-equivalent (FTE) physician	Effective Not Effective	
	Current ratio	Effective Not Effective	
	Debt/equity ratio	Effective Not Effective	
	Net revenue per FTE physician	Effective Not Effective	
	Gross collection ratio	Effective Not Effective	
	Net collection ratio	Effective Not Effective	
	Days in A/R	Effective Not Effective	
	A/R aging	Effective Not Effective	

Check all that apply	Measure	Circle one	Describe action needed
	Payroll ratio	Effective Not Effective	
	Payroll cost per FTE physician	Effective Not Effective	
	Employee turnover ratio	Effective Not Effective	
	Overhead ratio	Effective Not Effective	
	Overhead per FTE physician	Effective Not Effective	
	Medical and surgical supplies ratio	Effective Not Effective	
	Medical and surgical supplies per FTE physician	Effective Not Effective	
	Other:	Effective Not Effective	

Questions to consider	YES	NO If no, why not?	NOT APPLICABLE (note reason)
Are these measures compared to the prior period, budget, forecast, or other prospective data?			
Is the data "drilled down" as necessary to further understand problem areas?			
Are problem areas identified and action taken to resolve them?			

05.C Benchmarking

Are the following areas compared to industry benchmarks?

Check all that apply	Area	Circle one	Describe action needed
	Revenue	Effective Not Effective	
	Expenses	Effective Not Effective	
	A/R aging	Effective Not Effective	
	Payer mix	Effective Not Effective	
	Collection rate by payer	Effective Not Effective	
	Productivity	Effective Not Effective	
	Profitability	Effective Not Effective	
	Net collection ratio	Effective Not Effective	
	Overhead	Effective Not Effective	
	Other:	Effective Not Effective	

Questions to consider	YES	NO If no, why not?	NOT APPLICABLE (note reason)
Are these measures "drilled down" as necessary to further understand problem areas?			
Are problem areas identified and action taken to resolve them?			
Are the limitations of benchmarking recognized, understood, and communicated to the board?			
Is industry-accepted benchmark data used?			

05.D Communicating Financial Information

Questions to consider	YES	NO If no, why not?	NOT APPLICABLE (note reason)
Is financial information reported to the board on a regular basis?			

Does the board receive, at a minimum, the following information in a concise and easy-to-understand format?

Check all that apply	Item	Circle one	Describe action needed
	Income Statement	Effective Not Effective	
	Balance Sheet	Effective Not Effective	
	Charges	Effective Not Effective	
	Payments	Effective Not Effective	
	Adjustments	Effective Not Effective	
	A/R aging	Effective Not Effective	
	Other:	Effective Not Effective	

Questions to consider	YES	NO If no, why not?	NOT APPLICABLE (note reason)
Are reports formally reviewed by the board including discussion of variances and required action on problem areas?			

TASK 06: DIRECT THE PAYROLL PROCESS

Whether you outsource payroll for your practice or produce it in-house, oversight is paramount to ensure the process is correct – from hours worked and pay issued, to completing and filing the necessary taxes, to monitoring benefits and completing various required audit filings. What types of protocols do you have in place to ensure employees are paid for hours worked and at the correct rate? How do you maintain time off, insurance, and other benefits? How do you make certain the practice is compliant with federal, state, and other requirements relating to compensation? Answer these questions to assess your effectiveness.

06.A Paying Employees

Questions to consider	YES	NO If no, why not?	NOT APPLICABLE (note reason)
Is there a secure, automated system to document time and attendance?			
Does the system include accruals of sick leave, vacation time, personal leave, paid time off, bereavement leave, and so on for time earned and used, as well as balances?			
Are systems in place to keep compensation rates updated in payroll software?			
Is direct deposit used?			

06.B Reporting System to Gather Employee Work Hours

Questions to consider	YES	NO If no, why not?	NOT APPLICABLE (note reason)
Are time and attendance reported by employees within the required time frame?			
Are overtime and paid time off (vacation, sick, personal, paid time off, bereavement, holiday, etc.) policies in place?			
Is overtime monitored and controlled?			
Are other categories of paid time (sick, vacation, personal, paid time off, bereavement, etc.) reported by employees within the required time frame?			
Is there a system to deal with noncompliant employees (for example, wait until the next payroll date)?			

06.C Accurate Record-Keeping for Payroll

Questions to consider	YES	NO If no, why not?	NOT APPLICABLE (note reason)
Are time and attendance approved?			
Are payroll hours, accrual balances, and rates of pay verified and approved by an administrator, manager, or other?			
Are codes used to record various types of time worked (regular, overtime, holiday, vacation, personal, sick, paid time off, bereavement, etc.)?			
Is all paid time used properly calculated and coded?			
Are payroll records maintained as required by state and federal law?			
Are lost, uncashed, and returned payroll checks properly investigated and handled (for example, reason documented; payment stopped; if applicable, check voided with general ledger entries reversed, overpayment of payroll tax addressed with accountant, reissue completed)?			

06.D Regulatory Compliance for Payroll Filing

Questions to consider	YES	NO If no, why not?	NOT APPLICABLE (note reason)
Are all state and federal required tax filings completed and filed on time?			
Are payroll taxes paid via electronic funds transfer?			
Are payroll taxes paid on time?			
Are worker compensation filings completed accurately and on time?			
Is deferred compensation paid accurately and on time?			
Are W-2 forms individually cross-checked to payroll records?			
Are W-2 forms prepared by an individual who is not involved with the payroll process?			
Are returned W-2 forms processed by an individual who is not involved with the payroll process?			

Questions to consider	YES	NO If no, why not?	NOT APPLICABLE (note reason)
Are W-2 forms prepared, issued, and filed on time?			
Are 1099 forms prepared as required per tax law?			
Are 1099 forms issued and filed on time?			
Is employee payroll file information maintained per federal requirements?			

06.E Payroll Recorded Benefits

Questions to consider	YES	NO If no, why not?	NOT APPLICABLE (note reason)
Is documentation regarding employee voluntary deductions in place?			
Are necessary records maintained for determination of eligibility, monies contributed, and calculation of payouts for retirement plan (for example, pension, profit sharing, or 401(k))?			
Are pre- and post-tax options set up appropriately?			

06.F Payroll Audits by Tax Agencies, Insurers, or Government Entities

Questions to consider	YES	NO If no, why not?	NOT APPLICABLE (note reason)
Are externally requested payroll audits completed accurately and on time?			

TASK 07: ESTABLISH AND MAINTAIN THE ORGANIZATION'S BANKING, INVESTMENT, AND OTHER FINANCIAL RELATIONSHIPS

Good practice administrators know they can't do the job alone. Having a knowledge base that ranges from in-depth to overview level about the full range of information related to managing a practice is required, along with the understanding that external advisers are necessary. One needs to know when those advisers are needed and when they are not. Answer the following questions about your adviser relationships to see how you are doing in this area.

07.A Relationships with Advisers

Check all of the professionals with whom you have a working relationship.

Check all that apply	Professional	Circle one	Describe action needed
	Banker	Effective Not Effective	
	Accountant	Effective Not Effective	
	Auditor	Effective Not Effective	
	Consultant	Effective Not Effective	
	Insurance agent	Effective Not Effective	
	Attorney (corporate)	Effective Not Effective	
	Attorney (human resources)	Effective Not Effective	

Check all that apply	Professional	Circle one	Describe action needed
	Attorney (Stark law)	Effective Not Effective	
	Attorney (other):	Effective Not Effective	
	Investment adviser	Effective Not Effective	
	Financial planner	Effective Not Effective	
	Real estate agent	Effective Not Effective	
	Retirement plan adviser	Effective Not Effective	
	Other:	Effective Not Effective	

Questions to consider	YES	NO If no, why not?	NOT APPLICABLE (note reason)
Are these relationships evaluated on a periodic basis in terms of satisfaction, service, cost, and so on?			

07.B Review of Financial Relationships

Questions to consider	YES	NO If no, why not?	NOT APPLICABLE (note reason)
Are financial relationships (banking, investment, etc.) reviewed on a regular basis with the board to determine satisfaction, service, cost, and so on?			

TASK 08: DEVELOP RELATIONSHIPS WITH INDIVIDUAL INSURANCE CARRIERS TO OPTIMIZE CONTRACT NEGOTIATIONS AND MAINTENANCE OF EXISTING CONTRACTS

Having good insurance company contracts with appropriate fee schedules and terms has the potential to make or break a practice. The needs of a practice change over time. The terms of a contract that you negotiated last year and were suitable then may not be suitable now. Are you reviewing your contracts on a periodic basis to make certain they still fit your needs? As a part of that process are you auditing correctness and timeliness of payments? How are your negotiating skills and your relationships with payer representatives? When an agreement was signed, the payer may have been one of the best with regard to reimbursement, terms, and protocols, but now perhaps that is not the case. Are you equipped to renegotiate with the payer? The answer is more likely to be yes if, among other things, you have developed and maintained relationships with various insurance payer employees. Success with the payers is all about creating win–win outcomes. Answer these questions to determine how you're doing with payer contracts and relationships.

08.A Payer Contracts and Audit of Payments

Questions to consider	YES	NO If no, why not?	NOT APPLICABLE (note reason)
Are copies of all payer contracts on file?			
Is a summarization of key terms for each contract on hand for quick reference?			
Are all payer contracts reviewed annually?			
Are all payer reimbursements formally audited each year?			
Referencing Worksheet FM-1: Payer Analysis, does no single payer represent more than 20 percent of revenue?			
Are results of contract review and practice fee/payer fee schedule analysis reported to the board?			

08.B Payer Performance

Questions to consider	YES	NO If no, why not?	NOT APPLICABLE (note reason)
Is timeliness of payments by payers analyzed on a periodic basis?			
Is correctness of payments by payers analyzed on a periodic basis?			
Are payer denials analyzed on a periodic basis?			
Is payer "hassle factor" analyzed on a periodic basis?			
Is payer responsiveness analyzed on a periodic basis?			
If there are state clean claim laws, do payers pay interest as required?			
If there are no state clean claim laws, is there communication with appropriate authorities, as required?			

08.C Contracts

Is a common checklist that includes the following considerations used when preparing for negotiation or renegotiation?

Check all that apply	Consideration	Circle one	Describe action needed
	Practice dominance in area	Effective Not Effective	
	Amount of competition	Effective Not Effective	
	Level of patient satisfaction	Effective Not Effective	
	Level of referring physician satisfaction	Effective Not Effective	
	Special programs (evening hours, weekend hours, disease management, etc.)	Effective Not Effective	
	Relationships with large area employers	Effective Not Effective	
	Relationships with area insurance brokers	Effective Not Effective	
	Payer product line	Effective Not Effective	
	Other:	Effective Not Effective	

Questions to consider	YES	NO If no, why not?	NOT APPLICABLE (note reason)
Is each payer assessed using the same checklist?			
Are financial and nonfinancial elements identified that are mandatory, desired, and not necessary?			
Are practice profitability data (such as profitability by contract) on hand prior to starting the negotiating process?			
Are payer performance assessment data (such as administrative complexity, service level, and hassle factor) on hand prior to starting the negotiating process?			

Are the following potential areas of risk analyzed in each contract?

Check all that apply	Area	Circle one	Describe action needed
	Type of plan and products (for example, list of products, rates)	Effective Not Effective	
	Medical necessity (for example, decision-making authority, prior authorization)	Effective Not Effective	
	Indemnification (reciprocal hold-harmless clause, etc.)	Effective Not Effective	

Check all that apply	Area	Circle one	Describe action needed
	Claims payment (time frames, etc.)	Effective Not Effective	
	Provider manual (for example, changes, written consent, notification on material changes)	Effective Not Effective	
	Termination and renewal (length of agreement, notice period, etc.)	Effective Not Effective	
	Access to medical records (for example, which records, access to financial data, time lines)	Effective Not Effective	
	Appeals and denials (procedures, time frames, etc.)	Effective Not Effective	
	Compensation (type of payments, for example)	Effective Not Effective	
	Governing law (state, arbitration, etc.)	Effective Not Effective	
	Other:	Effective Not Effective	

Questions to consider	YES	NO If no, why not?	NOT APPLICABLE (note reason)
Are you knowledgeable about the types of reimbursement for each contract and product line?			
Are you knowledgeable about the scope of services the practice is responsible for delivering?			
Are you able to manage costs for the scope of services?			
Is stop-loss insurance in place?			
Is legal assistance obtained for contract review?			
When implementing a new plan and/or products, is operational planning completed?			
After implementing a new plan and/or products, is review completed after six months?			
Are terms and reimbursement renegotiated as necessary?			
Are payer reimbursement and hassle factor issues addressed with the payer representative?			

Questions to consider	YES	NO If no, why not?	NOT APPLICABLE (note reason)
If unsuccessful, are issues addressed with the payer provider relations manager?			
If still unsuccessful, are issues addressed with the state medical society and/or local independent practice association or physician–hospital organization?			
If issues remain unresolved, is consideration given to dropping the plan and/or product line?			
Are plans and/or products terminated as appropriate?			

08.D Negotiation Skills

Are you skilled at these elements of negotiating?

Questions to consider	YES	NO If no, why not?	NOT APPLICABLE (note reason)
Preparing necessary data			
Meeting face to face			
Aware of your negotiating style and how it is perceived			
Focusing on your goals and objectives			
Defining the deal breakers			
Displaying a professional demeanor			
Taking an inventive approach			
Persevering on key issues			
Other:			

Questions to consider	YES	NO If no, why not?	NOT APPLICABLE (note reason)
Do you have plans to obtain education and training in areas of negotiation weakness?			

08.E Personal Contacts with Payers

Questions to consider	YES	NO If no, why not?	NOT APPLICABLE (note reason)
Is respect for the payer balanced with the practice's needs?			
Is there focus on building and maintaining payer relationships?			
Are interactions courteous?			
Is the focus on achieving win–win results?			
Is emotion kept out of the equation?			
Is genuine interest shown for the payer's position?			
Are there appropriate contacts at each plan?			

BOTTOM LINE—FINANCIAL MANAGEMENT

Managing a practice's finances is a complicated task today. Reimbursement rates have not kept pace with inflation, requiring practices to do more with less. Responsibility for revenue, expenses, and everything in between now requires more tools and insight. Sound protocols must be used on a daily basis, reviewed periodically, and updated as needed. Financial management is a key task for today's medical practice administrator. Make certain to keep your skill level up, and take the time to focus regularly on the financial aspect of your practice.

Financial Management
Supplemental Notes

(copy as needed)

Task	Notes

Financial Management
Action Items

(copy as needed)

Task	Action	Responsible Party	Due Date	Priority

FM-1 PAYER ANALYSIS

Payer/plan	Unit Volume	Charges	Payments	Adjustments	A/R Aging 0–30	31–60	61–90	91–120	120+	TOTAL
Choose 1 indicator:			SAMPLE							
___ # of patients										
___ % of visits										
___ % of CPT codes										
___ Other ___										
Aetna	2419	328,763	289,666	76,021	56,985	35,982	19,004	3,001	854	115,826
BCBS	1209	205,389	176,432	45,980	45,093	15,830	5,410	1,002	529	67,864
Medicare B	5732	875,999	456,249	389,305	149,025	55,983	12,987	5,942	1,094	225,031
Welfare	2010	280,641	100,245	169,851	55,012	16,934	7,301	4,931	413	84,591
TOTAL	11370	1,690,792	1,022,592	681,157	306,115	124,729	44,702	14,876	2,890	493,312
	% OF UNIT VOLUME	% OF CHARGES	% OF PAYMENTS	% OF ADJUSTMENTS	% OF A/R AGING					
Aetna	21.28%	19.44%	28.33%	11.16%	49.20%	31.07%	16.41%	2.59%	0.74%	23.48%
BCBS	10.63%	12.15%	17.25%	6.75%	66.45%	23.33%	7.97%	1.48%	0.78%	13.76%
Medicare B	50.41%	51.81%	44.62%	57.15%	66.22%	24.88%	5.77%	2.64%	0.49%	45.62%
Welfare	17.68%	61.60%	9.80%	24.94%	65.03%	20.02%	8.63%	5.83%	0.49%	17.15%

FM-1 PAYER ANALYSIS

Payer/plan	Unit Volume Choose 1 indicator: ___ & of patients ___ % of visits ___ % of CPT codes ___ Other ___	Charges	Payments	Adjustments	A/R Aging 0–30	31–60	61–90	91–120	120+	TOTAL
TOTAL										
	% OF UNIT VOLUME	% OF CHARGES	% OF PAYMENTS	% OF ADJUSTMENTS	% OF A/R AGING					

FM-2 ADMINISTRATIVE COMPLEXITY WORKSHEET – INDIVIDUAL

Overall Summary

Payer _____

RATE EACH ELEMENT USING THE SCALE PROVIDED

	1	2	3	4	5
	POOR	FAIR	AVERAGE	ABOVE AVERAGE	EXCELLENT
Overall Administrative Hassle					
Claim Processing Timeliness					
Accuracy of Claim Processing					
Website					
Customer Service					
Response Time					
Referral Process					
Prior Authorization Process					
Benefit Verification Process					
Formulary					
Allowables					
Contracting Process					

FM-3 ADMINISTRATIVE COMPLEXITY WORKSHEET – PRACTICE

Overall Summary

Payer _____

RATE EACH ELEMENT USING THE SCALE PROVIDED

	1	2	3	4	5
	POOR	**FAIR**	**AVERAGE**	**ABOVE AVERAGE**	**EXCELLENT**
Overall Administrative Hassle					
Claim Processing Timeliness					
Accuracy of Claim Processing					
Website					
Customer Service					
Response Time					
Referral Process					
Prior Authorization Process					
Benefit Verification Process					
Formulary					
Allowables					
Contracting Process					

FM-4 FEE ANALYSIS WORKSHEET

CPT CODE	FEE	COST	PAYER 1	PAYER 2	PAYER 3	PAYER 4	PAYER 5	PAYER 6	PAYER 7 PRODUCT 1	PAYER 8 PRODUCT 2
			EFF DATE OF ALLOWABLE	EFF DATE OF ALLOWABLE	EFF DATE OF ALLOWABLE	EFF DATE OF ALLOWABLE	EFF DATE OF ALLOWABLE	EFF DATE OF ALLOWABLE	EFF DATE OF ALLOWABLE	EFF DATE OF ALLOWABLE
			1/1/xxxx	7/1/xxxx	1/1/xxxx	9/1/xxxx	12/15/xxxx	1/1/xxxx	6/1/xxxx	7/15/xxxx
99202	180.00	167.23	175.34	159.45	95.34	121.54	179.91	70.57	182.99	182.99
99203	255.00	201.22	248.09	229.00	133.09	164.32	240.81	101.85	257.21	257.21
99204	395.00	306.21	389.67	78.00	187.45	261.56	380.30	156.96	401.11	401.11
99212	105.00	74.23	99.23	86.36	54.21	71.78	97.30	41.02	104.23	104.23
99213	175.00	135.99	167.42	155.90	81.89	121.56	168.61	68.55	171.22	171.22
99214	260.00	109.31	253.12	239.67	127.91	174.71	249.71	102.61	259.99	259.99

SAMPLE

FM-4 FEE ANALYSIS WORKSHEET										
CPT CODE	FEE	COST	PAYER 1	PAYER 2	PAYER 3	PAYER 4	PAYER 5	PAYER 6	PAYER 7	PAYER 8
									PRODUCT 1	PRODUCT 2
			EFF DATE OF	EFF DATE OF	EFF DATE OF	EFF DATE OF	EFF DATE OF	EFF DATE OF	EFF DATE OF	EFF DATE OF
			ALLOWABLE	ALLOWABLE	ALLOWABLE	ALLOWABLE	ALLOWABLE	ALLOWABLE	ALLOWABLE	ALLOWABLE

CHAPTER 3

Human Resource Management

How do you use human resources to achieve and enhance organizational performance? Start by assessing the practice's current situation.

Traditionally, human resource (HR) management has primarily been concerned with recruiting, retaining, training, developing, and using human resources. However, rapid changes in social, technological, economic, and political factors and labor laws have transformed HR management to the point where the objectives of the organization, employee, and society often intermingle. In this environment, the healthcare industry presents special challenges to HR management because it is a dynamic, enormous, diverse, labor-intensive, complex industry. Dynamic and diverse also describe the people who work in medical practices. Their expectations drive many HR policies and processes, putting a hot spotlight on the following assessment questions to ensure competitiveness.

- How does the practice coordinate the recruitment and orientation process of clinical and nonclinical staff? Recruitment can take advantage of computer technology, especially the Internet, then move right into orientation with computer assists such as the practice's website. Yet, traditional techniques remain powerful.
- How does the practice manage the retention of clinical and nonclinical staff? Healthcare players compete intensely for qualified staff, requiring as much attention to retention as to recruiting.
- How does the group develop and monitor an effective staffing strategy? Knowing how many staff and of which kind to yield quality care and service while creating a profitable practice has become more than a numbers exercise; staffing must be carefully tied to the strategic plan.

- How does the group develop, implement, and evaluate performance management programs for clinical and nonclinical staff? Motivating staff to perform competently and successfully today requires a partnership between management and the persons themselves.
- How does the group develop and implement compensation and benefit plans? Compensation, including benefits, incentives, and reward programs, remains a key motivator for staff, and pay for performance for the practice brings new expectations from external players.
- How does the group provide systems, processes, and structure for administrative and clinical training for medical providers, employees, and students (if the practice has students)? The rapid changes in technology, procedures, and regulations mean that training is a forever responsibility using many media and methods.
- How does the practice establish systems and processes for awareness, education, and compliance with employment laws and regulations? HR management always has had to contend with legal issues related to personnel, but today the laws and regulations pervade everything from patient care to interpersonal relations.
- How do administrators provide personal commitment to enhance their knowledge, skills, and abilities in healthcare? Only a highly motivated administrator will stay abreast of changes and guide the practice into a successful future.

Now, more specifically assess the group's HR practices to learn if they are on track with industry best practices.

TASK 01: COORDINATE THE RECRUITMENT AND ORIENTATION PROCESS OF CLINICAL AND NONCLINICAL STAFF

After the practice's strategic plan and related operating plan have determined the kinds and numbers of staff needed, a recruitment plan goes into play. There may be intense competition for qualified people to fill certain positions, so classic methods must be supplemented by creative approaches. What methods does the group use? Recognizing that the Internet has totally revolutionized ways to recruit, is the practice maximizing all possible computer-based recruiting? At the same time, traditional methods such as internal posting remain necessary and useful. What works best for the practice? Once recruitment is successful, how is selection handled? Is there an orientation plan in place for both clinical and nonclinical staff? Answer these questions to find out how the group is doing in the area of recruitment and retention.

01.A Recruitment Sources and Techniques

Note all the sources used to recruit clinical and nonclinical staff.

Check all that apply	Source	Circle one	Describe action needed
	Clinical schools' placement and alumni offices	Effective Not Effective	
	Professional associations and publications	Effective Not Effective	
	Job-listing websites featuring healthcare positions	Effective Not Effective	
	Job posting on internal website and bulletin boards	Effective Not Effective	
	Employee referral program with incentives	Effective Not Effective	
	Clinical-specific employment/recruitment services and headhunters	Effective Not Effective	
	Physician referrals	Effective Not Effective	
	Local schools	Effective Not Effective	

Check all that apply	Source	Circle one	Describe action needed
	Walk-ins and write-ins	Effective Not Effective	
	Intern programs	Effective Not Effective	
	Temporary staffing/ employment agencies and recruiters	Effective Not Effective	
	Health and other job fairs	Effective Not Effective	
	Advertisements in healthcare publications	Effective Not Effective	
	Local newspapers, flyers, and bulletin boards	Effective Not Effective	
	Patients and vendors	Effective Not Effective	
	Other:	Effective Not Effective	

Specify top recruiting challenges in the Supplemental Notes worksheet.

01.B Meeting Skill Mix and Staff Needs

Check all the techniques that are in place to ensure recruitment is targeted to the skills and staff needed to fit the group and culture.

Check all that apply	Technique	Circle one	Describe action needed
	There is a recruiting general plan plus specifics for each position.	Effective Not Effective	
	There is a recruiting budget for clinical and nonclinical staff.	Effective Not Effective	
	Bonuses, finder's fees, and other incentives such as tuition reimbursement are included in the budget.	Effective Not Effective	
	Skill-set requirements are specified for each position including required competencies.	Effective Not Effective	
	Culture-match requirements are specified for clinical and nonclinical staff.	Effective Not Effective	
	Completion dates are specified for each recruited position.	Effective Not Effective	
	Responsibilities and assignments are specified for each phase of recruitment and each type of position.	Effective Not Effective	
	Interview question and rating forms are developed for each position and used by a team of interviewers.	Effective Not Effective	

Check all that apply	Technique	Circle one	Describe action needed
	Orientation topics are noted in the interview such as group mission, vision, goals, culture, and physician/ staff performance management.	Effective Not Effective	
	Other:	Effective Not Effective	

01.C Customer- and Patient-Focused Skills

Check all processes used to ensure emphasis on customer service during recruiting, selection, and hiring.

Check all that apply	Process	Circle one	Describe action needed
	The recruitment plan is focused on customer service by incorporating leaders' customer service expectations.	Effective Not Effective	
	Interview methods are used to elicit candidate attitudes and skills related to customer care.	Effective Not Effective	
	Candidates are asked to discuss their approach to customer–patient interactions.	Effective Not Effective	
	Candidates are asked to tell a story about how they faced a customer-service challenge and gained customer satisfaction.	Effective Not Effective	
	Candidates are requested to discuss their approach to customer–staff interactions as part of an effective team.	Effective Not Effective	
	Other:	Effective Not Effective	

01.D Job Scopes and Job Descriptions

What methods are used to define job scopes and job descriptions?

Check all that apply	Method	Circle one	Describe action needed
	The job scope is identified to include what interpersonal relationships are involved, difficulty level, and the impact of error as well as essential functions and responsibilities.	Effective Not Effective	
	A variety of job analysis methods are used to identify work performed; required work traits; and how work relates to data, people, and things.	Effective Not Effective	
	Job analysis results are verified by pertinent supervisors and department managers.	Effective Not Effective	
	A consultant(s) is used to help with job classification and job analysis.	Effective Not Effective	
	Other:	Effective Not Effective	

What methods are used to develop job descriptions?

Check all that apply	Method	Circle one	Describe action needed
	Verified job analysis results are used as a basis for descriptions.	Effective Not Effective	
	A standard format is used.	Effective Not Effective	
	The description is begun with the job title and a general summary of duties.	Effective Not Effective	
	Details are provided on supervision, relationships, physical demands, working conditions, equipment used, and essential and marginal functions.	Effective Not Effective	
	Qualifications are specified including knowledge, skills, abilities, education, experience, and requirements such as licensure and/or certification.	Effective Not Effective	
	Draft descriptions are reviewed and approved by job holders, supervisors, department heads, and the management team.	Effective Not Effective	
	Other:	Effective Not Effective	

01.E Interviewing Skills

Check all techniques that are used to ensure interviews gather necessary information and meet regulatory requirements.

Check all that apply	Technique	Circle one	Describe action needed
	More than one interviewer is used to facilitate effective gathering of information and comparison to eliminate potential bias.	Effective Not Effective	
	Effective interviewing is ensured by training interviewers on their role and the need for self-awareness in interview-acceptable behavior, and management of the process.	Effective Not Effective	
	Interviewers are provided with thorough information on position requirements and information vital for hiring decisions.	Effective Not Effective	
	Interviewers are trained on potential regulatory problems regarding religion, race, arrest record, birthdates, health, disability, and so on.	Effective Not Effective	
	Appropriate interview methods are used for each situation such as screening, one-on-one, group, situational, or search committee.	Effective Not Effective	
	Legally approved application forms are provided for applicants to complete, and they are used by HR and supervisors to identify whom to interview.	Effective Not Effective	

Check all that apply	Technique	Circle one	Describe action needed
	Applications are used along with standardized interview forms to gather information during interviews.	Effective Not Effective	
	Tests are administered as appropriate such as written (aptitude, proficiency, personality, security, integrity) and performance.	Effective Not Effective	
	A ranking form is used with each applicant for comparison purposes and as documentation if an unfair hiring practice complaint is filed.	Effective Not Effective	
	Other:	Effective Not Effective	

01.F Selection Process

What methods are used to ensure the best-possible hiring decisions?

Check all that apply	Method	Circle one	Describe action needed
	All candidates are asked to sign a consent for reference section on the application form and for background, criminal investigation, and credit checks.	Effective Not Effective	
	Interviewers are asked to identify three to five top candidates and to consider any EEO, ADA, or other legal requirements.	Effective Not Effective	
	HR staff is asked to deal with pre-employment steps such as confirming education and handling background, criminal, and credit checks.	Effective Not Effective	
	HR staff and/or the hiring manager are asked to conduct reference checks using standardized forms and are trained on specific protocols.	Effective Not Effective	
	All information is compiled and discussed by an HR specialist and hiring manager to reach selection recommendations in rank order.	Effective Not Effective	
	The person who is authorized to make an offer makes a brief call to the top candidate to ascertain interest. If that candidate is not interested, others are contacted as necessary.	Effective Not Effective	

Check all that apply	Method	Circle one	Describe action needed
	A written offer of employment is reviewed to eliminate unwanted contractual obligations and to note any contingencies such as a health exam.	Effective Not Effective	
	On acceptance of offer, a welcoming/orientation (probation) plan is put in place to introduce the new employee to practice staff, facilities, history, and culture.	Effective Not Effective	
	Other:	Effective Not Effective	

TASK 02: MANAGE THE RETENTION OF CLINICAL AND NONCLINICAL STAFF

After staff members have been selected, an equally important and unending task begins: motivating people so carefully chosen to stay with the practice and to perform successfully. Practice policies related to compensation, discrimination, safety and security, continuing education, performance, and discipline all affect how staff members rate the organization as a place to work. Does the practice's culture engage employees?

Are there processes in place to prevent and resolve any conflicts quickly? Is the compensation plan fair? If competitors offer more attractive rewards and incentives or promotions and options, or if the policies seem out of date and inflexible, turnover will skyrocket. How is turnover analyzed? Are records kept on personnel matters? Is a labor relations strategy in place? Is employee satisfaction surveyed and how? Is there assistance for employees with personal problems? Most important, interpersonal relationships – how people are treated by supervisors and coworkers – will swing the balance between staying and leaving. A carefully structured orientation program begun in the welcoming meeting and continuing throughout the early months of employment leads the way to retention and successful performance.

02.A Employee Motivation, Teamwork, and Performance

Check all the methods used to establish a culture that promotes employee engagement and encourages top performers to stay.

Check all that apply	Method	Circle one	Describe action needed
	Management recognizes the correlation between employee engagement and productivity.	Effective Not Effective	
	Policies are developed and updated, including competitive pay and benefit plans, in line with current trends and with consideration given to employee expectations.	Effective Not Effective	
	Resources, such as equipment, materials, and workspace, as well as training, are provided so employees can do their jobs well and be successful.	Effective Not Effective	
	The organization's mission, vision, and performance expectations are communicated at orientation and regularly thereafter.	Effective Not Effective	
	Employee-specific rewards and incentives such as thank-yous, cards, tickets, and so on are provided by supervisors to show appreciation.	Effective Not Effective	
	Continuing education is provided to ensure job competency and to prepare for career opportunities.	Effective Not Effective	
	Other:	Effective Not Effective	

02.B Healthy Workplace, Conflict Resolution, and Grievance Processes

Note the policies and practices that are in place covering safety and security issues and conflict.

Check all that apply	Policy/Practice	Circle one	Describe action needed
	Compliance with OSHA regulation is ensured via manager and employee training, posting information, and establishing a safety committee	Effective Not Effective	
	Policies are in place to prevent health hazards and injuries in the workplace such as back problems caused by improper lifting, and related training is provided.	Effective Not Effective	
	Possible exposure to disease-related hazards such as bloodborne pathogens are prevented with safety equipment and training.	Effective Not Effective	
	Compliance with workplace violence regulations as well as other employee security issues such as terrorism is covered in policies and training.	Effective Not Effective	
	Conflict resolution training is provided for supervisors and managers including role plays demonstrating proven strategies and facilitation techniques.	Effective Not Effective	
	Workplace behavior is defined in a code of conduct and communicated at orientation and regularly thereafter to everyone in the organization.	Effective Not Effective	

Check all that apply	Policy/Practice	Circle one	Describe action needed
	A formal, documented, and legally approved grievance process is provided to resolve employee discontent and improve morale and productivity.	Effective Not Effective	
	The grievance process is focused on defining the grievance and taking specific procedural steps with a third party such as setting time limits and behaviors for the employee.	Effective Not Effective	
	Other:	Effective Not Effective	

02.C Employee Turnover and Improvement Strategies

What analysis mechanisms are used related to the turnover rate?

Check all that apply	Mechanism	Circle one	Describe action needed
	The turnover rates and trends are tracked by time period and job position.	Effective Not Effective	
	Practice turnover rates are compared with industry survey report data on turnover (MGMA, specialty-specific society, other).	Effective Not Effective	
	Discussion and analysis are initiated if group rates do not match or exceed the median to help determine reasons.	Effective Not Effective	
	An employee satisfaction survey and other possible measurement techniques are used.	Effective Not Effective	
	A hypothesis is developed on key reasons and related improvement strategies.	Effective Not Effective	
	Other:	Effective Not Effective	

02.D Employee Satisfaction Surveys

What methods are used to measure employee satisfaction?

Check all that apply	Method	Circle one	Describe action needed
	Exit interview surveys are conducted and the results are analyzed by management.	Effective Not Effective	
	Trends are analyzed related to reasons for employees' decisions to leave, adequacy of rewards, training, compensation, and management concerns.	Effective Not Effective	
	Hypotheses are developed regarding employee likes and dislikes, work processes, and interpersonal relationships.	Effective Not Effective	
	Pros and cons of the employee satisfaction survey are discussed by HR and management to prevent unrealistic expectations.	Effective Not Effective	
	Employees are surveyed regarding compensation, scheduling, training, relationships, and culture.	Effective Not Effective	
	Survey results are analyzed by management and improvement strategies are developed.	Effective Not Effective	
	Survey results and improvement strategies are communicated to all employees and implemented in accordance with the report.	Effective Not Effective	
	Other:	Effective Not Effective	

02.E Employee Assistance Program

Note if an employee assistance program (EAP) is in place in the following ways.

Check all that apply	Method	Circle one	Describe action needed
	An EAP is offered to help employees address personal issues that may affect performance.	Effective Not Effective	
	An EAP is emphasized to management as a way to reduce employee risks, recruitment costs, and increase employee productivity.	Effective Not Effective	
	An EAP is built into the benefits plan as an income-equivalent payment to improve the quality of life.	Effective Not Effective	
	An EAP is communicated and promoted to employees as confidential, third-party counseling and work-life service.	Effective Not Effective	
	Other:	Effective Not Effective	

02.F Personnel Record-Keeping

Check all methods used for employee record-keeping.

Check all that apply	Method	Circle one	Describe action needed
	Employee data is documented and retained for legal, research, and management/employee report purposes.	Effective Not Effective	
	Staff meetings and in-services are documented to record attendance and information provided.	Effective Not Effective	
	There is compliance with government reporting laws related to labor relations, health and safety, benefits, civil rights, ADA, pay, age, and immigrant status.	Effective Not Effective	
	There is compliance with requirements to keep certain documents separate from employee files.	Effective Not Effective	
	A policy is developed and implemented specifying access and confidentiality of personnel documents and protecting employee privacy.	Effective Not Effective	
	There is a designated person for personnel record-keeping, reporting, and record retention.	Effective Not Effective	
	There is a designated person who is expected to provide reports to government agencies and management and to facilitate discussion on trends and challenges.	Effective Not Effective	
	Other:	Effective Not Effective	

02.G Labor Relations

Check all methods used to educate about and deal with labor relations.

Check all that apply	Method	Circle one	Describe action needed
	Education and information are provided to management about labor laws such as the Taft–Hartley Act regarding the right to unionize, strike, and picket.	Effective Not Effective	
	Legal counsel familiar with labor law is used for education and for dealing with labor issues.	Effective Not Effective	
	If currently unionized, policies are in place to comply with laws and to communicate and negotiate with union representatives.	Effective Not Effective	
	If not unionized, mechanisms are in place to address local and industry union activities, organizing tactics and targets, and employer legal rights.	Effective Not Effective	
	An alert system is in place to identify early warning signals of union involvement.	Effective Not Effective	
	A preventive program is established to reduce the possibility of unionization including competitive wages, updated employee policies, and participation.	Effective Not Effective	
	Other:	Effective Not Effective	

TASK 03: DEVELOP AND MONITOR AN EFFECTIVE STAFFING STRATEGY

In these changing times, relying on traditional staffing patterns and practices is folly. Shifting technologies, government regulations, healthcare trends, integration with larger systems, and creating ancillary services all demand a different way of looking at staffing. How does the group identify and analyze staffing needs related to the many roles in the practice? Is a job classification system in place? How does the group correlate numbers of staff needed with skills needed? Is there enough workspace, and is it appropriate? Is benchmark data considered for effective staffing? Most importantly, a staffing plan must match the group's strategic plan and its focus on vision and the future.

03.A Staffing Needs and Expectations

Note the methods used to build a staffing plan.

Check all that apply	Method	Circle one	Describe action needed
	The strategic plan and operating budget serve as the basis for gathering information about physician–owner expectations related to staffing.	Effective Not Effective	
	The staffing plan incorporates needs related to service types, patient acuity, and operation hours.	Effective Not Effective	
	Industry data (MGMA, specialty society, other) are used related to staffing levels per FTE physician for multispecialty (5.06–5.79), general surgery (2.86), and so on.	Effective Not Effective	
	Variables related to ancillary services, physician needs and preferences, workflow, and other factors are considered.	Effective Not Effective	
	The impact of technology to reduce or increase the number and type of staff needed is taken into consideration.	Effective Not Effective	
	Other:	Effective Not Effective	

03.B Physician and Staff Roles

Check the ways in which realistic pictures of physician and staff roles are captured.

Check all that apply	Method	Circle one	Describe action needed
	Data about all the roles played by physicians are gathered through observation and research as well as self-reporting.	Effective Not Effective	
	Data about all the roles played by staff members are gathered through observation and research as well as self-reporting.	Effective Not Effective	
	Research is conducted via industry data (MGMA, specialty society, etc.) to ascertain current as well as future roles of physicians and staff.	Effective Not Effective	
	Findings are integrated into a comprehensive staffing plan of realities related to multiple roles played, often beyond job descriptions.	Effective Not Effective	
	A widespread review of how the team works together to support medical care, service to patients, and EHR usage is conducted.	Effective Not Effective	
	Other:	Effective Not Effective	

03.C Job Classification

How are job classification systems used to facilitate staffing planning?

Check all that apply	Method	Circle one	Describe action needed
	A job classification process is used to group jobs together for use in planning, recruiting, training, paying, and staffing.	Effective Not Effective	
	Job/position analysis methods are used to gather and update current, realistic information about each position.	Effective Not Effective	
	Job descriptions are reviewed and updated by those performing the positions including physicians handling both clinical and administrative duties.	Effective Not Effective	
	A review by department managers and senior managers is conducted to ensure the staffing plan considers working conditions and customer needs.	Effective Not Effective	
	Other:	Effective Not Effective	

03.D Staff Mix of Skills

Check those processes that are in place to integrate the skill mix needed into the staffing plan.

Check all that apply	Process	Circle one	Describe action needed
	The staffing plan considers the types of skills needed for the number of locations and hours of operation for scheduling purposes.	Effective Not Effective	
	The staffing plan includes cross training (especially for administrative staff) to maximize the skill mix.	Effective Not Effective	
	The plan is in line with the numbers and the skill mix needed, both currently and in the immediate future for recruiting and training purposes.	Effective Not Effective	
	The mix takes into account clinical and administrative needs as well as meeting customer service expectations.	Effective Not Effective	
	Other:	Effective Not Effective	

03.E Workspace and Staffing Levels

What methods are used to correlate space planning with staffing planning?

Check all that apply	Method	Circle one	Describe action needed
	An analysis of workspace is conducted in terms of its impact on staffing levels.	Effective Not Effective	
	Workspace needs such as optimal work flow, technology requirements, flexibility, safety, and visibility are balanced with staffing levels.	Effective Not Effective	
	Current trends and customer expectations related to office and exam space such as optimal communication, confidentiality, and accessibility are considered.	Effective Not Effective	
	The size of the workspace is adjusted in line with the staffing level, allowing for flexibility and growth and in consideration of achieving group goals.	Effective Not Effective	
	Other:	Effective Not Effective	

03.F Benchmark Data

Check the methods in which benchmark data are gathered and used to build the staffing plan.

Check all that apply	Method	Circle one	Describe action needed
	Benchmark data are compiled from various industry sources (MGMA, specialty society, other).	Effective Not Effective	
	Data are used to compare current group policies with competitive information to determine trends and impacts on staffing.	Effective Not Effective	
	The staffing plan is based on data related to numerous factors including specialty, ownership, practice size, and future plans.	Effective Not Effective	
	Benchmark data are broken down by types of personnel needed to ensure an appropriate mix of skills needed for physician support.	Effective Not Effective	
	Other:	Effective Not Effective	

TASK 04: DEVELOP, IMPLEMENT, AND EVALUATE PERFORMANCE MANAGEMENT PROGRAMS FOR CLINICAL AND NONCLINICAL STAFF

Managing performance expectations begins when interviewing top candidates by briefly conveying key elements of the group's performance-oriented culture. By the end of the formal orientation period, agreed-upon expectations with related measurements should be developed by each person and his or her manager. Policies developed by the board should cover the performance management process including review of the organization as a whole. Does the practice have performance standards, professional development plans, periodic reviews, and evaluation tools? Are there policies in place related to promotions and terminations? What are the processes used to manage performance and behavior? Is performance documentation maintained in personnel records? Does the group use systems, methods, and tools to facilitate performance success? The desired outcome: Performance evaluations celebrate success!

04.A Performance Management System

What steps are used to ensure performance-enhancing elements are included in the system?

Check all that apply	Step	Circle one	Describe action needed
	Orientation (probation) performance is evaluated and a decision is made about whether to retain the person.	Effective Not Effective	
	All individual performance plans are correlated with the medical practice's overall business and quality goals.	Effective Not Effective	
	Individual goals and objectives are agreed on by each person and manager, and responsibility for ongoing monitoring is emphasized.	Effective Not Effective	
	Goals are documented on a written performance planning form that directly correlates with the performance evaluation form.	Effective Not Effective	
	Language used on the forms is chosen from job descriptions in terms of essential functions as well as customer service, attitude, and teamwork.	Effective Not Effective	

Check all that apply	Step	Circle one	Describe action needed
	A formal performance review is scheduled annually, and informal reviews are scheduled periodically throughout the year, including ongoing improvement tips from the manager.	Effective Not Effective	
	Assessment of key clinical skills such as CPR recertification and nonclinical skills such as an EMR skill check are done annually.	Effective Not Effective	
	Performance rewards are built into the salary and incentive plan with critical attention on how and when raises are given.	Effective Not Effective	
	Employee development and career opportunity policies and plans are put in place and publicized to the staff.	Effective Not Effective	
	Performance information is reflected in disciplinary and termination policies.	Effective Not Effective	
	Other:	Effective Not Effective	

04.B Job Promotions

Note how job promotions are handled via policies and procedures.

Check all that apply	Method	Circle one	Describe action needed
	A promotion-from-within policy is in place to benefit employee morale, productivity, and retention and to decrease recruiting costs.	Effective Not Effective	
	Success elements are built into the program including merit pay, job posting, job bidding (if applicable), skills inventory, staff coordination, and employee development.	Effective Not Effective	
	A policy and program based on consideration of legal factors such as use of employee records, record-keeping, and possible discrimination is in place.	Effective Not Effective	
	Identification of possible candidates for promotion, transfer, training, and development opportunities is emphasized to supervisors.	Effective Not Effective	
	Other:	Effective Not Effective	

04.C Managing Performance and Behavior

What methods are used to manage and evaluate performance?

Check all that apply	Method	Circle one	Describe action needed
	Consideration is given to a variety of evaluation methods including critical incident rating, peer review, and criterion-based.	Effective Not Effective	
	The primary method chosen puts the emphasis on the performance of specific essential job functions and related goals.	Effective Not Effective	
	The primary method chosen also reflects general job-related factors and goals such as patient relations.	Effective Not Effective	
	Responsibility is put on the direct supervisor to observe behavior and performance, guide improvement, and evaluate.	Effective Not Effective	
	Individuals are encouraged to manage their own performance and self-assessment and to seek mentoring, training, and resources as needed.	Effective Not Effective	
	An employee code of conduct is communicated consistently to set performance expectations and prevent disciplinary issues.	Effective Not Effective	
	Other:	Effective Not Effective	

04.D Performance Documentation and Personnel Records

Note the steps that are taken to record performance-related information.

Check all that apply	Step	Circle one	Describe action needed
	Emphasis is given to ensuring employee files and records include documents pertinent to performance for management and legal reasons.	Effective Not Effective	
	The importance of record-keeping and carefully documented files is stressed to all levels of management as a means to prevent legal litigation.	Effective Not Effective	
	A checklist is used to ensure the employee file includes documents related to hiring, training, promotions and transfers, discipline, layoffs, and terminations.	Effective Not Effective	
	Clarity is provided regarding documentation needed about behavior and performance and if the employee's signature is needed on items such as critical incident reports and warnings.	Effective Not Effective	
	Other:	Effective Not Effective	

04.E Discipline and Termination

Check all methods used to handle discipline and termination.

Check all that apply	Method	Circle one	Describe action needed
	Policies are in place related to employee conduct, grievances and disputes, discipline, and employee termination.	Effective Not Effective	
	Managers are well trained on all aspects of employee discipline and separation including legal issues such as employment at will.	Effective Not Effective	
	Training is provided to ensure managers understand that disciplinary action is their own as well as HR's responsibility, including documentation.	Effective Not Effective	
	Responsibilities for resolving disciplinary issues are specified in the policy including their application to supervisors, managers, administrators, HR, and/ or union representatives.	Effective Not Effective	
	Grievance-handling methods such as conflict resolution, mediation, and arbitration are provided.	Effective Not Effective	
	Steps in progressive discipline are taught emphasizing corrective action steps administered in a fair, consistent, and timely manner.	Effective Not Effective	

Check all that apply	Method	Circle one	Describe action needed
	Training is provided on how and when to document corrective actions and when final corrective action or suspension steps are appropriate.	Effective Not Effective	
	Termination occurs after consultation with counsel and development of an action plan to avoid wrongful discharge issues.	Effective Not Effective	
	Immediate termination is initiated by gross misconduct such as threat of or actual physical or verbal abuse of patients or coworkers.	Effective Not Effective	
	All types of employee separation are covered in a termination policy including resignation, layoff, severance pay, and exit interviews.	Effective Not Effective	
	Other:	Effective Not Effective	

TASK 05: DEVELOP AND IMPLEMENT STAFF COMPENSATION AND BENEFIT PLANS

Research on motivating employees has long indicated that money remains a key motivator. Even though pay is never enough to attract and retain employees, competitive compensation is necessary. Then other factors such as culture, interpersonal relationships, management emphasis on information sharing, and support are added to provide "psychic" pay. Compensation, including benefits, demands considerable administrative attention. Is the group's administration efficient and effective? Are market data such as wage and salary surveys used when determining compensation? Is there a range of benefit plans? How does the practice evaluate insurance, retirement, and severance benefits? How does it ensure confidentiality? How is compensation for clinical staff handled? One clue: Working with pay and benefit consultants is an excellent step to ensure the practice is in line with contemporary standards.

05.A Market Data and Wage/Salary Strategy

What methods are used to gather wage and salary data?

Check all that apply	Method	Circle one	Describe action needed
	Education and market data are provided to the board as needed to inform about competitive compensation and determine if the practice is on target.	Effective Not Effective	
	Local market data on supply and demand, schools graduating potential candidates, the cost of living, and the economy are gathered by an HR specialist.	Effective Not Effective	
	Informal compensation data are acquired via recruiting interviews and discussions with current staff.	Effective Not Effective	
	Research is conducted by HR or the administrator on regional and national trends related to compensation.	Effective Not Effective	
	Benchmark data are acquired via review of government and industry surveys (MGMA compensation surveys, specialty-specific surveys, etc.).	Effective Not Effective	
	Other:	Effective Not Effective	

05.B Compensation and Benefit Administration

Note methods that are in place to administer all aspects of compensation.

Check all that apply	Method	Circle one	Describe action needed
	The complexity of compensation administration is recognized via board support for consultants, staff specialists, and others.	Effective Not Effective	
	Compensation administration is specified by leaders to include pay, benefits, incentives, and nonmonetary rewards.	Effective Not Effective	
	Staff, consultants, and others are assigned specific responsibility for clinical and nonclinical pay, benefits, regulations, and legal records and reports.	Effective Not Effective	
	The compensation plan and administration reports are regularly reviewed and approved by the board, especially regarding their financial implications.	Effective Not Effective	
	Education and information on compensation administration are provided to managers and employees at least annually.	Effective Not Effective	
	Other:	Effective Not Effective	

05.C Retirement Benefit Plans

Check all types of retirement benefit plans offered.

Check all that apply	Plan	Circle one	Describe action needed
	Defined benefits	Effective Not Effective	
	Defined contribution	Effective Not Effective	
	401(k)	Effective Not Effective	
	403(b)	Effective Not Effective	
	Self-directed	Effective Not Effective	
	Employer-directed	Effective Not Effective	
	Profit-sharing	Effective Not Effective	
	Pension	Effective Not Effective	
	Other:	Effective Not Effective	

What methods are used to ensure effective administration of the plans?

Check all that apply	Method	Circle one	Describe action needed
	Consultant(s)	Effective Not Effective	
	Third-party administrator	Effective Not Effective	
	Compliance reporting	Effective Not Effective	
	Legal documents	Effective Not Effective	
	Investment management	Effective Not Effective	
	Management of contributions, distributions, and new participant paperwork	Effective Not Effective	
	Plan monitoring and review	Effective Not Effective	
	Other:	Effective Not Effective	

05.D Insurance, Retirement, and Severance Benefits

Check all types of insurance, retirement, and severance benefits that are offered.

Check all that apply	Benefit	Circle one	Describe action needed
	Health	Effective Not Effective	
	Disability, long term	Effective Not Effective	
	Disability, short term	Effective Not Effective	
	Dental	Effective Not Effective	
	Vision and hearing	Effective Not Effective	
	Post-retirement medical benefits	Effective Not Effective	
	Long-term care	Effective Not Effective	
	Life, AD&D	Effective Not Effective	
	Severance	Effective Not Effective	
	Other:	Effective Not Effective	

What severance pay policy factors determine the level of severance pay?

Check all that apply	Factor	Circle one	Describe action needed
	Employment status (full time vs. part time)	Effective Not Effective	
	Employee class (exempt vs. nonexempt, management vs. employee)	Effective Not Effective	
	Years of service	Effective Not Effective	
	Other:	Effective Not Effective	

05.E Confidentiality of Compensation Data

Note ways in which confidentiality is ensured.

Check all that apply	Method	Circle one	Describe action needed
	Confidentiality is covered in the compensation policy including whether it is open or closed as related to sharing pay grades and ranges.	Effective Not Effective	
	Wage and salary information is limited to those who have a need to know.	Effective Not Effective	
	Physicians and staff are encouraged to maintain confidentiality regarding pay and income.	Effective Not Effective	
	Salary increase information such as cost-of-living increases and bonus distribution is provided to all staff at the same time when appropriate.	Effective Not Effective	
	Individual salary increase information is provided on an individual, private basis at an appropriate time such as at a performance evaluation or promotion.	Effective Not Effective	
	Other:	Effective Not Effective	

05.F Clinical Staff Compensation

Note ways in which medical provider – including physician – compensation is handled.

Check all that apply	Method	Circle one	Describe action needed
	The clinician compensation structure is set to reflect the practice's culture, history, legal requirements and structure, costs, external influences, goals, and recruiting and retention needs.	Effective Not Effective	
	Provider knowledge and skills are taken into account such as years of training, years of experience, specialty, and dual board certification.	Effective Not Effective	
	Productivity is rewarded consistent with the practice's mission, values, and goals.	Effective Not Effective	
	Provider compensation is communicated in simple, understandable, legally approved language.	Effective Not Effective	
	Equity ownership is offered to physicians in stock options or direct ownership.	Effective Not Effective	
	Physicians are encouraged to plan for retirement and wealth accumulation via financial planning.	Effective Not Effective	
	Other:	Effective Not Effective	

TASK 06: PROVIDE SYSTEMS, PROCESSES, AND STRUCTURE FOR ADMINISTRATIVE AND CLINICAL TRAINING FOR MEDICAL PROVIDERS, EMPLOYEES, AND STUDENTS

Continuing education via various vehicles is essential for a medical practice to become and remain successful. Clinical and nonclinical staff expect professional development through education and training, which may lead to career opportunities. Training is a costly yet vital investment; the lack of training generates its own costs in lost productivity and errors. How does the practice foster a culture of learning and professional development? Who oversees training? Are training programs effective? How does the practice deal with the time and budget investments necessary for training? Note: Professionals well versed in adult learning techniques are critical to achieve desired outcomes from training.

06. A Culture of Learning and Professional Development

What methods are used to help clinical and nonclinical staff stay current with change?

Check all that apply	Method	Circle one	Describe action needed
	The philosophy stated by leadership specifies ongoing learning as a key value, reinforced by actions related to such items as budget and time available.	Effective Not Effective	
	Commitment to the value of continuing education for competitiveness in recruiting and retention is reflected in internal and external messages.	Effective Not Effective	
	Future plans for the group are built on an expectation of a solid foundation of human-capital knowledge to better perform current and future jobs.	Effective Not Effective	
	There is an awareness of and focus on electronic technology to allow for different learning styles, best use of time, and flexibility.	Effective Not Effective	
	Other:	Effective Not Effective	

06.B Training Oversight

Note methods used to oversee every type of training for every type of staff.

Check all that apply	Method	Circle one	Describe action needed
	Education and license/ certification requirements are specified in job descriptions.	Effective Not Effective	
	There is an overall annual education plan in place.	Effective Not Effective	
	Training is categorized by orientation, supervisory and management, technical skills, career development, certification, and cross training.	Effective Not Effective	
	A formal orientation program is mandated for all new hires to provide comprehensive, consistent introduction to the group and their jobs.	Effective Not Effective	
	Department managers are charged with responsibility for ensuring proficiency via acquisition of new knowledge and maintenance of skills.	Effective Not Effective	
	Other:	Effective Not Effective	

06.C Training Program Array

Check all the methods that are used to provide training.

Check all that apply	Method	Circle one	Describe action needed
	Training effectiveness is promoted by providing a variety of training options to help ensure a positive environment for learning.	Effective Not Effective	
	Management staff is educated on effective on-the-job training techniques and participates in train-the-trainer courses.	Effective Not Effective	
	Electronic media such as video and audiotapes, computer media including software, and online resources are used to gain new knowledge and skills.	Effective Not Effective	
	Interactive hands-on training in a "skills lab" is provided to build certain skills, both technical and customer service.	Effective Not Effective	
	Workshops, group discussions, lectures, and role playing are offered as options as well as outsourced training and outside conferences.	Effective Not Effective	
	Books, journal subscriptions, and online website access are provided as part of the professional development plan.	Effective Not Effective	
	Other:	Effective Not Effective	

06.D Adult Learning Styles

Note how adult learning styles are taken into account.

Check all that apply	Method	Circle one	Describe action needed
	Training is based on adult styles of learning and provided in challenging, productive, self-guided ways.	Effective Not Effective	
	Learning by doing is emphasized via on-the-job training, role plays, and simulations.	Effective Not Effective	
	Education is built on didactic techniques including lesson plans, reading and homework assignments, class interactions, feedback, and skill testing.	Effective Not Effective	
	Mentoring and coaching is provided by carefully chosen exceptional performers trained in supportive techniques.	Effective Not Effective	
	Technology is maximized to facilitate self-directed learning.	Effective Not Effective	
	A variety of group interaction options is offered including forums, small groups, games and exercises, and online workshops with dialog.	Effective Not Effective	
	Other:	Effective Not Effective	

06.E Training Policies and Procedures

What items are covered in the training policy?

Check all that apply	Item	Circle one	Describe action needed
	Training budget	Effective Not Effective	
	Training plan for both clinical and nonclinical staff	Effective Not Effective	
	Specific and general training	Effective Not Effective	
	Time off for training	Effective Not Effective	
	Mandatory and optional training	Effective Not Effective	
	Paid attendance	Effective Not Effective	
	Continuing education requirements for professional and licensed staff	Effective Not Effective	
	Frequency of training	Effective Not Effective	
	Staff requirements such as qualifications, time availability, and so on	Effective Not Effective	
	Other:	Effective Not Effective	

TASK 07: ESTABLISH SYSTEMS AND PROCESSES FOR AWARENESS, EDUCATION, AND COMPLIANCE WITH EMPLOYMENT LAWS AND REGULATORY STANDARDS

Like all organizations, medical practices are subject to universally applied employment laws and regulatory standards. In addition, there are some laws that target the healthcare industry. Failure to comply imposes severe penalties. Does the group have an updated employee handbook? How is education related to laws and regulations handled? How does the practice ensure compliance with laws and regulations ranging from the Civil Rights Act to the Equal Pay Act to Affirmative Action? These responsibilities are ongoing and serious. In particular, supervisors must receive ongoing training about their responsibilities related to these legal matters.

07.A Employee Handbook

Check all items related to handbook administration.

Check all that apply	Item	Circle one	Describe action needed
	The employee handbook is distributed and discussed at orientation and updated at least annually.	Effective Not Effective	
	Simplified versions of key, complex HR policies are presented in the handbook to facilitate communication.	Effective Not Effective	
	An introduction and welcoming statement is featured at the front of the handbook.	Effective Not Effective	
	The practice's mission, vision, values statements, and employee code of conduct are included in the handbook.	Effective Not Effective	
	Key HR policies are summarized such as pay administration, time off, leave time, and safety and health, with referral to the HR specialist for more detail.	Effective Not Effective	

Check all that apply	Item	Circle one	Describe action needed
	The practice's Equal Employment Opportunity/Affirmative Action statement is included.	Effective Not Effective	
	An employment-at-will statement and signature sheet are included.	Effective Not Effective	
	The employee's rights and responsibilities are stated.	Effective Not Effective	
	Employee benefits services such as an EAP, flu shots, and professional development are outlined.	Effective Not Effective	
	A handbook receipt signature form is included.	Effective Not Effective	
	Other:	Effective Not Effective	

07.B Staff Education and Training on Legal Matters

What methods are used to ensure employees are knowledgeable about laws and regulations?

Check all that apply	Method	Circle one	Describe action needed
	The required U.S. Department of Labor, state, and other government posters are posted on employee bulletin boards.	Effective Not Effective	
	Key laws specifically related to healthcare jobs such as OSHA and Health Insurance Portability and Accountability Act (HIPAA) are stressed during orientation and ongoing training.	Effective Not Effective	
	Printed materials from the Department of Labor and other sources are made available.	Effective Not Effective	
	Immediate education and training are provided to supervisors and all staff when new laws, regulations, or updates are issued.	Effective Not Effective	
	Lawyers and consultants are used as needed to educate senior management and supervisors on mandates, compliance, documentation, and reporting.	Effective Not Effective	

Check all that apply	Method	Circle one	Describe action needed
	Leaders are educated on the range of laws: wages and benefits, safety and health, sexual orientation, employment at will, and discrimination.	Effective Not Effective	
	Emphasis is on record-keeping and reporting as well as professional licensure and certification requirements.	Effective Not Effective	
	Other:	Effective Not Effective	

07.C Compliance with Laws

Check off all laws and regulations that are covered in the training and information provided AND with which the practice is compliant.

Check all that apply	Law/Regulation	Circle one	Describe action needed
	Fair Labor Standards Act (FLSA), regulating such employment matters as hours of work, overtime	Effective Not Effective	
	Americans with Disabilities Act (ADA), ensuring equal employment opportunities, nondiscrimination, accommodations	Effective Not Effective	
	Family and Medical Leave Act (FMLA), providing unpaid, job-protected leave up to 13 weeks to eligible employees	Effective Not Effective	
	Occupational Safety and Health Act, protecting employees from harm on the job	Effective Not Effective	
	Civil Rights Act, specifying nondiscrimination due to race, age, color, gender, national origin, religion, and related affirmative action	Effective Not Effective	
	Immigration Reform and Control Act, controlling unauthorized U.S. immigration including employer sanctions and penalties	Effective Not Effective	
	National Labor Relations Act, specifying the right of workers to join unions without management retaliation	Effective Not Effective	

Check all that apply	Law/Regulation	Circle one	Describe action needed
	Equal Pay Act, prohibiting sex-based pay discrimination	Effective Not Effective	
	Age Discrimination in Employment Act, prohibiting employment discrimination against people age 40 years and older	Effective Not Effective	
	Vocational Rehabilitation Act, promoting rehabilitation for injured veterans including job training and opportunities	Effective Not Effective	
	Vietnam Era Veterans' Readjustment Assistance Act, requiring federal contractors to provide equal job opportunity for Vietnam veterans	Effective Not Effective	
	Pregnancy Discrimination Act, preventing discriminatory acts related to pregnancy, childbirth, and related medical conditions	Effective Not Effective	
	Other:	Effective Not Effective	

TASK 08: PROVIDE PERSONAL COMMITMENT TO ENHANCE KNOWLEDGE, SKILLS, AND ABILITIES IN HEALTHCARE ADMINISTRATION

"Growing" oneself in knowledge, skills, and abilities remains a forever task for all administrators for professional, career, and personal reasons. Medical practice administrators exist in an ever-changing, challenging environment where the "need to know" about what's happening in their world is primary for the survival and success of themselves and their practices. How are management, leadership, and interpersonal skills enhanced? What types of continuous learning are used? In what ways are ethical standards, behavior, and decision making portrayed? Are written and presentation skills up to date? Are time and stress management skills effective? How are self-confidence and integrity displayed? It is up to the practice administrator to acquire the skills needed to deal with the heavy-duty responsibilities of the job and work with leadership to respond to change in ways that are economical, affordable, and compliant.

08.A Management/Leadership Skill Development

What methods are used to enhance team performance and effectiveness?

Check all that apply	Method	Circle one	Describe action needed
	Administrator leadership is measured by effective relationships with the board and clinical/nonclinical staff and the goals achieved.	Effective Not Effective	
	The administrator emphasizes teamwork via regular discussions with all managers to build knowledge and skills.	Effective Not Effective	
	Frank discussion is used to communicate when the administrator must be the leader vs. one of the team.	Effective Not Effective	
	Interpersonal skills are demonstrated by the administrator to enhance group performance.	Effective Not Effective	
	Other:	Effective Not Effective	

08.B Continuous Learning

Check all of the ways you acquire advanced professional knowledge.

Check all that apply	Method	Circle one	Describe action needed
	The administrator sets personal goals for career and professional development.	Effective Not Effective	
	The administrator schedules time and develops a budget to accomplish goals.	Effective Not Effective	
	The administrator joins and participates in professional and business associations and community organizations.	Effective Not Effective	
	The administrator networks and develops relationships with others in the industry.	Effective Not Effective	
	The administrator reads industry, business, and consumer publications and uses other resources to stay current with changes.	Effective Not Effective	
	The administrator uses Internet resources such as reliable websites to access sources of specific, credible knowledge.	Effective Not Effective	
	The administrator enrolls in on-site or online advanced education courses or degree programs at colleges and universities.	Effective Not Effective	

Check all that apply	Method	Circle one	Describe action needed
	The administrator participates in professional certification programs to demonstrate a commitment to professionalism and leadership.	Effective Not Effective	
	Other:	Effective Not Effective	

08.C Ethics

What methods do you use to facilitate ethical standards, behavior, and decision making?

Check all that apply	Method	Circle one	Describe action needed
	Leadership is provided in the development of a code of ethics reflecting higher standards than technically correct legal or "right" actions.	Effective Not Effective	
	The administrator plays a key role in the communication of ethical standards throughout the organization.	Effective Not Effective	
	Enforcement and vigilance related to standards are demonstrated via monitoring and follow-through.	Effective Not Effective	
	Unethical behavior caused by policy or procedure conflicts between competing goals is prevented or eliminated (for example, inappropriate patient abandonment).	Effective Not Effective	
	Ethical behavior standards are adhered to every day with every duty and interaction.	Effective Not Effective	
	Other:	Effective Not Effective	

08.D Interpersonal Skills and Self-Awareness

Note ways in which you gain interpersonal skills and ensure self-awareness.

Check all that apply	Method	Circle one	Describe action needed
	Self- or other-administered tests are used to aid awareness of behavioral style and other personal characteristics.	Effective Not Effective	
	Informal feedback is sought from coworkers as well as family and friends on "how do you see me."	Effective Not Effective	
	A "know myself" picture is discussed with mentors and team to double-check self-awareness.	Effective Not Effective	
	Tests such as 360-degree evaluation and others are used to measure interaction effectiveness and team success.	Effective Not Effective	
	Interpersonal skill training courses are attended including role playing and feedback to/ from participants.	Effective Not Effective	
	Other:	Effective Not Effective	

08.E Communication Skills

Check the techniques and tools you use to ensure a high level of communication skills.

Check all that apply	Technique/Tool	Circle one	Describe action needed
	Courses on business writing communication skills are taken.	Effective Not Effective	
	Written communications are critiqued by instructors, certifiers, and editors on a regular basis.	Effective Not Effective	
	Public speaking courses are taken including voice training as necessary.	Effective Not Effective	
	Workshops on presentation tools and skills are taken including the use of technology such as Microsoft® PowerPoint, audio/videotapes, and a web-based presence.	Effective Not Effective	
	Speaking and presentation skills are practiced in "safe" situations such as local clubs and organizations.	Effective Not Effective	
	Use of presentation skills is planned before meetings and critiqued afterward by self or others.	Effective Not Effective	
	Communication skills training is offered to managers and staff and attended by the administrator to enhance the group's skill level.	Effective Not Effective	
	Other:	Effective Not Effective	

08.F Stress and Time Management

How do you ensure the best use of your time and reduce stress?

Check all that apply	Method	Circle one	Describe action needed
	Time management courses are taken and books are read to learn about key elements such as prioritizing, planning, and monitoring.	Effective Not Effective	
	Daily consideration is given to all aspects of time management including planning, allocating and scheduling, delegating, monitoring, and analysis.	Effective Not Effective	
	There is a balance between goals and roles vs. time and related urgencies.	Effective Not Effective	
	A variety of tools is used including clock, calendar, planner, and computer-assisted time-management devices.	Effective Not Effective	
	The impact of no or poor time management on stress is recognized and taken into account in planning.	Effective Not Effective	
	Stress management courses are taken and books are read to learn about psychological and physiological aspects.	Effective Not Effective	
	Skills are developed to sort out the range of stressors from unpredicted, external events and crises to everyday internal annoyances and to prioritize them accordingly.	Effective Not Effective	

Check all that apply	Method	Circle one	Describe action needed
	Coping skills are learned including preventive techniques such as worst-case planning scenarios, goal setting, and problem solving.	Effective Not Effective	
	Personal stress is acknowledged and dealt with through relaxation techniques, time outs, burnout analysis, and resolution of the matter.	Effective Not Effective	
	Stress and time management courses are offered to staff with participation by the administrator.	Effective Not Effective	
	Other:	Effective Not Effective	

08.G Self-Confidence and Personal Integrity

Note methods used to develop self-confidence and demonstrate personal integrity.

Check all that apply	Method	Circle one	Describe action needed
	Self-confidence is developed by taking steps to gain competence and experience on an ongoing basis.	Effective Not Effective	
	Self-confidence is maintained by staying current with changes to the healthcare world via continuing education and networking.	Effective Not Effective	
	Self-confidence is tested by taking well-orchestrated risks and learning what works or does not work and moving on.	Effective Not Effective	
	Personal integrity is based on acceptance of professional responsibility and a leadership role.	Effective Not Effective	
	Personal integrity is demonstrated through behavior: daily actions that are in line with the ethical code, and follow-through that is consistent. (In other words, "I do what I say.")	Effective Not Effective	
	Personal integrity is cemented by admission of mistakes and correction of missteps.	Effective Not Effective	
	Other:	Effective Not Effective	

BOTTOM LINE—HUMAN RESOURCE MANAGEMENT

People are the key resource of any medical group practice, thus human resource management is of highest importance to administrators. HR management today is concerned not only with traditional personnel functions such as recruiting and retention, but also with strategic planning, quality improvement, and performance management for clinical and nonclinical staff. Technology can help to build employee databases, enable training, and gather and report information required by the government. However, because HR is all about people, an understanding of human psychology and interpersonal skills is paramount.

Human Resource Management
Supplemental Notes
(copy as needed)

Task	Notes

Human Resource Management
Action Items
(copy as needed)

Task	Action	Responsible Party	Due Date	Priority

CHAPTER 4

Information Management

Information management is crucial to the successful operation of a practice. From computers to telephones to e-mail, society has become and will continue to be information driven. That change is significant to the practice of medicine. Patients, particularly younger patients who grew up in the information age, increasingly expect to be able to interact with their physician via electronic methods. Additionally, with reimbursements shrinking and costs rising, there is a need to focus on more effective and efficient ways to complete tasks and communicate. Technology has come a long way and advances will continue to occur. Practice administrators need to stay abreast of what's available and plan – both financially and operationally – to adopt new technologies. This chapter covers the multitude of means by which you communicate externally with patients, outside physicians, and other organizations, as well as internally within the practice. Do you have effective internal communication? What about a technology plan for your practice?

Technology is expensive. The practice's ability to realize the benefits and value from a successful implementation are limited if technology is not fully applied. Do you have a budget and implementation plans for major system upgrades such as computer and telephone systems? While practices have always been concerned with privacy, now patient privacy and security are legal requirements. Increasingly, the media reports about breaches and theft of confidential information. How secure are your systems? Practices also need to be concerned with day-to-day management of one of their most important systems: the medical record. How effective is the management of your practice's medical records? What about state and federal reporting? Are you knowledgeable? Are you compliant? Complete this section to determine how you measure up in the area of information management.

TASK 01: DEVELOP AND MAINTAIN APPROPRIATE INTERNAL COMMUNICATION PATHWAYS FOR CLINICAL AND NONCLINICAL STAFF

Practices need multiple means to communicate with patients, both receiving and sending. Internally, efficient methods are needed to exchange information. What methods do you use? Are they current technologies, or are you using old methods – ones that might be costing you in terms of productivity? Technology will never replace face-to-face communication. Meeting management is an important skill set for an administrator to possess. How do your skills rate? And how are the interpersonal communication skills of the providers and staff in your practice? What are you doing to facilitate development of those skills? Technology is interrelated. For instance, a practice might have a fantastic website, but patients and prospective patients can't find it because it is not optimized for search engines, or because the staff has not been trained and encouraged to drive patients to it. Or, a new information-on-hold service is adopted, but because of the way it is interfaced with the phone system, callers on hold can't hear it. Administrators need to understand the interrelationship of technologies. How well versed are you on the multitude of types of technology for practices? Answer these questions to find out how you're doing in the area of communication.

01.A Communications Systems for Patients

Note methods by which your practice and patients communicate back and forth.

Check all that apply	Method	Circle one	Describe action needed
	Mail (letters, postcards, patient statements, etc.)	Effective Not Effective	
	Telephone	Effective Not Effective	
	Voice mail	Effective Not Effective	
	Answering service	Effective Not Effective	

Check all that apply	Method	Circle one	Describe action needed
	Pager	Effective Not Effective	
	Cell phone	Effective Not Effective	
	Text	Effective Not Effective	
	Face to face	Effective Not Effective	
	Interpreters	Effective Not Effective	
	Recordings (audio/video, information-on-hold, educational videos, etc.)	Effective Not Effective	
	Fax	Effective Not Effective	
	Website	Effective Not Effective	

Check all that apply	Method	Circle one	Describe action needed
	E-mail	Effective Not Effective	
	Telemedicine	Effective Not Effective	
	Patient surveys	Effective Not Effective	
	Educational seminars	Effective Not Effective	
	Open house	Effective Not Effective	
	Automated test results system	Effective Not Effective	
	Kiosk	Effective Not Effective	
	Printed materials (post-op instructions, practice brochure, disease-specific flyers, etc.)	Effective Not Effective	
	Signage (disease/treatment posters, copay reminders, etc.)	Effective Not Effective	
	Other:	Effective Not Effective	

Mail Processing

Check all that apply	Method	Circle one	Describe action needed
	A postage meter is on site.	Effective Not Effective	
	Hospital or other mailroom services are provided.	Effective Not Effective	
	First-class stamps are purchased at the post office.	Effective Not Effective	
	First-class stamps are purchased online.	Effective Not Effective	
	Click-N-Ship services are used.	Effective Not Effective	
	Other:	Effective Not Effective	

Questions to consider	YES	NO If no, why not?	NOT APPLICABLE (note reason)
Is the postage meter up to date and in good working order?			
Is there a service agreement on file?			
Is service response time prompt?			
Is the hospital or other mailroom service timely?			
Are there minimal losses and delays through the hospital or other mailroom services?			
If stamps are purchased, are claims and statements produced and mailed through a clearinghouse or other service? (In other words, postage is not manually placed on statements and claims by practice staff.)			
Is an appropriate quantity of stamps maintained to ensure the expense is incurred in the period the stamps are used and to maximize efficiency by minimizing trips to the post office or time spent completing online purchasing?			
Is a sufficient quantity of postage consistently kept on hand to process mail promptly?			
Is return mail handled promptly?			

Telephone System

Questions to consider	YES	NO If no, why not?	NOT APPLICABLE (note reason)
Does the practice use a telephone system?			
Is the phone system up to date and in good working order?			
Is a service agreement in place?			
Is service response time prompt?			
Is the phone system integrated among all locations?			
Is there an appropriate number of incoming and outgoing lines?			
Is a line usage analysis conducted periodically?			
Is there an appropriate number of extensions?			

Questions to consider	YES	NO If no, why not?	NOT APPLICABLE (note reason)
Is there an automated attendant?			
Is there a minimal number of options for callers to choose from with minimal depth of branching?			
Is the frequency of call reasons sequential in options (for example, if an appointment request is the most frequent call, it is Option 1; if a prescription refill is the second most frequent call, it is Option 2)?			
Are options presented in a simple and straightforward manner?			
Is voice mail available for all users?			
Do callers receive information while on hold?			
Is there a dial-by-name directory?			
Is there a hunt feature?			

Questions to consider	YES	NO If no, why not?	NOT APPLICABLE (note reason)
Is there a transfer feature?			
Is there a call forwarding feature?			
Is there an intercom feature?			
Is there a paging feature?			
Are calls answered promptly, without excessive ringing?			
Is the staff properly trained to correctly and accurately route and respond to calls?			
Is voice mail handled throughout the day on a same-day basis with guidelines for timeliness (every two hours, once in the morning, and once in the afternoon, for example)?			
Are hold times reasonable and minimal?			

Fax System

Questions to consider	YES	NO If no, why not?	NOT APPLICABLE (note reason)
Is the fax server, including outgoing fax capability, available from the user's desktop workstation?			
Is the fax equipment up to date and in good working order?			
Is there a service agreement in place?			
Is service response time prompt?			
Are the fax capacity and speed sufficient?			
Are documents processed in a timely manner?			
Are patient-related faxes processed directly into the EHR?			
Do systems exist for handling confidential faxes?			

Answering System

Questions to consider	YES	NO If no, why not?	NOT APPLICABLE (note reason)
Is an answering service used when the practice is closed?			
Are callers automatically transferred to the answering service?			
Is the service cost effective?			
Is the service timely?			
Are messages received in a timely manner and tracked for resolution?			
Are messages accurate and complete?			
Are patient call-backs completed in a timely manner?			

Personal Devices

Questions to consider	YES	NO If no, why not?	NOT APPLICABLE (note reason)
Do the providers have digital pagers and/or cell phones?			
Are the cell phones "smart" phones?			
Are cell phone standards in place (type of phone, budget, plan, etc.)?			
Is there a policy of no family plans, or are providers required to pay for the family portion?			

Website

Questions to consider	YES	NO If no, why not?	NOT APPLICABLE (note reason)
Does the practice have a website?			
Is the website reviewed and updated on a regular basis?			

Does the website contain the following information?

Check all that apply	Item	Circle one	Describe action needed
	Providers and other clinicians	Effective Not Effective	
	Staff	Effective Not Effective	
	Telephone extensions	Effective Not Effective	
	Specialties	Effective Not Effective	
	Services	Effective Not Effective	
	Locations	Effective Not Effective	
	Directions	Effective Not Effective	
	Hours	Effective Not Effective	
	Insurance plans	Effective Not Effective	

Check all that apply	Item	Circle one	Describe action needed
	Pertinent office policies and procedures (both clinical and nonclinical)	Effective Not Effective	
	Patient education	Effective Not Effective	
	Clinical trials	Effective Not Effective	
	Current information about the practice	Effective Not Effective	
	Links to websites with related medical information	Effective Not Effective	
	Other:	Effective Not Effective	

Can patients contact the practice via the website in a secure, HIPAA-compliant manner to accomplish the following tasks?

Check all that apply	Task	Circle one	Describe action needed
	Schedule appointments and request appointment changes	Effective Not Effective	
	Request prescription refills (subject to practice protocols regarding refills)	Effective Not Effective	
	Request medical records (to the extent allowed by privacy regulations)	Effective Not Effective	
	Register	Effective Not Effective	
	Complete visit information (past medical, social, family history and/or history of present illness)	Effective Not Effective	
	Request referrals	Effective Not Effective	
	Ask medical questions	Effective Not Effective	
	Access diagnostic test results	Effective Not Effective	
	Print and acknowledge the Notice of Privacy Practices	Effective Not Effective	
	Other:	Effective Not Effective	

Questions to consider	YES	NO If no, why not?	NOT APPLICABLE (note reason)
Alternatively, can patients print medical records or request forms to mail to the practice?			
As a last option, can patients print registration forms to complete in advance of appointments?			
Are communications through the website secure?			
Are all communications through the website answered within 24 hours?			
Is there an automated system to obtain normal test results?			
Is the system cost effective?			
Is the system efficient?			
Are results of patient tests delivered in a timely manner?			
Is a system in place to determine which patients do not retrieve results?			

Patient Surveys

Questions to consider	YES	NO If no, why not?	NOT APPLICABLE (note reason)
Are patient surveys used to measure patient satisfaction on a regular basis?			
Are results benchmarked both internally and externally?			
Is action taken on results as needed?			
Are results reported to the appropriate internal departments and individuals (practice owners/administration/ board, staff, etc.)?			

Interpreters

Questions to consider	YES	NO If no, why not?	NOT APPLICABLE (note reason)
Are interpreters used as required by state and/or federal law?			
Are there adequate resources to obtain interpreters?			
Are rates reviewed to ensure they are competitive?			

Printed Materials

Questions to consider	YES	NO If no, why not?	NOT APPLICABLE (note reason)
Are printed materials current, complete, and accurate?			
Are printed materials professional in appearance?			
When medical in nature, is distribution of printed materials documented in the patient's chart?			
Is cost-effective pricing obtained?			
Are cost and benefit evaluated for all printed materials?			

Signage

Questions to consider	YES	NO If no, why not?	NOT APPLICABLE (note reason)
Is signage clear and understandable at an eighth-grade reading level?			
Are signs professional in appearance?			
Is excessive signage avoided?			

Patient Education

Questions to consider	YES	NO If no, why not?	NOT APPLICABLE (note reason)
Are educational seminars and open houses focused on topics of interest?			
Are education events held in locations that are easily accessed?			
Are education events held at convenient times?			
Are education events promoted in appropriate venues?			
Are education events well attended?			
Is a post-event evaluation completed?			
Does the evaluation include a cost–benefit analysis?			
Are educational recordings used in the office professional?			
If medical in nature, do recordings include necessary information?			
Are viewing and/or listening recorded in the patient's medical record?			

Telemedicine

Questions to consider	YES	NO If no, why not?	NOT APPLICABLE (note reason)
Is telemedicine used?			
Does the practice transmit and review images and/or monitor remote (home) devices (glucometers, blood pressure devices, etc.)?			
Is there adequate reimbursement to cover operational costs and clinician time?			
Are store-and-forward (asynchronous) applications appropriately secured and backed up?			
Is an annual review of teleprocedures with major payers conducted to determine changes in reimbursement policies?			

E-Mail

Questions to consider	YES	NO If no, why not?	NOT APPLICABLE (note reason)
Is the practice's e-mail secure?			
Is e-mail answered in a timely manner using the same guidelines as voice mail?			
Do e-answers include necessary disclaimer language?			
Are e-mail threads incorporated into the patients' charts?			

Copier

Questions to consider	YES	NO If no, why not?	NOT APPLICABLE (note reason)
Is the office copier networked?			
Is the copier speed sufficient?			
Are the copier features adequate?			
Does the copier feature in-boxes?			
Is a service contract in place?			
Are the cost and service adequate?			

01.B Communication Systems for Clinical and Nonclinical Staff

Note methods for internal and nonpatient external communication.

Check all that apply	Method	Circle one	Describe action needed
	Intranet and Internet (internal/external e-mail, web access, EHR, etc.)	Effective Not Effective	
	Face-to-face meetings (organization-wide, departmental, evaluations, etc.)	Effective Not Effective	
	Stakeholder surveys	Effective Not Effective	
	Meetings and seminars	Effective Not Effective	
	Training and educational workshops	Effective Not Effective	
	Policy and procedure manuals	Effective Not Effective	
	Telephone	Effective Not Effective	
	Voice mail	Effective Not Effective	
	Pager (with or without digital messages)	Effective Not Effective	

Check all that apply	Consideration	Circle one	Describe action needed
	Cell phone (with texting)	Effective Not Effective	
	Fax	Effective Not Effective	
	Mail	Effective Not Effective	
	Other:	Effective Not Effective	

Questions to consider	YES	NO If no, why not?	NOT APPLICABLE (note reason)
Is a strategy in place for communicating with the community?			
Does the practice participate in opportunities to educate the community about specialty-specific medical matters?			
Is the practice involved in community health matters?			
Is a public relations plan in place, including the use of news releases and media coverage?			
Does the EHR include task functionality?			
Is the practice involved in a health information exchange?			
Is there 24/7 secure remote access to the practice's computer systems including the practice management system, EHR, e-mail, and so on?			
Is there a private telephone line(s) for physician-to-physician communication?			
Are physician-to-physician calls answered and processed in a timely manner?			

01.C Communication Pathways

Questions to consider	YES	NO If no, why not?	NOT APPLICABLE (note reason)
Are there patient, internal, and external communication plans?			
Do these plans include verbal and written communication?			
Are the plans broken down by audience on a need-to-know basis?			
Are the plans reviewed and updated regularly?			
Does each plan include key and pertinent information?			
Does the patient plan include, for example, policies and procedures, system improvements, and events?			
Does the internal plan include, for example, orientation information, ongoing reports, policies and procedures, system improvements, events, general corporate communication, and public relations matters?			
Does the external plan (nonpatient) include, for example, surveys, emergency room coverage at hospitals, and referring physician communications?			
Does the patient plan address medical literacy issues?			

Does the internal communication plan include a combination of the following?

Check all that apply	Method	Circle one	Describe action needed
	Newsletter	Effective Not Effective	
	Suggestion box	Effective Not Effective	
	Intranet	Effective Not Effective	
	Company-wide e-mail blast	Effective Not Effective	
	Phone tree	Effective Not Effective	
	Social media	Effective Not Effective	
	Staff meetings	Effective Not Effective	
	Other:	Effective Not Effective	

Does the external plan for stakeholder communications include the following methods of surveys? Check all in use and note alternatives to consider.

Check all that apply	Method	Circle one	Describe action needed
	Mail	Effective Not Effective	
	E-mail	Effective Not Effective	
	Telephone	Effective Not Effective	
	In person	Effective Not Effective	
	Focus groups	Effective Not Effective	
	Other:	Effective Not Effective	

Questions to consider	YES	NO If no, why not?	NOT APPLICABLE (note reason)
Are survey results benchmarked internally and externally?			
Is action taken on results as needed?			
Are results reported to appropriate internal departments and individuals (practice owners/administration/ board, staff, etc.)?			

Questions to consider	YES	NO If no, why not?	NOT APPLICABLE (note reason)
Are communication pathways appropriate to deliver information (timely, efficient, clear, concise, type of medium, chain of communication, grievance path, etc.)?			
Are pathways periodically reviewed and analyzed to ensure optimization of information delivery?			

Questions to consider	YES	NO If no, why not?	NOT APPLICABLE (note reason)
Is a range of channels analyzed and reviewed when communicating new information?			
Are messages communicated in a consistent, standard format or template?			
Are messages consistently professional?			
Do communications reflect a service-oriented culture?			

Have the following been addressed to create a service-oriented culture?

Check all that apply	Method	Circle one	Describe action needed
	Telephone etiquette	Effective Not Effective	
	Reception etiquette	Effective Not Effective	
	E-mail etiquette	Effective Not Effective	
	Determination of appropriate media to use	Effective Not Effective	
	Dealing with difficult people	Effective Not Effective	
	Bedside manner	Effective Not Effective	
	Interpersonal relationships	Effective Not Effective	
	Other:	Effective Not Effective	

01.D Meeting Management

Questions to consider	YES	NO If no, why not?	NOT APPLICABLE (note reason)
Are designated individuals (administrator, managers, supervisors, etc.) responsible for meeting organization and management?			
Do these individuals possess the necessary meeting management skills?			
Are these individuals capable in the area of meeting facilitation?			
Are meeting guidelines in place (for example, based on Robert's Rules of Order)?			
Is a meeting leader identified whose role is to call the meeting to order, preside over the meeting, ask for motions and votes, adjourn the meeting, and so on?			
Is a meeting facilitator identified whose role is to review the meeting guidelines, act as a neutral party, create a safe environment, focus on resolution, obtain clarifying information, and so on?			

Questions to consider	YES	NO If no, why not?	NOT APPLICABLE (note reason)
Are meetings scheduled during nonclinical time slots?			
Are meeting dates and times communicated to participants in advance?			
Is there a clear purpose for all meetings?			
Are expectations of the outcomes of the meetings realistic?			
Do meetings allow for participation by all attendees?			
Do all attendees have a stake in the issues (a contribution to make, need to know, etc.)?			
Do meetings start and finish on time?			
Is there a clear agenda for all meetings?			
Is the agenda distributed in advance to participants, allowing sufficient time for review?			

Do meeting agendas include the following?

Check all that apply	Item	Circle one	Describe action needed
	Description of each item listed	Effective Not Effective	
	Action to be taken	Effective Not Effective	
	Start and finish times for each item	Effective Not Effective	
	Name of presenter	Effective Not Effective	
	Supporting materials	Effective Not Effective	
	Other:	Effective Not Effective	

Questions to consider	YES	NO If no, why not?	NOT APPLICABLE (note reason)
Does the agenda flow appropriately? That is, does it start with routine matters, move to more time-consuming issues, and close with more straightforward items?			
Is a meeting recorder identified?			
Are meeting minutes prepared and distributed in a timely manner?			

Do meeting minutes include the following?

Check all that apply	Item	Circle one	Describe action needed
	Date of meeting	Effective Not Effective	
	Start and finish times	Effective Not Effective	
	Name of person preparing the minutes	Effective Not Effective	
	Participant names	Effective Not Effective	
	Topics	Effective Not Effective	
	Pertinent discussion	Effective Not Effective	
	Decisions	Effective Not Effective	
	Follow-up items	Effective Not Effective	
	Names of persons responsible for follow-up items	Effective Not Effective	
	Anticipated completion dates	Effective Not Effective	
	Other:	Effective Not Effective	

Questions to consider	YES	NO If no, why not?	NOT APPLICABLE (note reason)
Are follow-up items tracked?			
Is action taken and are items brought to a conclusion?			

Review the following list of meeting-room elements. Check off those in use and note those to consider.

Check all that apply	Item	Circle one	Describe action needed
	Sufficient seating	Effective Not Effective	
	Comfortable seating	Effective Not Effective	
	Table space for participant meeting materials	Effective Not Effective	
	Comfortable temperature	Effective Not Effective	
	Necessary equipment (projector, laptop, extra bulbs, outlets, taped-down extension cords, easel/pad/markers/pins/tape, etc.)	Effective Not Effective	
	Projected materials and speaker visible to all participants	Effective Not Effective	
	Food and beverages, as required	Effective Not Effective	

Check all that apply	Item	Circle one	Describe action needed
	Nearby bathrooms	Effective Not Effective	
	Appropriate lighting	Effective Not Effective	
	Other:	Effective Not Effective	

01.E Development of Interpersonal Communication Skills

Questions to consider	YES	NO If no, why not?	NOT APPLICABLE (note reason)
Are there effective interpersonal communication skills among staff and providers?			
Is there ongoing training and development for all in this area?			
Is there a training and development plan in place for those with a weak skill set in this area?			

01.F Interplay among and Options for Internal Communications Systems and Channels

Are the options for and interplay among internal and external communications systems and channels (fax server, smart cell phones, 24/7 systems access, etc.) optimized using the following methods?

Check all that apply	Method	Circle one	Describe action needed
	Auto-forward of office voice mail to cell phone	Effective Not Effective	
	E-mail/smart phone integration	Effective Not Effective	
	Auto-generated patient contacts documented in the EHR (automated appointments, confirmation calls, diagnostic test result deliveries via patient portal, and e-statement distribution documented in the billing system, etc.)	Effective Not Effective	
	Other:	Effective Not Effective	

TASK 02: DEVELOP A TECHNOLOGY PLAN THAT ESTABLISHES THE CRITERIA FOR SELECTION AND IMPLEMENTATION OF INFORMATION TECHNOLOGY, INCLUDING COMPUTER SYSTEMS, INTERNET STRATEGIES, AND TELECOMMUNICATIONS

Planning for the future is an important part of the administrator's job. Technology is complex and can be costly. What is state of the art today will not be in the coming years. What's the status of your technology plan? How up to date is your knowledge about technology? A poorly planned electronic health record project can lead to low morale, decreased productivity, below average patient service, and much more. How do you go about selecting and implementing technology to ensure that you not only purchase what is right for your practice, but what is also cost effective and appropriately serviced by the vendor? Systems are not optimized unless people know how to operate them – the basics as well as features that will increase productivity and efficiency. How do you go about ensuring everyone in your practice has the right skill level to work with the technology in place as well as new technology as it is adopted? Complete this section to find out.

02.A Technology Plan and Budget

Questions to consider	YES	NO If no, why not?	NOT APPLICABLE (note reason)
Is an information system needs assessment – both business and clinical – completed periodically?			
Does the assessment include evaluation of all aspects of the practice?			

Indicate which of the following potential and existing applications are included in the needs assessment.

Check all that apply	Application	Circle one	Describe action needed
	Practice management	Effective Not Effective	
	Refund management and A/P integration	Effective Not Effective	
	Check and credit/ debit card transaction processing	Effective Not Effective	
	Remote deposit management	Effective Not Effective	
	E-mail	Effective Not Effective	
	Insurance eligibility and benefits verification	Effective Not Effective	
	Patient statement processing (electronic and paper)	Effective Not Effective	
	Claims processing and scrubbing	Effective Not Effective	
	Databases and office applications	Effective Not Effective	

Check all that apply	Application	Circle one	Describe action needed
	Personnel performance management	Effective Not Effective	
	Inventory and A/P integration	Effective Not Effective	
	Transcription	Effective Not Effective	
	Waste and recycling	Effective Not Effective	
	Utilities	Effective Not Effective	
	Electronic health record	Effective Not Effective	
	Medical device and lab instrumentation connectivity to the EHR	Effective Not Effective	
	Telephone message tracking and monitoring	Effective Not Effective	
	Prescribing	Effective Not Effective	
	Disease management	Effective Not Effective	

Check all that apply	Application	Circle one	Describe action needed
	Website	Effective Not Effective	
	Electronic patient monitoring devices	Effective Not Effective	
	Patient education	Effective Not Effective	
	Telehealth	Effective Not Effective	
	Other:	Effective Not Effective	

Questions to consider	YES	NO If no, why not?	NOT APPLICABLE (note reason)
Does the assessment include inventory of hardware currently in use (computers including servers and workstations, routers, fax/copier/printer units, PDAs/smart phones, etc.)?			
Does the assessment include an inventory of software applications (practice management system, EHR, picture archiving and communication system [PACS], laboratory information system [LIS], patient registries, reference applications, patient education software, e-mail, antivirus software, spyware, workstation tools, A/P, human resources, payroll, etc.)?			
Is an assessment of technology security issues included?			
Does the assessment address needs related to external stakeholders (insurance companies, labs, pharmacies, hospitals, diagnostic centers, vendors, etc.)?			
Does the assessment incorporate gap analysis?			
Does the assessment include information technology (IT) trending?			
Does the assessment incorporate an assessment of change management issues?			

Questions to consider	YES	NO If no, why not?	NOT APPLICABLE (note reason)
Is a three- to five-year IT plan in place?			
Is the plan aligned with practice strategic goals and objectives?			
Is the plan reviewed periodically and updated as needed?			
Does the plan identify responsible parties and time lines?			
Does the plan identify overall infrastructure and external connectivity?			
Does the plan identify information requirements and practice priorities?			
Does the plan include a budget?			
Is the plan communicated within the practice?			

02.B Types of Information Technology Systems and Applications

Are you knowledgeable about the following electronic systems?

Check all that apply	System	Circle one	Describe action needed
	Practice management (registration, appointments, billing, etc.)	Effective Not Effective	
	Automated payments (electronic remittance advice through practice management system, third-party integrated solution, etc.)	Effective Not Effective	
	Real-time insurance verification and batch verification through clearinghouse	Effective Not Effective	
	Referral and authorization management	Effective Not Effective	
	Real-time claims adjudication	Effective Not Effective	
	Automated registration (kiosk, practice website, etc.)	Effective Not Effective	
	Electronic health record	Effective Not Effective	
	Patient registries	Effective Not Effective	
	State immunization registries	Effective Not Effective	

Check all that apply	System	Circle one	Describe action needed
	E-prescribing and medication management, including formulary management and drug interaction checking	Effective Not Effective	
	Document management	Effective Not Effective	
	Exchange of clinical information between providers and hospitals	Effective Not Effective	
	Patient viewing of medical record through the practice portal	Effective Not Effective	
	Electronic record summary for patient	Effective Not Effective	
	Accounting	Effective Not Effective	
	Payroll and HR management	Effective Not Effective	
	E-mail	Effective Not Effective	
	Practice website and patient portal services	Effective Not Effective	
	Patient satisfaction survey	Effective Not Effective	
	Other:	Effective Not Effective	

Are you knowledgeable about the following features and benefits of integrated systems?

Check all that apply	Feature/Benefit	Circle one	Describe action needed
	One set of master files is shared by the practice management system and EHR.	Effective Not Effective	
	The shared database supports reports including the practice management EHR data.	Effective Not Effective	
	There may be lower ongoing costs as one technology base is needed.	Effective Not Effective	
	Other:	Effective Not Effective	

Questions to consider	YES	NO If no, why not?	NOT APPLICABLE (note reason)
Are you knowledgeable about the features and benefits of the Certification Commission for Health Information Technology (CCHIT), including specialty-specific (child health and cardiology, for example) certifications?			
Are you knowledgeable about the features and benefits of meaningful use, including the Certified Health IT Product List?			

02.C Information Technology Selection, Procurement, and Installation

Questions to consider	YES	NO If no, why not?	NOT APPLICABLE (note reason)
Is there an IT selection committee?			
Is the committee comprised of a combination of the administrator and end users including nursing, medical records, front desk and billing, staff representatives, and physician leaders?			
Is there buy-in within the practice?			
Has there been a comprehensive analysis to determine required features, equipment, and so on?			
Are workflow changes planned in advance for increased effectiveness?			
Are potential vendors researched?			
Is a process in place for requesting proposals from vendors?			
Are multiple references checked via telephone and site visits?			
Questions to consider	YES	NO If no, why not?	NOT APPLICABLE (note reason)

Are contracts negotiated?			
Are implementation and payment schedules negotiated and included in the contract?			
Are costs and payment terms negotiated and included in the contract?			
Are support parameters (system setup and training; conversion of existing electronic data, and a transition plan for paper medical charts) negotiated and included in the contract?			
Are response time and service level agreements negotiated and included in the contract?			
Are upgrades and interface maintenance negotiated and included in the contract?			
Do you have a good relationship with the sales staff?			
Does the sales staff understand the practice's needs?			
Is the sales staff attentive and prompt?			
Does the sales staff provide necessary technical support during the procurement process?			

02.D Technology Implementation

Questions to consider	YES	NO If no, why not?	NOT APPLICABLE (note reason)
Is there an implementation plan, including a time line?			
Is the plan created with input from key individuals involved with the project?			
Is installation timely?			
Does the training schedule cover necessary skills and knowledge?			
Do all staff and providers receive training on the modules they will use?			
Is a workflow redesign completed?			
Is the workflow redesign created with representation from all departments?			
Is the workflow redesign communicated back to department members?			
Is the workflow redesign integrated into the practice processes?			

Questions to consider	YES	NO If no, why not?	NOT APPLICABLE (note reason)
Is the workflow redesign evaluated and assessed post-implementation, with necessary modifications?			
Are practice owners, administration, department managers, and providers kept informed throughout the process?			
Are designated vendor contacts in place?			
Are support hours sufficient?			
Is response time appropriate?			

02.E Maintenance of Technology Systems, Equipment, and Services

Questions to consider	YES	NO If no, why not?	NOT APPLICABLE (note reason)
Do you stay abreast of technology trends and developments?			
Is an analysis of future needs conducted?			
Is a scheduled replacement cycle for computer workstations created?			
Is there ongoing analysis and maintenance of technology systems in use?			

Note which of the following items receive routine analysis and maintenance.

Check all that apply	Item	Circle one	Describe action needed
	Personal computers	Effective Not Effective	
	Laptops	Effective Not Effective	
	Tablets	Effective Not Effective	
	Thin clients	Effective Not Effective	
	Monitors	Effective Not Effective	
	Servers	Effective Not Effective	
	Cabling	Effective Not Effective	
	Wireless	Effective Not Effective	
	Hub, router, etc.	Effective Not Effective	

Check all that apply	Item	Circle one	Describe action needed
	Telephone system	Effective Not Effective	
	Cell phones	Effective Not Effective	
	Pagers	Effective Not Effective	
	Web portal	Effective Not Effective	
	E-mail	Effective Not Effective	
	Website	Effective Not Effective	
	Applications and software	Effective Not Effective	
	Technical support	Effective Not Effective	
	Other:	Effective Not Effective	

02.F Training and Support

Questions to consider	YES	NO If no, why not?	NOT APPLICABLE (note reason)
Are technology training needs assessed on an ongoing basis?			
Do the staff and providers have the necessary skill sets to use technology systems?			
Are users able to maximize use of system features?			
Is there ongoing, as-needed technology training for clinical and nonclinical staff?			
Do new hires receive technology training?			
Is technology training customized based on skill level and applications used?			
Is nontechnology on-site training provided for clinical and nonclinical staff without a professional development budget?			

Do you consider the variety of training approaches available and analyze their effectiveness? Select all approaches that are used in your organization.

Check all that apply	Approach	Circle one	Describe action needed
	Lecture	Effective Not Effective	
	Demonstration	Effective Not Effective	
	Hands-on	Effective Not Effective	
	Self-directed	Effective Not Effective	
	One-on-one	Effective Not Effective	
	Online	Effective Not Effective	
	Train-the-trainer	Effective Not Effective	
	On-site	Effective Not Effective	
	Off-site	Effective Not Effective	
	Other:	Effective Not Effective	

Do you have a budget for providers, management, and clinical/nonclinical staff to obtain the necessary professional development?

Check all that apply	Position	Circle one	Describe action needed
	Physicians	Effective Not Effective	
	Midlevel providers	Effective Not Effective	
	Practice administrator	Effective Not Effective	
	Department managers	Effective Not Effective	
	Nurses	Effective Not Effective	
	Technicians (note types)	Effective Not Effective	
	Other:	Effective Not Effective	

Which of the following professional development options do you take advantage of?

Check all that apply	Option	Circle one	Describe action needed
	Professional journals	Effective Not Effective	
	Webinars and podcasts	Effective Not Effective	
	Audio conferences	Effective Not Effective	
	Online educational courses	Effective Not Effective	
	Professional association offerings	Effective Not Effective	
	Academic institutions	Effective Not Effective	
	Books	Effective Not Effective	
	Portable electronic media	Effective Not Effective	
	Other:	Effective Not Effective	

Questions to consider	YES	NO If no, why not?	NOT APPLICABLE (note reason)
Are guidelines for professional development in place (topics, travel, timing, length, cost, etc.)?			
Are cost and time issues considered when planning training?			
Are post-training analyses conducted to assess the success rate?			
Is a program in place to share training skills and knowledge among clinical and nonclinical staff?			

TASK 03: PLAN AND DESIGN A TECHNOLOGY SECURITY PROCESS TO PROTECT PATIENT AND PRACTICE DATA SYSTEMS

To protect the privacy of patient information, systems must be secure. A working knowledge of the types of technological threats that exist now, and awareness of the new ones on the horizon, are both required. The passage of HIPAA formalized how patient information is protected. Do you have a privacy plan? What about a security plan? Are privacy and security practiced daily? Do you have a contingency operating plan including back-up and recovery as well as an emergency mode operation plan? Various technology disasters noted in the news lead one to think about our potential disasters closer to home. Have you thought about what you might do if a severe storm took out one or more of your communication systems? How quickly could you be back in business? A technology disaster plan would help direct your response and control downtime. Internet viruses and the like can severely damage the ability to use web-based technology functions. Do you have systems in place to monitor and assess these threats? What about risks related to employee use of practice systems? Do you have policies in place to address these concerns? In daily news there are reports about the theft of laptops and other devices containing employee and patient data. What steps are you taking to prevent the theft of your devices that contain confidential data? Answer these questions to find out how your practice measures up.

03.A Security Processes and Standards

Questions to consider	YES	NO If no, why not?	NOT APPLICABLE (note reason)
Is a firewall in place?			
Is antivirus software used on servers and workstations?			
Is intrusion protection and detection in place?			
Is spyware and malware detection in place on servers and workstations?			
Are all protections consistently up to date?			
Is the system encrypted?			
Does the practice have a written policy against opening and forwarding e-mails and documents from unknown sources?			
Does the practice have a written policy against downloading applications (free or not) without prior approval by manager?			
Is website access limited to sites related to job duties and responsibilities?			

Questions to consider	YES	NO If no, why not?	NOT APPLICABLE (note reason)
Is provider and staff access limited to applications that are needed?			
Is access terminated after a reasonable period of inactivity?			
Is user access monitored and audited?			
Are access and transactions logged (additions, changes, deletions, etc.)?			
Are access issues recorded and resolved?			
Are individual passwords used?			
Is password protection used at the program level?			
Are passwords at least six characters and do they require a combination of letters, numbers, and special characters?			
Are different passwords used for different applications?			

Questions to consider	YES	NO If no, why not?	NOT APPLICABLE (note reason)
Are policies in place regarding changing of passwords every 90 days?			
Are policies in place regarding not sharing passwords, with appropriate penalties for infractions?			
Are policies in place about keeping written passwords in a secure place?			
Is annual training provided on password protocols?			
Is new employee training provided on password protocols?			
Are passwords and access terminated immediately upon employee termination?			
Do disciplinary procedures address consequences on access and password issues?			

Questions to consider	YES	NO If no, why not?	NOT APPLICABLE (note reason)
Is password authentication used?			
Are staff and providers educated about technology security and reporting security issues?			
Are staff and providers not allowed to install outside software and hardware (free or not), including removable hard drives and USB devices?			
Is there a back-up power supply?			
Is the back-up power supply checked on a regular basis to ensure it is in good working order?			

Questions to consider	YES	NO If no, why not?	NOT APPLICABLE (note reason)
Is the server in a secure area?			
Is a fire extinguisher nearby?			
Is everyone aware of the importance of physical security?			
Does the practice have a good working relationship with a technology security consultant?			
Is the service cost effective?			
Is the service timely?			

03.B Information Integrity, Security, and Confidentiality

Questions to consider	YES	NO If no, why not?	NOT APPLICABLE (note reason)
Is a written privacy plan in place along with a process to review it annually?			
Is there a designated privacy officer?			
Are the required privacy forms used?			
Are complaint protocols in place?			
Are complaint records maintained?			
Are anonymous reporting mechanisms in place?			
Is a disciplinary system in place?			
Are providers and staff trained in privacy?			

Questions to consider	YES	NO If no, why not?	NOT APPLICABLE (note reason)
Are new providers and staff trained in privacy?			
Is annual privacy training conducted for all staff?			
Is training documented?			
Do all sign a confidentiality statement?			
Are safeguards in place to protect health information?			
Does the practice have a Notice of Privacy Practices?			
Is it provided to each patient?			
Is a written acknowledgment of receipt of the Notice of Privacy Practices obtained from each patient?			

Questions to consider	YES	NO If no, why not?	NOT APPLICABLE (note reason)
Are copies of all versions of the Notice of Privacy Practices maintained?			
Are business associate agreements in place?			
Are business associate agreements updated to reflect the HIPAA Security Rule?			
Are business associate agreements updated to reflect the Health Information Technology for Economic and Clinical Health Act?			
Are mitigation and reporting conducted as required after disclosure of protected health information (PHI)?			
Is disciplinary action taken when breaches occur?			
Is the practice compliant with privacy documentation and retention requirements?			
Does the practice adhere to state privacy laws?			

Questions to consider	YES	NO If no, why not?	NOT APPLICABLE (note reason)
Does the practice have a specific written security plan in place?			
Is development and implementation of the security plan documented?			
Is there ongoing monitoring of the security plan and protocols?			
Is there a designated security officer?			
Are gap analysis and risk assessment conducted?			
Are technical, administrative, and physical safeguards addressed?			
Do operational systems support security (computer screens are not visible to the public, privacy screens are used, patient paperwork is not placed in locations visible to the public, etc.)?			
Are other physical aspects of the security rule addressed as required (limiting access to the server room, limiting access into the facility, patient escort policies, etc.)?			
Is a reasonable standard applied in the instance of addressable standards?			

Questions to consider	YES	NO If no, why not?	NOT APPLICABLE (note reason)
Are providers and staff trained in security?			
Are new providers and staff trained in security?			
Is annual security training conducted for all staff?			
Are policies in place to prevent, detect, and report security concerns?			
Are known security incidents identified?			
Are security breaches responded to, mitigated, and corrected?			
Are the security plan and policies regularly updated?			
Is disciplinary action taken for breaches?			
Is there a plan and protocols to respond to emergencies, disasters, and other events that are related to PHI?			
Are repairs and changes to physical security documented?			

03.C Database Management and Maintenance

Is a periodic database management needs assessment completed, including the following items?
Note those that are used in your practice.

Check all that apply	Item	Circle one	Describe action needed
	Current systems are adequate.	Effective Not Effective	
	Current systems are efficient.	Effective Not Effective	
	Current systems are easy to use.	Effective Not Effective	
	There are different computers or servers for different database systems.	Effective Not Effective	
	An access control list and audit procedures are in place.	Effective Not Effective	
	The hardware and network infrastructure is adequate to access applications.	Effective Not Effective	
	The hardware and network infrastructure is adequate to run applications.	Effective Not Effective	
	The system has the ability to store additional data.	Effective Not Effective	

Check all that apply	Item	Circle one	Describe action needed
	The speed of the system is sufficient.	Effective Not Effective	
	There is clear responsibility for oversight.	Effective Not Effective	
	Users are identified.	Effective Not Effective	
	Needs with regard to data extraction and manipulation are assessed.	Effective Not Effective	
	There is a policy regarding data retention periods and archiving.	Effective Not Effective	
	Vendor support is appropriate.	Effective Not Effective	
	Vendor costs are competitive.	Effective Not Effective	
	Other:	Effective Not Effective	

If database management applications are not in use, are the current systems for storage, access, and manipulation of data adequate?

Questions to consider	YES	NO If no, why not?	NOT APPLICABLE (note reason)
Is the server(s) backed up daily?			
Is a back-up log kept?			
Is back-up verified?			
Is a tape rotation system in place?			
Are tapes replaced routinely?			
Are tapes stored in a secure place off site?			
Is a year-end tape kept as a permanent record?			
Is a log kept of software loaded onto the system?			

Questions to consider	YES	NO If no, why not?	NOT APPLICABLE (note reason)
Are updates and modifications loaded as required and in a timely manner?			
Are updates and modifications logged?			
Are system issues logged and resolved?			
Are regular and periodic database management completed?			
Are steps taken to ensure the accuracy and completeness of data?			
Are new users set up with specific rights needed to perform their duties?			
Is a plan in place to recover lost and/or damaged data?			

03.D Technology Disaster and Contingency Management Planning

Questions to consider	YES	NO If no, why not?	NOT APPLICABLE (note reason)
Are technology disaster and contingency operations plans in place?			
Is downtime for disasters estimated?			
Are employee costs related to recovery estimated?			
Are IT costs related to repair and/or replacement estimated?			
Is lost revenue estimated?			
Are costs related to recreating a back-up gap (if any) estimated?			
Is the location of the original software known and included in the plan?			
Has the ease of restoring systems been assessed?			

Questions to consider	YES	NO If no, why not?	NOT APPLICABLE (note reason)
Is at least one phone line separate from the main phone system?			
Are communication servers separate from the data servers?			
Has insurance to cover loss and theft of equipment been purchased?			
Is a list of employees (with cell phone numbers) that have personal e-mail and Internet access maintained and kept off site?			
Is the disaster and contingency operations plan documented both electronically and on paper?			
Is the plan available to all, both on and off site?			
Is the plan tested on a regular basis?			

03.E Security Audit Procedures

Questions to consider	YES	NO If no, why not?	NOT APPLICABLE (note reason)
Does the staff possess an overall understanding of security threats?			
Are physical threat protocols audited regularly (facility security, device and media control, workstation use and security, etc.)?			
Are technical threat protocols audited regularly (controls, audit controls, data integrity controls, etc.)?			
Are administrative threat protocols audited regularly (back-up plans, disaster recovery plans, emergency operations plans, etc.)?			
Is ongoing skill and knowledge training about threats provided?			

03.F Employee Personal Use of Practice Technology

Questions to consider	YES	NO If no, why not?	NOT APPLICABLE (note reason)
Are policies in place regarding personal use of practice technology?			
Do the policies address the practice ownership of information (voice mail, e-mail, etc.)?			
Do the policies address disciplinary action for misuse?			
If access is allowed during nonworking periods, are inappropriate websites prohibited?			

03.G Theft or Loss of Technology Equipment

Questions to consider	YES	NO If no, why not?	NOT APPLICABLE (note reason)
Are policies in place regarding taking computer software, hardware, and data off site?			
Do the policies include data storage media such as flash drives, portable hard drives, and so on?			
Is logoff required during breaks and at the end of the day?			
Does automatic logoff occur upon nonuse of the computer?			
Do password-controlled screen savers come up when automatic logoff occurs?			
Is data on equipment permanently erased before the equipment is disposed of (computers, flash drives, fax machines, high-end printers, etc.)?			
Are employee backgrounds verified through references and background checks before hiring?			
Are all employees required to sign off on the confidentiality policy?			
When outsourcing, is vendor commitment to confidentiality verified?			

TASK 04: MANAGE MEDICAL INFORMATION SYSTEMS INCLUDING MEDICAL RECORDS, MEDICATION ADMINISTRATION, AND HEALTHCARE-RELATED DOCUMENT STORAGE

Medical records provide important details about current care as well as history, and they support billing functions. Patients have the right to privacy of their medical information, making HIPAA compliance a key concern for practices. Are you compliant with the original legislation as well as the updates? If you're not yet using an EHR, you have continuously increasing volumes of paper charts. If you are using one, your quantity of charts has stabilized or been eliminated. Regardless, issues exist with regard to storage, retention, and retrieval, as well as destruction. Do you have systems in place to address these concerns? Do you have a working knowledge of retention laws affecting your practice? How well versed are you with regard to regulations about prescribing? Are you certain that your providers follow the law? Read and respond to the following to determine how you're doing with these aspects of practice management.

04.A Release, Update, and Maintenance of Confidential Information

Questions to consider	YES	NO If no, why not?	NOT APPLICABLE (note reason)
Is written authorization obtained when required (for reasons not related to treatment, payment, or operations)?			
Is separate authorization obtained when required (for psychotherapy, etc.)?			
Does the release form meet HIPAA requirements?			
When releasing medical records, does the practice adhere to the "minimum only" principle?			
Are HIPAA rules followed regarding the use of medical information and disclosures for marketing purposes?			
Are disclosures documented?			
Is PHI de-identified prior to release when possible?			
Are patients' rights to inspect and copy PHI honored?			
Are protocols in place to address patients' requests to amend their PHI?			

04.B Record Storage, Retrieval, and Destruction

Questions to consider	YES	NO If no, why not?	NOT APPLICABLE (note reason)
Do you follow state regulations regarding medical record retention?			
Are protocols in place for medical records storage?			
Are protocols in place for retrieval of archived medical records?			
Are procedures in place for the destruction of medical records?			

04.C Fault Tolerance (in accordance with standards for continuous availability) for Technological Systems

Questions to consider	YES	NO If no, why not?	NOT APPLICABLE (note reason)
Has an assessment for hardware and software fault tolerance been completed?			
Are your requirements determined?			

Note all fault tolerance systems you currently have in place.

Check all that apply	System	Circle one	Describe action needed
	Redundancy	Effective Not Effective	
	Hotswap	Effective Not Effective	
	Rolling upgrades	Effective Not Effective	
	System performance	Effective Not Effective	
	Availability logs with routine monitoring	Effective Not Effective	
	Intrusion protection	Effective Not Effective	
	Device tracking	Effective Not Effective	
	Asset tracking and license management	Effective Not Effective	
	Other:	Effective Not Effective	

04.D Prescribing, Transmission, and Monitoring of Patient Medications

Questions to consider	YES	NO If no, why not?	NOT APPLICABLE (note reason)
Do you follow state and federal prescribing regulations (for example, tamper-proof prescription pads)?			
Do you follow state and federal prescribing regulations for written and electronic prescriptions?			
Do you follow state and federal prescribing regulations for transmission of electronic prescriptions?			
Does the practice have a license to dispense medications?			
Does the practice follow state regulations regarding dispensing medications?			
Is there a written policy for dispensing medications?			
Is the policy within the scope of practice for the staff?			
Are systems in place to monitor patient response to and compliance with medications?			

04.E Security of Protected Health Information

Questions to consider	YES	NO If no, why not?	NOT APPLICABLE (note reason)
Is exposure to internal and external data breaches routinely assessed?			
Are configuration settings and file systems locked down?			
Are other steps not already noted taken to secure PHI? Note what they are:			

TASK 05: DEVELOP AND IMPLEMENT PROCESSES TO COMPLY WITH MANDATED REPORTS OF SPECIFIED PATIENT ISSUES TO REGULATORY AGENCIES

Tracking certain disease states enables society to focus on public health safety, including prevention, control, and management. By reporting certain conditions, vaccinations, and so on, practices aid in this endeavor. Are you aware of what you need to report, when and how you need to report, and the significance of the reporting? Answer the following to find out.

05.A Reporting of Medical Conditions

Questions to consider	YES	NO If no, why not?	NOT APPLICABLE (note reason)
Do you have knowledge of conditions that must be reported per state and federal requirements (child abuse, communicable diseases, dog bites, etc.)?			
Do you have knowledge of optional reporting to state and federal agencies (for example, Physician Quality Reporting Initiative)?			
Are you aware of specific reporting requirements (what, when, where, why, how)?			
Are all state and federal reporting requirements met?			

05.B Reporting to Disease, Vaccine, and Other Registries

Questions to consider	YES	NO If no, why not?	NOT APPLICABLE (note reason)
Is the practice set up to automatically receive physician reporting information from the state and the U.S. Department of Health?			
Is the information reviewed on a regular basis?			
Do you work with providers and access other resources to gain a clinical understanding of diseases, vaccinations, and so on that require reporting?			

05.C Requirements for Biohazard and Epidemic Responses

Questions to consider	YES	NO If no, why not?	NOT APPLICABLE (note reason)
Do you have knowledge of state and federal response requirements for biohazard and epidemic situations?			
Are you aware of specific response requirements (what, when, where, why, how)?			
Does the practice meet response requirements?			

BOTTOM LINE—INFORMATION MANAGEMENT

Information management and technology drive a multitude of activities in practices. From computer systems to use of the Internet to cell phones and more, technology affects what you do and how you do it. As technology applications increase and change - for example, EHR systems and health information exchanges - so will the need to effectively manage data. Technological advancements occur rapidly and administrators need to stay abreast of what's new to operate in the most efficient manner they can. Efficiency, in turn, has the potential to positively affect the bottom line.

Information Management
Supplemental Notes
(copy as needed)

Task	Notes

Information Management
Action Items
(copy as needed)

Task	Action	Responsible Party	Due Date	Priority

CHAPTER 5

Organizational Governance

How do you ensure effective governance and leadership through policies, long-term strategies, and the strategic direction of the organization? This aspect of your job is perhaps the most important and you need to address multiple aspects of it. Is your legal structure appropriate? There are many new models today, thus having experienced lawyers – and accountants – on your team is critical. Are you comfortable facilitating organizational governance matters? Remember, "governance" is a societal mechanism of control involving authority, administration, and direction. Is your practice's board of directors effective? As administrator, you need to keep an eye on board composition and orientation, bylaws, committees, records and history, meeting management, and succession planning. Do you feel you are effectively integrating the corporate mission into the organization's culture? Brochures, posters, and other marketing materials are not enough. You and the leaders must walk the talk. How do you ensure there is an updated strategic plan – that is implemented? It's hard enough to ensure one is developed, much less put it to work. And how about the big one – handling compensation for physicians and mid-level providers? New ways of thinking about clinical compensation need to be communicated effectively. How are you helping the group's leaders to gain leadership management skills and use them to improve staff performance? Reinforcing standards of conduct and performance expectations must become everyday matters. How are you assisting the physicians to grow as leaders? Workshops on topics like conflict resolution help. And finally, are you and the leaders participating in advocacy efforts? Getting involved in industry, government, and community affairs helps the group to survive and thrive.

TASK 01: FACILITATE THE ESTABLISHMENT AND MONITORING OF THE APPROPRIATE CORPORATE LEGAL STRUCTURE FOR THE ORGANIZATION

Medical practices choose the type of legal structure that fits the organization's goals and culture and provides both legal and tax benefits as well as liability protection. State laws related to corporations specify the requirements related to each type of structure, and federal laws also dictate responsibility and compliance in specific areas. Retaining a law firm experienced with the legalities of medical practice and an accounting firm with experience in healthcare taxation issues is vital when establishing a structure. Then these advisers should continue to monitor these matters to keep up with changes internally and externally. Maintaining legal and taxation compliance is a critical governance matter as is ensuring appropriate shareholder agreements, physician contracts, and management control over time.

01.A Types of Legal Structures

Check the type of legal structure that is used by the practice.

	Sole proprietorship
	Professional corporation (PC)
	General corporation
	Business corporation
	"C" corporation
	"S" corporation
	Limited liability partnership (LLP)
	Limited liability company (LLC)
	Other:

Questions to consider	YES	NO If no, why not?	NOT APPLICABLE (note reason)
Is the structure still appropriate? If not, make a note to consider action.			

01.B Liability and Taxation Issues

Check the liability and taxation issues related to the chosen legal structure.

	Limited liability
	Tax on entity income paid by owners
	Double taxation
	Reasonable debt basis for pass-through losses and deductions
	Unreasonable compensation issues
	Exemption of certain fringe benefits
	Other:

Questions to consider	YES	NO If no, why not?	NOT APPLICABLE (note reason)
Is the structure still appropriate in terms of liability and taxation issues? If not, make a note to consider action.			

01.C Legal Compliance with Legal Structure

Check all federal and state laws with which you are in compliance.

	Tax law
	Physician self-referral/Stark law
	Anti-kickback law
	False claims law
	Antitrust laws
	Other:

01.D Impact of Legal Structure on the Governance System and Culture of the Organization

Check the methods that are in place to match the legal structure with the organizational governance and culture.

Check all that apply	Method	Circle one	Describe action needed
	Bylaws and rules for governance are established.	Effective Not Effective	
	Discussions are held at least annually on philosophy and goals.	Effective Not Effective	
	The leadership model is documented (for example, how the primary leader is designated).	Effective Not Effective	
	The responsibilities and rights of leadership positions are in writing.	Effective Not Effective	
	Other:	Effective Not Effective	

01.E Attorney Expertise

How do you ensure legal expertise?

Check all that apply	Method	Circle one	Describe action needed
	An outside attorney is used to eliminate conflicts of interest.	Effective Not Effective	
	Multiple lawyers and law firms are consulted to obtain diverse expertise on risk management, malpractice, compliance, employment/contract law, and so on.	Effective Not Effective	
	The law firm(s) used is respected, ethical, and efficient.	Effective Not Effective	
	To the extent possible, the firm(s) is not associated with key referring physicians or facilities (avoiding a conflict of interest).	Effective Not Effective	
	A system is in place to monitor legal fees and billing.	Effective Not Effective	
	Other:	Effective Not Effective	

01.F Shareholder Agreements and Physician Contracts

Check to ensure all of these topics are covered in the shareholder agreements.

Check all that apply	Topic	Circle one	Describe action needed
	Owner initial and additional investments	Effective Not Effective	
	Director and officer definitions	Effective Not Effective	
	Voting rights	Effective Not Effective	
	Decision making and control	Effective Not Effective	
	Rights and duties	Effective Not Effective	
	Conditions of change of composition	Effective Not Effective	
	Share transfers	Effective Not Effective	
	Salaries and draws	Effective Not Effective	
	Employment	Effective Not Effective	

Check all that apply	Topic	Circle one	Describe action needed
	Exit clauses	Effective Not Effective	
	Restrictive covenant	Effective Not Effective	
	Indemnification	Effective Not Effective	
	Termination	Effective Not Effective	
	Arbitration	Effective Not Effective	
	Governing law	Effective Not Effective	
	Waiver	Effective Not Effective	
	Survival	Effective Not Effective	
	Notices	Effective Not Effective	
	Other:	Effective Not Effective	

Check to ensure all of these topics are covered in the physician contracts.

Check all that apply	Topic	Circle one	Describe action needed
	Term	Effective Not Effective	
	Duties	Effective Not Effective	
	Restrictive covenant	Effective Not Effective	
	Termination	Effective Not Effective	
	Compliance with regulations and laws	Effective Not Effective	
	Confidential information	Effective Not Effective	
	Assignment of contract	Effective Not Effective	
	Amendments to the agreement	Effective Not Effective	
	Governing law	Effective Not Effective	
	Compensation	Effective Not Effective	
	Benefits	Effective Not Effective	
	Other:	Effective Not Effective	

01.G Impact of Independent Practice Associations, Hospitals, and Ancillary Providers

Note if the practice has moved to a new organizational model such as an integrated delivery system.

Check all that apply	Model	Circle one	Describe action needed
	Hospital	Effective Not Effective	
	Practice management company	Effective Not Effective	
	IPA network	Effective Not Effective	
	Other:	Effective Not Effective	

TASK 02: FACILITATE ORGANIZATIONAL GOVERNANCE STRUCTURE AND MAINTAIN PROPER CORPORATE RECORD-KEEPING OF STRATEGIC DECISIONS

Assurance that the medical practice's governance structure can succeed occurs via appropriate implementation of such governance mechanisms as the board of directors, committees, meeting management, and bylaws. Such leadership tools enhance discussion and decision making. Making and keeping records of decisions helps ensure that the goals and plans of the group are carried out successfully. The age, size, and organizational model of the practice will shape how governance evolves over the years.

02.A Development of a Committee Structure to Meet Organizational Needs

Check ways in which the practice complies with bylaw language related to committees.

Check all that apply	Method	Circle one	Describe action needed
	Committee structure is in line with bylaw requirements.	Effective Not Effective	
	Operational concerns are addressed by committees rather than the board.	Effective Not Effective	
	Physician input is gathered by committees in an organized, not ad hoc, way.	Effective Not Effective	
	Future leaders are involved in committees to learn the governance processes.	Effective Not Effective	
	Other:	Effective Not Effective	

02.B Types of Committees

What types of committees are implemented in the practice?

Check all that apply	Committee	Circle one	Describe action needed
	Finance and budget	Effective Not Effective	
	Personnel	Effective Not Effective	
	Quality review	Effective Not Effective	
	Research	Effective Not Effective	
	Recruiting	Effective Not Effective	
	Financial performance	Effective Not Effective	
	Business operations	Effective Not Effective	
	Ad hoc	Effective Not Effective	
	Other:	Effective Not Effective	

02.C Roles and Responsibilities of the Board of Directors and Committees

Note the documented responsibilities for the practice's board and committees.

Check all that apply	Responsibility	Circle one	Describe action needed
	Mission development	Effective Not Effective	
	Goal development and monitoring	Effective Not Effective	
	Recruitment of CEO, selection, evaluation, and interaction	Effective Not Effective	
	Quality care monitoring	Effective Not Effective	
	Interaction with external constituents such as community, government, and media	Effective Not Effective	
	Organizational performance monitoring	Effective Not Effective	
	Development of strategic vision and plans	Effective Not Effective	
	Evaluation of the board	Effective Not Effective	
	Other:	Effective Not Effective	

02.D Board Composition and Procedural Rules

Check board positions and procedures that are implemented in accordance with bylaws.

Check all that apply	Position/Procedure	Circle one	Describe action needed
	Board positions are in place and described as, for example, president, vice president, secretary, and treasurer.	Effective Not Effective	
	The size of the board is in line with the bylaws.	Effective Not Effective	
	The term of board members is specified as the number of years to serve, whether terms are staggered, and so on.	Effective Not Effective	
	Meetings are scheduled as specified (for example, monthly, quarterly).	Effective Not Effective	
	Outside advisers are invited to participate in discussions of legal, financial, or other matters as needed.	Effective Not Effective	
	Retreats are scheduled for assessment and planning.	Effective Not Effective	
	Other:	Effective Not Effective	

02.E Adherence to Corporate Bylaws Including Annual Review

What mechanisms are in place to ensure alignment with the bylaws?

Check all that apply	Mechanism	Circle one	Describe action needed
	There is ongoing monitoring of bylaw compliance to prevent legal action by shareholders and dissatisfaction of group members.	Effective Not Effective	
	An annual review of bylaws is conducted, with special attention to factors changed during the year.	Effective Not Effective	
	A regular board review is conducted to ensure board members are knowledgeable of the bylaw requirements.	Effective Not Effective	
	Other:	Effective Not Effective	

02.F Orientation and Ongoing Board and Committee Members

Check the types of board and committee education that are provided.

Check all that apply	Type	Circle one	Describe action needed
	Orientation is provided at the start of board or committee service and includes a review of board history, meeting minutes, past major decisions, job descriptions, and so on.	Effective Not Effective	
	Access to external educational programs (for example, governance workshops) is provided.	Effective Not Effective	
	Joint attendance is required at programs to build member relationships and teamwork.	Effective Not Effective	
	Other:	Effective Not Effective	

02.G Record-Keeping and Record Retention

Check record-keeping and retention policies that are in place to comply with practice and legal issues.

Check all that apply	Policy	Circle one	Describe action needed
	Type of record: for example, financial, employee, property, tax returns, medical records	Effective Not Effective	
	Type of media: electronic, paper, and so on	Effective Not Effective	
	Location of record	Effective Not Effective	
	Retention length of time	Effective Not Effective	
	Authority to order record destruction	Effective Not Effective	
	Methods of destruction specified	Effective Not Effective	
	Authority to access records	Effective Not Effective	
	Other:	Effective Not Effective	

02.H Organizational History

Note the types of records used to capture the history of the organization.

Check all that apply	Record	Circle one	Describe action needed
	Records featuring organizational culture elements, events, and accomplishments	Effective Not Effective	
	Records providing a context for current board discussions, policy development, and staff training	Effective Not Effective	
	Records required to meet regulatory and legal requirements	Effective Not Effective	
	Other:	Effective Not Effective	

02.I Board/Committee Meeting Management and Board Evaluation

What methods are used to encourage effective meetings and evaluations?

Check all that apply	Method	Circle one	Describe action needed
	Consistent policies across locations and departments on meeting rules	Effective Not Effective	
	Board leader emphasis on significance of meetings and on examining issues (operational, strategic, professional, and so on)	Effective Not Effective	
	Encouragement of board and committee members to spend an average of 120–200 hours per year preparing for meetings	Effective Not Effective	
	Meetings are regularly scheduled with written agendas including goals and objectives	Effective Not Effective	
	Meetings are conducted by leaders using proven meeting management techniques and tools	Effective Not Effective	
	Provision of materials in advance pertaining to informational and consent agenda items not requiring debate to save time	Effective Not Effective	
	Positioning of "quick" items (for example, approval of minutes) at the front of the agenda followed by items requiring discussion	Effective Not Effective	
	Annual evaluation of board performance conducted in a serious manner, perhaps by an outsider	Effective Not Effective	
	Other:	Effective Not Effective	

02.J Effective Succession Planning

Note ways used to provide for the organization's future through succession planning.

Check all that apply	Method	Circle one	Describe action needed
	Identification and mentoring of younger members with potential interest in board leadership	Effective Not Effective	
	Transition plan for physician leaders including consideration of younger physicians' motivation for leadership roles	Effective Not Effective	
	Transition plan for organizational structure factors such as leader term limits and leader vs. clinical time allocation	Effective Not Effective	
	Specification of elected vs. appointed roles, compensation for leader roles, cultural expectations	Effective Not Effective	
	Other:	Effective Not Effective	

TASK 03: LEAD THE INTEGRATION OF THE CORPORATE MISSION STATEMENT INTO ALL ASPECTS OF THE ORGANIZATION'S CULTURE

"The way we do things here," the classic definition of organizational culture, evolves from the way founders set the initial scene for the medical practice to change over time in tune with group dynamics and trends. Culture determines the variables of vision and values as well as shaping goals. Strategies fail if they are not in line with the current cultural context. A mission statement basically defines what purpose the organization serves now. It should clearly delineate not only what the medical practice does, but more importantly, its reason for being, a reason (for example, "help people be healthy") recognized as beneficial by society. The vision statement extends the mission statement by specifying what the organization is known for today and what it seeks to achieve for tomorrow such as, for example, the best practices in quality healthcare. Values, sometimes defined as belief statements, state the guiding principles or philosophy of an organization – what the organization stands for (for example, putting the patient first).

03.A Effectively Communicate the Organization's Mission, Vision, and Values to Influence the Strategic Direction

Check ways that are used to ensure communication of the mission, vision, and values.

Check all that apply	Method	Circle one	Describe action needed
	Both formal and informal organizational communication methods are used (for example, e-mail, memos, meetings).	Effective Not Effective	
	Guidance for physicians is provided on articulating the mission, vision, and values and showing understanding of customer needs and satisfaction.	Effective Not Effective	
	The mission, vision, and values statements are reviewed and updated regularly for clarity and currency based on internal and external feedback.	Effective Not Effective	
	Physicians are responsible for formulating statements; the administrator is responsible for emphasizing importance and encouraging participation.	Effective Not Effective	
	Statements are circulated throughout the organization and used as a basis for group and one-on-one discussions to ensure knowledge and support.	Effective Not Effective	
	The mission, vision, and values are communicated during recruiting, for all positions.	Effective Not Effective	
	Other:	Effective Not Effective	

03.B Provide Leadership, Innovative Thinking, and Change Management

Note principles and techniques that are applied to encourage joint leadership.

Check all that apply	Principle/Technique	Circle one	Describe action needed
	A collaborative model is used to promote executive teamwork between physicians and administrative staff.	Effective Not Effective	
	Innovation is inspired by using creativity-generation techniques and tools in joint sessions.	Effective Not Effective	
	Change management skill building is offered on negotiation, persuading, planning, implementing, and conflict management.	Effective Not Effective	
	Ongoing development of change leaders' ability to communicate vision, create urgency, and facilitate team process is provided.	Effective Not Effective	
	The delegation of a change leader role to administrator may be offered as a possibility.	Effective Not Effective	
	Other:	Effective Not Effective	

03.C Understand Organizational Culture, Including Patterns of Behavior, Shared Values, Traditions, Politics, Power, and Group Interaction

What ways are used to ensure knowledge of the organization's culture?

Check all that apply	Method	Circle one	Describe action needed
	Awareness is encouraged by spotlighting business and employee strengths and weaknesses, information and resources.	Effective Not Effective	
	Knowledge about competitors (medical practices, hospitals) is shared including strengths and weaknesses.	Effective Not Effective	
	Job descriptions featuring roles and responsibilities are shared to reinforce expected patterns of behavior.	Effective Not Effective	
	Corporate "storytelling" is used to showcase shared values and traditions.	Effective Not Effective	
	Organizational politics, power, and group interactions are recognized as key cultural elements to manage effectively.	Effective Not Effective	
	Other:	Effective Not Effective	

03.D Uphold and Advocate Ethical Standards, Behavior, and Decision Making

Note which of the following techniques are used to emphasize business ethics throughout the organization.

Check all that apply	Technique	Circle one	Describe action needed
	The importance of the organization's ethical conduct toward patients, employees, community, and other stakeholders is stressed.	Effective Not Effective	
	Attention is paid to ethical behavior at all levels including integrity, participation, stewardship, and decisions made at the best level.	Effective Not Effective	
	A strong moral compass is highlighted as a powerful force, especially during times of crisis.	Effective Not Effective	
	The administrative focus is on building a culture of trust and collaboration.	Effective Not Effective	
	Systems and resources are available to facilitate issue resolution and align goals, actions, and performance evaluations with values.	Effective Not Effective	
	Other:	Effective Not Effective	

03.E Foster a Culture of Trust and Respect

Ascertain emphasis on trust and respect by checking techniques that are used to foster this outcome.

Check all that apply	Technique	Circle one	Describe action needed
	Top leaders recognize the importance of building trust and respect by demonstrating values via decisions and actions.	Effective Not Effective	
	Decisions are made after consideration of the betterment of the group, individuals, and all stakeholders.	Effective Not Effective	
	Board resolutions are presented and communicated publicly.	Effective Not Effective	
	A healthy, dynamic culture is maintained by regularly evaluating the existing culture.	Effective Not Effective	
	Ceremonies are used to celebrate completion of established goals and phases.	Effective Not Effective	
	Other:	Effective Not Effective	

03.F Manage the Intricate Interrelationships of the Organization, Staff, and Stakeholders

Assess the practice's status in terms of managing complex relationships by checking methods that are in place.

Check all that apply	Method	Circle one	Describe action needed
	Identification by leadership of multiple stakeholders: for example, patients, clinical and business staff, external players	Effective Not Effective	
	Recognition of overlap among relationships and possible conflicts among stakeholders	Effective Not Effective	
	Strategies developed for physicians and administrator to manage relationships effectively and dynamically	Effective Not Effective	
	Other:	Effective Not Effective	

TASK 04: LEAD DEVELOPMENT OF THE ORGANIZATION'S STRATEGIC PLAN AND ITS IMPLEMENTATION

Strategic planning is a complex and ongoing process of organizational development and change. It requires discipline to produce fundamental decisions and actions that shape and guide what an organization is – what it does and why it does it, always with a focus on the future. Although some practices, especially small ones, never take the time for planning, this can be a fatal mistake. Survival depends on awareness of the environment and appropriate adjustment. As a continuous process, strategic planning aims to keep the practice aligned with the vision of where it wants to be, its mission, and how it will implement its plans. Goals and objectives are key as is the environmental context of the external world; strategies must be creative and the communication/measurement process is critical.

04.A Understand Components of a Strategic Plan, Including Mission, Vision, Values, Goals, and Objectives

Note leadership awareness of strategic plan components and definitions by checking items that are in place.

Check all that apply	Component/Definition	Circle one	Describe action needed
	The mission statement is tied to success as measured by leadership and stakeholders.	Effective Not Effective	
	The vision statement provides direction about a desired future and the behaviors necessary to achieve it.	Effective Not Effective	
	The values statement clarifies beliefs and guidelines for making choices about behavior.	Effective Not Effective	
	Goals broadly define targets that the organization uses to prioritize activities.	Effective Not Effective	
	Objectives expand goals into specific focus areas and success measures (for example, market share, innovation, productivity, profitability).	Effective Not Effective	
	Stakeholders are questioned by leaders to gather information on the environment, future, organization, and strategies to accomplish.	Effective Not Effective	
	Other:	Effective Not Effective	

04.B Conduct SWOT Analysis (strengths, weaknesses, opportunities, and threats)

Check tools used to conduct an analysis of organizational status and environment.

Check all that apply	Tool	Circle one	Describe action needed
	A SWOT matrix tool is used to capture information on current strengths, weaknesses, opportunities, and threats.	Effective Not Effective	
	There is clear identification of strengths (resources available), weaknesses (flaws), opportunities (favorable environment), and threats (unfavorable).	Effective Not Effective	
	An analysis is used to reveal where the group should focus resources; the information is then used to develop goals and objectives.	Effective Not Effective	
	Other:	Effective Not Effective	

04.C Facilitate Group Self-Assessment and Stakeholder Needs Assessment

Verify assessment mechanisms by checking the processes that are used.

Check all that apply	Process	Circle one	Describe action needed
	A structured method is used for analysis.	Effective Not Effective	
	Stakeholders are questioned and research conducted on the current status of the organization.	Effective Not Effective	
	A questionnaire is used to assess organizational issues possibly impeding future plans.	Effective Not Effective	
	Discussions are used to assess physician commitment to the organization.	Effective Not Effective	
	Leaders review successful planning meetings held in the past.	Effective Not Effective	
	Other:	Effective Not Effective	

04.D Understand Market Trends

Note ways that are used to gather information on customer needs, external environment developments, and competitor moves.

Check all that apply	Method	Circle one	Describe action needed
	Patient (existing and potential) demographics are captured via internal and external data.	Effective Not Effective	
	Customer needs and desires are gathered via patient satisfaction surveys, focus groups, and other survey tools plus one-on-one casual conversations.	Effective Not Effective	
	Patient satisfaction data is also collected from referring physician satisfaction and hospital/ facility staff satisfaction surveys.	Effective Not Effective	
	Information is gathered consistently on competitors, referring physicians, and healthcare trends.	Effective Not Effective	
	The direction of the practice is guided by the practice's strategic plans for expansion (for example, adding services or technology/operation changes).	Effective Not Effective	
	Other:	Effective Not Effective	

04.E Facilitate Board Monitoring and Review

Check methods that are in place to ensure implementation of strategic plans and evaluation of progress and outcomes.

Check all that apply	Method	Circle one	Describe action needed
	The board delegates implementation of the strategic plan to management.	Effective Not Effective	
	The administrator's oversight emphasis is equally on fulfillment of the practice's mission and vision and on market needs.	Effective Not Effective	
	Goals, objectives, time frames, resources needed, and responsibilities are incorporated into the action plans of the practice.	Effective Not Effective	
	Monthly, quarterly, and annual review of progress on goal and responsibility fulfillment is conducted by the administrator.	Effective Not Effective	
	Other:	Effective Not Effective	

04.F Facilitate Board Retreat and Meeting Management

Check methods that are used to ensure effective retreats and meetings.

Check all that apply	Method	Circle one	Describe action needed
	The meeting or retreat is scheduled annually to identify SWOT elements, market trends, and stakeholder needs.	Effective Not Effective	
	An agreement is developed to put major issues on the table at the session.	Effective Not Effective	
	Questionnaires and interviews are used in a fair and confidential manner to draw participants out and avoid defensiveness.	Effective Not Effective	
	An agenda is developed to outline where the group wants to go, the issues to address, and time frames for accomplishment.	Effective Not Effective	
	Decisions are recorded and prioritized with responsibilities for outcomes and reporting noted.	Effective Not Effective	
	An outside facilitator is used to act as a referee and resource to stimulate thinking and move the group toward decisions.	Effective Not Effective	
	Other:	Effective Not Effective	

TASK 05: ESTABLISH, COMMUNICATE, IMPLEMENT, AND MONITOR PRODUCTION AND COMPENSATION STANDARDS FOR PHYSICIAN AND MID-LEVEL PROFESSIONAL STAFF

Compensation, always a sensitive topic in any organization, remains a high priority for physicians and mid-level providers. Simply defined as "something given or received for services rendered," compensation (pay and benefits) remains a complex HR management function. A group's policies must reflect commitment to an equitable, balanced compensation system that places fair value on the work of all its people and rewards its primary clinicians appropriately. Without such commitment, a group's performance and productivity will suffer severely. In addition, individual considerations must balance with group priorities in terms of mission, strategic plan, and financial goals and do so in a changing environment. Physician pay plans in studied better-performing groups tend to have a strong production orientation. Rewards directly relate to work, physician responsibility, and performance outcomes and link the plan to the group's strategic plan and goals. Successful groups' compensation plans are simple and understandable, creating a clear relationship between the incentive structure and physician performance. Keep in mind that many compensation elements remain outside of the control of the practice (competitive compensation, payer rates, and government mandates such as pay for performance and Medicare fees, for example). Trends also affect a group's compensation system including the move to the consolidation of groups and the integration into larger systems with their own policies on how to compensate (for example, salaries for physicians and mid-level providers). Use of a compensation consultant helps ease the process.

05.A Ensure Linkage between the Compensation Plan and the Organization's Mission, Goals, and Culture

Check elements that are included in the group's physician pay plans.

Check all that apply	Element	Circle one	Describe action needed
	Links between physician productivity (measured by dollars, RVUs, etc.) and pay	Effective Not Effective	
	Performance thresholds related to production and the establishment of greater physician "ownership" of operating costs	Effective Not Effective	
	Team involvement in compensation policy development	Effective Not Effective	
	Processes ensuring effective communication and performance feedback linked to shared strategic goals	Effective Not Effective	
	Other:	Effective Not Effective	

05.B Implement an Effective Allocation System of Revenues and Expenses, Serving as a Performance Incentive and Feedback System for Physicians

Check the type of system and processes that are used for revenue and expense allocation.

Check all that apply	System/Process	Circle one	Describe action needed
	Direct method used to pass through revenue earned by physicians	Effective Not Effective	
	Indirect method, flow fund model	Effective Not Effective	
	Indirect method, separate incentive pool	Effective Not Effective	
	Performance-related revenue used for discretionary purposes	Effective Not Effective	
	Integrative method used to recognize physicians for high-quality, low-cost outcomes	Effective Not Effective	
	Other:	Effective Not Effective	

05.C Understand Components of an Effective Compensation System, Including Practice and Physician Goals, Rewarding Productivity, and Clarifying Physician Responsibility and Accountability

Note ways used to ensure an effective compensation system.

Check all that apply	Method	Circle one	Describe action needed
	Focus on rewarding individuals fairly for the work performed and expertise exhibited	Effective Not Effective	
	Alignment of individual incentives with those of the organization	Effective Not Effective	
	Reduction or elimination of undesirable behavior adversely affecting productivity and performance	Effective Not Effective	
	Preparation for the future evolution of the job or industry	Effective Not Effective	
	Compensation plan designed to motivate group/physicians to perform at a higher level	Effective Not Effective	
	Consideration and incorporation into plan of nonrevenue generating factors such as patient outcomes and satisfaction	Effective Not Effective	
	Other:	Effective Not Effective	

05.D Recognize Compensation Plan Considerations Including Practice Size, Practice Setting, Capitation, and On-Call Obligation

Check mechanisms that are used to take practice characteristics into consideration in the compensation plan.

Check all that apply	Mechanism	Circle one	Describe action needed
	A compensation committee is selected to include the most influential and respected group members.	Effective Not Effective	
	A mission and objectives for the committee are developed.	Effective Not Effective	
	Behavior is identified that the compensation plan will address and encourage.	Effective Not Effective	
	An approval process is described such as two thirds, unanimous, and so on.	Effective Not Effective	
	Issues are resolved throughout the process.	Effective Not Effective	
	Members are educated as needed on compensation considerations.	Effective Not Effective	
	A schedule is set at the onset for plan completion.	Effective Not Effective	

Check all that apply	Mechanism	Circle one	Describe action needed
	Feedback is solicited from group members and used to improve the process.	Effective Not Effective	
	Consideration is given to compensation for mid-level provider supervisors, part-time employees, newly hired physicians, and disabled employees.	Effective Not Effective	
	Other:	Effective Not Effective	

05.E Understand Types of Compensation Plans Including Individualistic Models, Team-Oriented Models, and Base Salary Plus Incentive

What methods are used to ensure knowledge of different types of compensation?

Check all that apply	Method	Circle one	Describe action needed
	Pros and cons of straight base salary are described to physicians and the compensation committee including when they are best used.	Effective Not Effective	
	Education is provided on a salary plus incentive plan including methodology and type of practice where best used.	Effective Not Effective	
	A description of 100 percent productivity plan characteristics is discussed in the committee.	Effective Not Effective	
	Other:	Effective Not Effective	

05.F Understand Revenue Allocation Methods Including Actual Collections, Gross/Net Charges, Work Relative Value Units, and Hybrid Measures

Check ways used to help the compensation committee and physicians learn about revenue allocation methods.

Check all that apply	Method	Circle one	Describe action needed
	Information is provided on RVU costing including tracking of revenues and costs.	Effective Not Effective	
	Clarification is given on resource-based relative value scale cost accounting.	Effective Not Effective	
	The cost per RVU, set as the bottom line for contract negotiation, is emphasized to physicians.	Effective Not Effective	
	Other:	Effective Not Effective	

05.G Understand Expense Allocation Methods Including Cost Accounting and Modified Cost Accounting

Note mechanisms that are in place to ensure knowledge of expense allocation terms and methods.

Check all that apply	Mechanism	Circle one	Describe action needed
	Cost information and education is provided to managers with focus on how it helps determine compensation.	Effective Not Effective	
	Cost accounting benefits are stressed such as improving productivity and comparing costs against indices.	Effective Not Effective	
	Education is provided on how cost accounting guides group income distribution to reduce disharmony among physicians.	Effective Not Effective	
	An explanation on methods used to determine costs of resources consumed during medical procedures is provided.	Effective Not Effective	
	Other:	Effective Not Effective	

05.H Understand Practice Buy-In, Buy-Out, and Transition Arrangements

Ascertain information provided to physicians on the following policies.

Check all that apply	Policy	Circle one	Describe action needed
	Information is provided to existing and potential physician members on buy-in provisions such as length of service before becoming eligible.	Effective Not Effective	
	Physicians are given an explanation of the terms of buy-out agreements.	Effective Not Effective	
	Legal counsel review of buy-in and buy-out requirements is discussed.	Effective Not Effective	
	Clearly communicated plans are in place to ensure a smooth transition from one leader to another.	Effective Not Effective	
	Other:	Effective Not Effective	

05.I Ensure Regulatory Compliance, Including Stark Law and Anti-Kickback Laws

Note processes that are in place to ensure compliance with regulations.

Check all that apply	Process	Circle one	Describe action needed
	Oversight ensuring compliance with Stark Law I regulations	Effective Not Effective	
	Income distribution methods in line with Stark Law II regulations	Effective Not Effective	
	Physicians prohibited from receiving compensation for certain designated health services (DHS)	Effective Not Effective	
	Strict restrictions on referrals of Medicare and Medicaid patients to ownership or investment entity	Effective Not Effective	
	Compliance with Stark law rules on acceptable profit-sharing options	Effective Not Effective	
	In line with other Stark Law II regulations such as being a legal entity of two or more physicians recognized by state law	Effective Not Effective	
	Communication to members of Stark law sanctions such as severe monetary penalties	Effective Not Effective	
	Adherence to anti-kickback laws	Effective Not Effective	

Check all that apply	Process	Circle one	Describe action needed
	Awareness that regulations can change (Red Flags Rules as of this writing), so there is continual scrutiny of any current or recently regulated areas of concern	Effective Not Effective	
	Other:	Effective Not Effective	

TASK 06: IMPLEMENT AND/OR SUPPORT ORGANIZATION LEADERSHIP MANAGEMENT OF CLINICAL STAFF CONDUCT AND PERFORMANCE EXPECTATIONS OR PROGRAMS

Like any profession, medical practices and their clinicians understand the need for professional standards to guide their behavior. They may be less comfortable about performance expectations because of years of independent decisions and actions. It's up to organization leadership management to ensure the clinical staff meets today's – and tomorrow's – standards and expectations. Written standards of conduct and expectations must be developed and implemented to serve as the basis for what is expected. This is essential for the continuance of group culture. A professional standards committee of department heads should establish a code of conduct. In turn, the department heads should be empowered to have procedures in place to deal with performance and behavioral issues.

06.A Document Professional Standards of Conduct and Expectations

Check mechanisms that are in place to ensure standards of conduct and expectations are documented.

Check all that apply	Mechanism	Circle one	Describe action needed
	A code of conduct is written and communicated.	Effective Not Effective	
	A disruptive behavior policy is developed and implemented.	Effective Not Effective	
	A compliance policy is in place.	Effective Not Effective	
	Conflicts of interest are specified, documented, and reviewed.	Effective Not Effective	
	A sexual and other harassment policy is clearly stated, publicized, and enforced.	Effective Not Effective	
	A harassment and intimidation policy is developed and carried out consistently.	Effective Not Effective	
	Other:	Effective Not Effective	

06.B Establish a Professional Standards Violation Policy for Physicians

Note ways that are in place to ensure physicians do not violate professional standards.

Check all that apply	Method	Circle one	Describe action needed
	Steps are outlined in a professional standards violation policy used to resolve complaints about inappropriate physician conduct.	Effective Not Effective	
	Collegial steps are highlighted in the policy to reflect peer influence among physicians.	Effective Not Effective	
	Behavioral changes are targeted as a means of addressing and motivating conduct consistent with professional standards.	Effective Not Effective	
	Adherence to the mission, vision, and core values is emphasized as the rationale for consistent professional conduct.	Effective Not Effective	
	Other:	Effective Not Effective	

06.C Effectively Communicate and Clarify Performance Expectations

What steps are taken to ensure physician performance?

Check all that apply	Step	Circle one	Describe action needed
	Performance standards are defined and mechanisms are in place to deal with those not meeting performance goals.	Effective Not Effective	
	Performance-related policies are spotlighted in clinical staff orientation and reviewed annually.	Effective Not Effective	
	A structured, consistent performance appraisal is in place for physicians rather than just peer review and evaluation.	Effective Not Effective	
	Performance expectations and measures such as production, costs, and relationships with patients, other providers, and staff are clearly defined.	Effective Not Effective	
	Data is collected and analyzed to ensure accurate calculations and to pinpoint trends.	Effective Not Effective	
	Data benchmarks such as MGMA benchmarking data, specialty society data, and others are used for comparison purposes.	Effective Not Effective	
	A plan of action is in place for improvement actions such as milestones and time frames for physician improvement.	Effective Not Effective	
	Other:	Effective Not Effective	

06.D Support Leadership, the Governing Body, or a Professional Standards Committee Regarding Conflicts of Interest, Performance Issues, and Disruptive Behavior

Note methods that are used to ensure physicians are in line with leadership on professional conduct, group norms and general standards, and culture.

Check all that apply	Method	Circle one	Describe action needed
	Equal emphasis is put on four key areas of potential physician behavior problems: clinical/ethical, behavioral, legal/regulatory, and economic.	Effective Not Effective	
	Clinical competence, quality of care and adverse outcomes, medical ethics, and adherence to medical staff bylaws are spotlighted.	Effective Not Effective	
	Behavioral issues are noted and handled quickly including immaturity, psychiatric diagnosis, substance abuse, and sexual or other harassment.	Effective Not Effective	
	Firm expectations related to legal and regulatory matters including coding compliance, avoiding malpractice issues, and inappropriate prescriptions are set, communicated, monitored, and addressed as necessary.	Effective Not Effective	
	Economic issues are watched closely including lack of individual productivity or overproduction, poor work ethic, and failure to do fair share of work.	Effective Not Effective	

Check all that apply	Method	Circle one	Describe action needed
	Problem-solving methods are in place and are used to solve bad-behavior issues.	Effective Not Effective	
	Other:	Effective Not Effective	

TASK 07: FOSTER THE GROWTH AND DEVELOPMENT OF PHYSICIAN LEADERS AS KNOWLEDGEABLE, PARTICIPATIVE STAKEHOLDERS

Medical practices must recognize the importance of their physician leaders developing and maintaining effective interpersonal relationships. Methods used may include mentoring, training, rewarding, and testing, including self-assessments. Administrators and physicians must trust each other, communicate openly, and keep the interests of the group in mind when decision making, while offering each other respect and support. Physicians, who once tended to be autocratic and autonomous, now are encouraged to share power by getting more involved in leadership, in mission and vision development, and in creating a strong team culture. Their commitment to the long-term success of the practice is key as is the necessity for them to understand the changing culture of business such as the move to patients as consumers and to consumer-directed healthcare. As the world keeps changing, so must the role of physician leaders to ensure viable medical practices and a healthy healthcare system.

07.A Work Effectively with Leadership to Foster a Team Culture

Check methods that are used to collaborate with physician and administrative leaders on ensuring a team culture.

Check all that apply	Method	Circle one	Describe action needed
	Education is offered on sound business practices and teamwork methods to enhance physician knowledge.	Effective Not Effective	
	Experiences are provided to show how leaders and administrators can work together to meet consumer quality-care needs.	Effective Not Effective	
	The importance of hiring the right people is stressed to physicians along with tips on how to make successful selection decisions together.	Effective Not Effective	
	Emphasis is put on collaborating on a hiring strategy to establish a workforce that is able and willing to fulfill the practice's vision.	Effective Not Effective	
	Focus is placed on working together to provide adequate training to ensure job competency and awareness of the mission, culture, and teamwork philosophy.	Effective Not Effective	
	Leaders and the administrator discuss appropriate employee empowerment and ways to develop a team orientation.	Effective Not Effective	
	Other:	Effective Not Effective	

07.B Ensure Effective Communication between Physicians and Administrative Staff

Check mechanisms that are used to facilitate communication among leaders.

Check all that apply	Mechanism	Circle one	Describe action needed
	Practice administrators and the board collaboratively establish effective communication channels.	Effective Not Effective	
	Information is shared regularly on business matters such as financials and physician production.	Effective Not Effective	
	A system is in place to alert leaders of out-of-the-ordinary changes or events with details on why, when, and implications.	Effective Not Effective	
	Informal conversations among leaders are encouraged to reinforce effective relationships and communication.	Effective Not Effective	
	Other:	Effective Not Effective	

07.C Foster the Development and Growth of a Physician/Administrator Team

Note ways that are employed to foster the physician/administrator team.

Check all that apply	Method	Circle one	Describe action needed
	Frank discussions are held between physician leaders and the administrator about working together effectively.	Effective Not Effective	
	Physicians and the administrator collaborate to set a course, obtain resources, and implement plans.	Effective Not Effective	
	The governance structure is designed to effectively establish policies together based on mutual commitment to the mission, vision, and values.	Effective Not Effective	
	Physicians and the administrator collaborate to create and maintain a culture that meets the needs of shareholders, employees, and patients.	Effective Not Effective	
	Other:	Effective Not Effective	

07.D Communicate, Educate, and Facilitate Understanding of Good Business Standards and Financial Practices

Check processes that are in place to enhance leader business expertise.

Check all that apply	Process	Circle one	Describe action needed
	Frank discussions are held with physicians on how their behavior affects group finances.	Effective Not Effective	
	Extensive data, full reporting, and rigorous analysis is provided to physicians on finances and production.	Effective Not Effective	
	Pathways for change and for error disclosure are provided to eliminate secrecy and suspicion.	Effective Not Effective	
	Physicians are savvy in financial data analysis shared with colleagues to link clinical practices with the bottom line.	Effective Not Effective	
	Business matters are stressed in leadership development with focus on carving out time for group discussions.	Effective Not Effective	
	Compensation is considered for physician leader availability and effort.	Effective Not Effective	
	Other:	Effective Not Effective	

07.E Facilitate Conflict Resolution

Note methods that are used to handle conflict quickly and well.

Check all that apply	Method	Circle one	Describe action needed
	Minimization of conflict is based on a clear mission, vision, job descriptions, strong leaders, and fair evaluations.	Effective Not Effective	
	There is an immediate leader response to conflict by bringing participants together privately, listening to concerns, and finding resolution.	Effective Not Effective	
	Focus is on commonalities, shared expectations, establishing future behavior requirements, and following up on actions.	Effective Not Effective	
	The meeting environment is taken into account; a comfortable setting is provided, and rules of engagement are established.	Effective Not Effective	
	Other:	Effective Not Effective	

07.F Demonstrate Professional Integrity

Check processes that are in place to ensure that behavior demonstrates integrity.

Check all that apply	Process	Circle one	Describe action needed
	Defined norms and standards of practice are in place and behavior is assessed to evaluate compliance.	Effective Not Effective	
	Clinician patient care is assessed to ensure it is carried out with integrity as measured by medical professional standards.	Effective Not Effective	
	Operations management is assessed to ensure it is carried out with integrity as measured by business professional standards.	Effective Not Effective	
	The rewards of professionalism are highlighted including personal satisfaction, credibility, respect, authority, and career opportunities.	Effective Not Effective	
	Other:	Effective Not Effective	

TASK 08: ENCOURAGE AND LEAD PARTICIPATION IN ADVOCACY ENDEAVORS AT LOCAL, STATE, AND NATIONAL LEVELS

Medical practices sit squarely in the middle of the chaos swirling around healthcare reform. Changes in reimbursement, technology, regulation, and business models, among other things, are yet to stabilize. The good news: physician leaders, administrators, and other staff still have time to get involved and have influence. Participation in the community, in the state, and in the nation can make a definite, significant difference by leading discussions, providing data, and stimulating problem solving, shaping societal decision making and regulations. First up: learning about the issues and the players. Then educate the staff about advocacy issues. This means a focus on helping employees understand what's on the table and how it will affect healthcare management – and possibly their jobs. The staff can serve as a very influential source of information in the community.

In particular, staff members need to know the views of their own leaders about possible changes in the healthcare delivery system and consequences.

08.A Understand How Social, Political, and Legal Issues Affect Access, Cost, and Quality of Healthcare

Indicate ways that are used to promote advocacy.

Check all that apply	Method	Circle one	Describe action needed
	Information for staff is updated regularly on social, political, and legal issues related to healthcare.	Effective Not Effective	
	Focus is on the regulatory impact on access, cost, and quality of healthcare.	Effective Not Effective	
	Specific examples of possible consequences of healthcare reform on the practice are presented.	Effective Not Effective	
	Alternative, perhaps contrary, debate-worthy arguments about reform are presented.	Effective Not Effective	
	Other:	Effective Not Effective	

08.B Participate in Local, State, and National Advocacy Efforts Affecting Healthcare Management

Check methods used to encourage participation in advocacy efforts.

Check all that apply	Method	Circle one	Describe action needed
	Leaders are encouraged to volunteer for local, state, and national advocacy efforts.	Effective Not Effective	
	Compensation and work responsibilities are adjusted to eliminate barriers to involvement.	Effective Not Effective	
	Physician perspective is spotlighted as significantly influential in discussions with government officials.	Effective Not Effective	
	Other:	Effective Not Effective	

08.C Educate Staff on Advocacy Issues

Note processes that are in place to inform employees on advocacy issues.

Check all that apply	Process	Circle one	Describe action needed
	Employees are informed about ways new regulations may affect them.	Effective Not Effective	
	Staff members are encouraged to inform and influence those involved in regulatory decisions.	Effective Not Effective	
	Employees are trained to answer patient questions in a well-informed manner about regulatory impacts on the practice.	Effective Not Effective	
	Other:	Effective Not Effective	

08.D Encourage and Participate in Community and Civic Activities

Ascertain methods that are used to reinforce the importance of local participation.

Check all that apply	Method	Circle one	Describe action needed
	Personal participation in community and civic affairs as a role model to stimulate others' involvement is encouraged.	Effective Not Effective	
	Leadership is encouraged to sponsor and/or support local healthcare activities such as community health fairs.	Effective Not Effective	
	Leaders are expected to perform healthcare community service such as serving on the hospital board or county public health commission.	Effective Not Effective	
	Other:	Effective Not Effective	

BOTTOM LINE—ORGANIZATIONAL GOVERNANCE

Organizational governance, properly done, ensures that the medical practice is led well in the present and the future. The organization's structure and policies are targeted to carry out the promise of the group's mission, vision, and values in an ethical manner. The leadership supports a workplace where physicians, administrators, and clinical/nonclinical staff understand and endorse the practice's goals and work together as teams to achieve objectives.

Organizational Governance
Supplemental Notes
(copy as needed)

Task	Notes

Organizational Governance
Action Items
(copy as needed)

Task	Action	Responsible Party	Due Date	Priority

CHAPTER 6

Patient Care Systems

The ability to create and maintain effective and efficient patient care systems is essential for an administrator. One can either make or break a practice based on this ability. How are your systems working? Patients are increasingly involved in their care, learning about their conditions through a variety of sources, including the Internet. Practices enhance that process by encouraging participation. Do your systems support patient participation? Since the advent of managed care, practitioners have had to develop systems to handle referrals. Missing referrals create delays in reimbursement and write-offs, affecting the bottom line. Another piece of the referral pie relates to how practices handle referrals from and to other physicians. Do your referral protocols work for or against the practice? All of us have at one time or another experienced situations in which a practitioner has been late. Does it happen at your practice? Does it occur often, or is it a rare event? Regardless, the disruption created is counterproductive – in a multitude of ways. How efficient is the patient flow in your practice? Patient service is a must today. Patients have choices as to where to obtain their care. A bad reputation on the part of the practice or provider can lead to a diminished practice. How good is your service? Management of pharmaceuticals and medical supplies (both billable and nonbillable) requires that the right items are in stock at the right time and at the right price. Do you have what your practitioners need? Complete this section to find out how well you are doing in the area of patient care systems.

TASK 01: ESTABLISH AND MONITOR BUSINESS PROCESSES TO ENSURE EFFECTIVE AND EFFICIENT CLINICAL OPERATIONS

Delivering quality care is a key goal for a medical practice. Some payers have tied quality to reimbursement in an effort to control costs. Practice administrators now have a two-fold purpose to work toward creating quality in their practices. Operational effectiveness is one place to start creating quality. It begins with standards. What are yours? Patient outcomes relate to quality as well. Do you have systems in place to measure them? The healthcare arena is constantly changing. At one time insurance covered catastrophic events and copays didn't exist. Since then we've experienced capitation, high-deductible plans, and more. Alternative approaches will continue to emerge. Are you staying abreast of new models for delivery of healthcare? Some practices make a choice to be involved in clinical trials. Do you understand the pros and cons of including a research aspect in your practice? Complete this section to find out how you're doing in the area of clinical operations.

01.A Clinical Quality of Care Standards

Questions to consider	YES	NO If no, why not?	NOT APPLICABLE (note reason)
Is the call coverage schedule satisfactory?			
Are physicians responsible for their own call coverage during office hours?			
Does a rotating schedule cover call in the evenings and overnight during the week and weekends?			
Is the call schedule fair and equitable?			
Is the call schedule arranged by each specialty and subspecialty?			
Are midlevel providers used for call coverage?			
Do physicians back up the midlevel providers?			
Is there a back-up physician for call coverage?			
Are sound systems in place for the answering service to reach the on-call physician through pager, cell phone, or other?			
Are the physicians on call geographically accessible?			

Questions to consider	YES	NO If no, why not?	NOT APPLICABLE (note reason)
Is medical record documentation completed by the end of the day?			
Are medical record entries accurate, complete, and legible?			
Are corrections made by drawing a single line through incorrect information – so that information is still readable – and dating and signing the entry?			
Is the EMR "locked" after chart documentation is complete?			
Regardless of note format, does the documentation detail appropriate vital signs and cover subjective and objective data, assessment, and plan?			
For paper charts, does each page of notes (front and back) include patient name, patient date of birth, and service date?			
Is the service date consistently correct?			

Questions to consider	YES	NO If no, why not?	NOT APPLICABLE (note reason)
Are the medical records (paper or electronic) well organized, making it easy to find information?			
Do the medical records contain sections for type of information (visit notes, operative reports, lab results, X-ray, correspondence, etc.)?			
Is the medical records department well organized?			
If paper charts are used, is storage convenient?			
If paper charts are used, is storage compliant with HIPAA guidelines?			
Is the filing system alpha or numeric and, if using paper charts, color coded?			
Is filing consistently up to date?			
Are there minimal misfiles?			

Questions to consider	YES	NO If no, why not?	NOT APPLICABLE (note reason)
Are paper charts periodically proofread to identify misfiles?			
Are protocols in place about not taking paper charts off site (other than directly to satellite offices)?			
Are protocols in place about returning paper charts to the chart area in a timely manner for refilling?			
Are noncurrent paper records archived to maximize use of space?			
Is the practice compliant with laws regarding medical record retention?			

01.B Patient Outcomes

Questions to consider	YES	NO If no, why not?	NOT APPLICABLE (note reason)
Are you knowledgeable about patient outcomes?			
Are outcomes to track identified?			
Do you have physician buy-in of outcomes to track?			
Are systems in place to track outcomes?			
Do the systems measure the effectiveness, cost, and patient satisfaction with treatment?			
Is outcome information reported to physician leaders?			
Is action taken to improve outcomes?			

01.C Emerging Models for Healthcare Delivery

Do you have knowledge of the following models for healthcare delivery?

Check all that apply	Model	Circle one	Describe action needed
	Integrated delivery systems	Effective Not Effective	
	Fully integrated EHRs such as between all healthcare institutions	Effective Not Effective	
	Regional health information exchange	Effective Not Effective	
	Primary care/specialist information exchange	Effective Not Effective	
	Clinical integration system	Effective Not Effective	
	Accountable care organization	Effective Not Effective	
	Joint ventures	Effective Not Effective	
	Community partnerships	Effective Not Effective	

Check all that apply	Model	Circle one	Describe action needed
	Shared practice	Effective Not Effective	
	Micropractice	Effective Not Effective	
	Patient-centered medical home	Effective Not Effective	
	Web-based care	Effective Not Effective	
	Telemedicine	Effective Not Effective	
	Meaningful use	Effective Not Effective	
	Hospital/doctor bundling	Effective Not Effective	
	Concierge practice	Effective Not Effective	
	Cash-only practice	Effective Not Effective	
	Other:	Effective Not Effective	

Questions to consider	YES	NO If no, why not?	NOT APPLICABLE (note reason)
Do leaders stay abreast of changes in delivery via professional reading, seminars, and so on?			
Do leaders consider the impact of other delivery models on the practice?			
Do leaders evaluate current vs. alternative delivery methods in terms of what represents the best for the practice?			

01.D Nurse Triage Systems

Questions to consider	YES	NO If no, why not?	NOT APPLICABLE (note reason)
Is a triage system in place?			
Are physician-approved written guidelines and protocols for triage in place?			
Do guidelines include call categorization (for example, routine, urgent, life threatening) and response time parameters for each?			
Are triage calls handled on a same-day basis?			

Questions to consider	YES	NO If no, why not?	NOT APPLICABLE (note reason)
Is triage responsibility centralized?			
Is the triage nurse qualified in terms of education, credentials, experience, and so on?			
Is the triage nurse appropriately trained?			
Are the physicians comfortable with the triage nurse's judgment?			
Are incoming calls briefly screened for appropriate transfer?			
Are patient situations not fitting triage guidelines routed to providers for disposition?			
Are triage call details documented using a physician-designed template in the medical record (for example, who, what, when, where, why, disposition, advice given, name, date, and time)?			

01.E Clinical Trials Research

Do you have a working knowledge of the following aspects of the clinical trials process?

Check all that apply	Aspect	Circle one	Describe action needed
	Selection process	Effective Not Effective	
	Financial assessment	Effective Not Effective	
	Contract and budget negotiations	Effective Not Effective	
	Accounting and billing	Effective Not Effective	
	Other:	Effective Not Effective	

Questions to consider	YES	NO If no, why not?	NOT APPLICABLE (note reason)
Does the practice have the time and flexibility to participate in clinical trials?			

Do participating physicians possess the following necessary qualities for success in clinical trials?

Check all that apply	Quality	Circle one	Describe action needed
	Organized	Effective Not Effective	
	Efficient	Effective Not Effective	
	Detail oriented	Effective Not Effective	
	Flexible	Effective Not Effective	
	Committed to research	Effective Not Effective	
	Other:	Effective Not Effective	

Questions to consider	YES	NO If no, why not?	NOT APPLICABLE (note reason)
Are the physicians knowledgeable about responsibilities associated with research, both written and unwritten (Food and Drug Administration Form 1572, ultimate responsibility of primary investigator, disclosure of conflicts of interest, etc.)?			
Is participant consent obtained prior to participation in the study?			
Does the consent process include informing the participant about risks and benefits as well as documentation of the process?			
Do all participants reconsent if new information arises about study medication?			
Is treatment of nonstudy illnesses and conditions avoided?			
Does the principal investigator attend all study-related meetings with the study sponsor?			
Is responsibility delegated for administrative aspects of the study (contract, finance and budget, regulatory documentation, training and setup, patient recruitment, etc.)?			

Questions to consider	YES	NO If no, why not?	NOT APPLICABLE (note reason)
Is staffing adequate to assume study-related tasks?			
Are drugs inventoried immediately after every patient visit?			
Is space adequate for the study (dedicated exam room, laboratory space, storage for associated paperwork, space for study coordinators and staff to complete paperwork, etc.)?			
Is study documentation stored in a secure area?			
If study volume is adequate, is an in-house auditing system used?			
Are time, effort, and profit associated with the study tracked?			
Is a legal review of the contract to participate in the study conducted?			
Does the administrator review the study budget?			
Do leaders determine if the study protocol is a good fit for the practice?			

TASK 02: PROVIDE RELEVANT AND ACCURATE RESOURCES TO ENHANCE PATIENTS' KNOWLEDGE, UNDERSTANDING, AND PARTICIPATION IN THEIR MEDICAL CARE

Many patients now arrive for their appointments having researched possible diagnoses and treatments and want active involvement in their care. In the practice setting, it is important to support that wish. Patient involvement starts with patient communication systems such as appointment confirmations, notifications, and financial counseling. Patient education is also part of this task, as are informed consent and disclosure of possible outcomes, treatment plans, and prescription management. The issue of termination of care also arises occasionally. How are you doing in these areas? Answer the following questions to find out.

02.A Patient Communication Procedures

Questions to consider	YES	NO If no, why not?	NOT APPLICABLE (note reason)
Are effective and efficient patient communication systems in place?			
Do the communication approaches suit all patient age groups?			
Are systems periodically assessed for effectiveness and changes made as necessary?			
Does the practice staff confirm appointments two days in advance?			
Is an automated system in place?			
Are appointment confirmation, cancellation (including reason), rescheduling, and so on recorded in the system?			

Questions to consider	YES	NO If no, why not?	NOT APPLICABLE (note reason)
Are cancellations and reschedules reviewed for medical necessity issues?			
Is a cancellation list used?			
Is the cancellation list automated?			
Are cancellations reviewed early in the morning and an attempt made to fill openings?			
Are early openings filled before later openings?			
Are the slots created from cancellations consistently filled?			
Are patient follow-up actions that are created as a result of visits, telephone calls, and other interactions consistently acted upon in a timely manner?			
Are actions noted and documented in the chart (who, what, when, where, and why as well as staff member name, date, and disposition)?			

Questions to consider	YES	NO If no, why not?	NOT APPLICABLE (note reason)
Are patient notifications documented in the chart (who, what, when, where, and why as well as staff member name, date and disposition)?			
Are financial counseling protocols in place?			
Are protocols compliant with related laws (Stark law, False Claims Act, HIPAA, etc.)?			
Are protocols applied fairly and evenly?			
Is patient financial counseling documented in the practice management system?			

02.B Patient Education

Questions to consider	YES	NO If no, why not?	NOT APPLICABLE (note reason)
Is a direction established within the practice with regard to patient education priorities and topics?			
Is a patient education program in place and materials coordinated between providers for the clinical portion and management for the administrative portion?			

Note the vehicles for delivery of patient education.

Check all that apply	Vehicle	Circle one	Describe action needed
	Brochures	Effective Not Effective	
	Flyers	Effective Not Effective	
	Videos	Effective Not Effective	
	Audio	Effective Not Effective	
	Website	Effective Not Effective	
	One-on-one training	Effective Not Effective	
	Seminars	Effective Not Effective	
	Other:	Effective Not Effective	

Questions to consider	YES	NO If no, why not?	NOT APPLICABLE (note reason)
Is patient education documented in the medical record (who, what, when, where, why, etc.)?			
Are patient literacy issues addressed in the patient education program?			
Is the staff informed about the program?			
Is the program evaluated on a periodic basis with modifications made as appropriate?			
Are patients surveyed for feedback on patient education effectiveness?			

02.C Informed Consent and Unanticipated Outcomes

Questions to consider	YES	NO If no, why not?	NOT APPLICABLE (note reason)
Is informed consent obtained when appropriate (for surgical procedure, treatment decision, and so on)?			

Does your informed consent form incorporate the following items?

Check all that apply	Item	Circle one	Describe action needed
	Patient name	Effective Not Effective	
	Date of birth	Effective Not Effective	
	Summary of patient condition (diagnosis)	Effective Not Effective	
	Nature of the decision or procedure	Effective Not Effective	
	Name of physician performing the procedure	Effective Not Effective	
	Facility where the procedure will be performed	Effective Not Effective	
	Benefits, risks, uncertainties, side effects, complications, and prognosis	Effective Not Effective	
	Alternative decisions or procedures	Effective Not Effective	

Check all that apply	Item	Circle one	Describe action needed
	Benefits, risks, uncertainties, side effects, complications, and prognosis of alternatives	Effective Not Effective	
	Statement of patient understanding	Effective Not Effective	
	Acknowledgment of acceptance of decision or procedure	Effective Not Effective	
	Other:	Effective Not Effective	

Questions to consider	YES	NO If no, why not?	NOT APPLICABLE (note reason)
Are patients competent and do they consent voluntarily?			
Is the reasonableness standard (physician, patient, subjective, etc.) applied?			
Is the practice compliant with pertinent laws regarding informed consent?			
Is informed consent discussed with the patient?			
Is informed consent documented contemporaneously in the medical record?			

02.D The Treatment Plan

Questions to consider	YES	NO If no, why not?	NOT APPLICABLE (note reason)
Is the treatment plan consistently communicated to the patient?			
Is the treatment plan communicated in a clear and easy-to-understand manner?			

Questions to consider	YES	NO If no, why not?	NOT APPLICABLE (note reason)
Are the options, pros and cons of each, risks, and other pertinent information communicated to the patient?			
Does chart documentation (note or template) consistently reflect communication of the treatment plan as well as the actual treatment plan?			
Is the diagnosis recorded using the highest level of specificity?			
Are methods in place to communicate with the deaf, blind, and non-English-speaking patients?			
Is the practice compliant with state and federal laws regarding communications with deaf, blind, and non-English-speaking patients?			
Are providers and staff aware of medical illiteracy?			
Are methods in place to address medical illiteracy in patient communication about the treatment plan?			

02.E Prescription and Refill Management

Questions to consider	YES	NO If no, why not?	NOT APPLICABLE (note reason)
Do the providers use electronic prescribing?			
Are electronic formularies used?			
Is electronic drug interactions software used?			
Is a prescription submission network used to forward prescriptions electronically to pharmacies?			
Is prescription eligibility checked electronically?			
Is prescription history, including over-the-counter medications, obtained?			
Are patients provided with an updated list of medications at each visit (including name, strength, dosage, and frequency)?			
Do providers prescribe based on medical necessity, not patient request or pressure?			

Questions to consider	YES	NO If no, why not?	NOT APPLICABLE (note reason)
Are prescriptions renewed only as appropriate given the medical condition and drug?			
Are patients appropriately instructed on drug use?			
Are prescription pads kept locked and secure, with only a daily "in use" quantity in the provider's possession?			
Does the practice follow state and federal prescribing laws?			
Is medication safety practiced?			
Are protocols in place for filling after-hours prescription requests?			
Is a log maintained of paper prescriptions that are picked up at a time other than at an appointment?			
Are protocols established and followed for times when someone other than the patient picks up a paper prescription?			

02.F Termination of Care and the Patient Relationship

Questions to consider	YES	NO If no, why not?	NOT APPLICABLE (note reason)
Are providers notified regarding excessive no-show and cancellation events?			
Are patients sent letters regarding excessive no-show and cancellation events (including an explanation of office protocols)?			
Is a policy in place regarding patient discharge?			
Does the policy cover steps to follow when discharging a patient?			

Does your patient discharge policy include the following reasons?

Check all that apply	Reason	Circle one	Describe action needed
	Repeated no-show events	Effective Not Effective	
	Nonpayment of patient bills	Effective Not Effective	
	Noncompliance	Effective Not Effective	
	Abusive (verbal or nonverbal) behavior	Effective Not Effective	
	Threatening behavior	Effective Not Effective	
	Litigation	Effective Not Effective	
	Other:	Effective Not Effective	

Questions to consider	YES	NO If no, why not?	NOT APPLICABLE (note reason)
Do all providers follow the policy consistently?			
Is the practice knowledgeable about and compliant with state law regarding termination of care?			
Is the practice knowledgeable about and compliant with federal law, state medical board issues, and community practices regarding termination of care?			
Does the practice not abandon patients who are discharged?			
Does the practice not discharge patients for reasons associated with discrimination (race, gender, sexual preference, religion, etc.)?			
Do the providers not offend referring physicians when discharging patients?			
Are issues leading up to discharge, attempts to educate the patient, and discharge documented?			

Questions to consider	YES	NO If no, why not?	NOT APPLICABLE (note reason)
Is a termination letter sent that includes reasons, events, a 30-day notice, and a medical records request form, and is it sent by certified mail, return receipt requested, as well as by regular mail?			
Has the practice's legal counsel reviewed and approved the letter?			

TASK 03: DEVELOP AND IMPLEMENT A REFERRAL MANAGEMENT PROCESS

The referral process encompasses referrals both from and to other physicians as well as from insurance payers. This section addresses how both are maximized to benefit practices. What processes do you have in place for referrals? Are you knowledgeable about payer requirements? What about follow-up – on missing referrals, for instance – and reporting – such as providing a summarization of care provided? Further, physicians need positive working relationships with referring physicians – crucial to both primary care and specialist physicians, each for different reasons. Tackle the section below to determine how your referral processes measure up.

03.A The Referral Process and Plan Requirements

Questions to consider	YES	NO If no, why not?	NOT APPLICABLE (note reason)
Do you have a good working knowledge of the physician referral process?			
Is a system in place to track physician referrals and analyze patterns?			
Are you knowledgeable about payer referral requirements (forms, participating provider lists, authorization protocols, etc.)?			
Do patients clearly understand the reason for referrals?			

03.B Referrals In and Out of the Practice

Questions to consider	YES	NO If no, why not?	NOT APPLICABLE (note reason)
Are the physicians accessible to and friendly with primary care physicians?			
Do the physicians take advantage of relationship-building opportunities that others create?			
Does the practice also create relationship-building opportunities?			

Review the following list of opportunities to interact with referring physicians. Check all that are used in your practice.

Check all that apply	Opportunity	Circle one	Describe action needed
	Grand rounds	Effective Not Effective	
	Physician lounge	Effective Not Effective	
	Committee meetings	Effective Not Effective	
	Attendance at regional physician meetings	Effective Not Effective	
	Attendance at state physician meetings	Effective Not Effective	
	Attendance at national physician meetings	Effective Not Effective	
	Social outings	Effective Not Effective	
	In-service presentations at regional meetings	Effective Not Effective	

Check all that apply	Opportunity	Circle one	Describe action needed
	In-service presentations at state meetings	Effective Not Effective	
	In-service presentations at national meetings	Effective Not Effective	
	Presence in clinical areas of hospital (floors, ER, etc.)	Effective Not Effective	
	Visits to other physician offices	Effective Not Effective	
	Other:	Effective Not Effective	

Is it easy for referring physicians to reach your practice? Check off all methods provided.

Check all that apply	Method	Circle one	Describe action needed
	Private line	Effective Not Effective	
	Physicians' e-mail addresses	Effective Not Effective	
	Physicians' cell phone numbers	Effective Not Effective	
	Other:	Effective Not Effective	

03.C Follow-Up and Reporting

Questions to consider	YES	NO If no, why not?	NOT APPLICABLE (note reason)
Are physician referral protocols in place?			
Are physician referrals documented in the chart?			
Does the practice provide and receive all necessary information (patient demographics, reason for referral, pertinent notes and test results, office contact information, special needs, etc.)?			
Are all physician referrals tracked to ensure care is delivered, and is follow-up conducted on a periodic, as-needed basis?			
Are communications from referring physicians handled promptly (calls, correspondence, etc.)?			
Are patients from referring physicians scheduled promptly?			
Are reports sent to referring physicians promptly?			
Is continuity of care ensured within the physician referral process?			

Questions to consider	YES	NO If no, why not?	NOT APPLICABLE (note reason)
Are insurance payer referral process protocols in place?			
Is the insurance referral work flow efficient?			
Are payer websites used for insurance referral activities (submission, confirmation, etc.)?			
Are patients reminded about insurance referral requirements when making and confirming appointments?			
Is receipt of referrals verified prior to appointments?			
Are patients who have not obtained insurance referrals prior to their appointments required to sign a waiver form?			
Is a payer-specific waiver form used when required, and is a generic waiver form used when the payer does not provide a form?			
Are protocols in place to address multiple waivers for a single patient?			
Are referrals recorded in the practice management system?			
Is the number of visits tracked when a referral authorizes multiple visits on a single referral?			

03.D Relationships with Referring Physicians

Questions to consider	YES	NO If no, why not?	NOT APPLICABLE (note reason)
Are good relationships with referring physicians developed, fostered, and maintained?			
Does the practice develop complementary relationships?			

Check the purposes for regular communication with referring physicians that occur in your practice.

Check all that apply	Purpose	Circle one	Describe action needed
	To find out about what's going on in the referring physicians' practices	Effective Not Effective	
	To provide updates about changes in the practice	Effective Not Effective	
	To hold an open house for referring physicians and their staffs	Effective Not Effective	
	To send information about new associates in the practice	Effective Not Effective	
	Patient reports (a notch above those provided by competitors) that require discussion	Effective Not Effective	

Check all that apply	Purpose	Circle one	Describe action needed
	Post care, patients are sent back to their referring physicians.	Effective Not Effective	
	Referring physicians and their staffs are thanked with personal notes, small and appropriate gifts, and so on.	Effective Not Effective	
	Education is provided for referring physicians about your specialty, preferably with continuing medical education credits.	Effective Not Effective	
	All physicians in the group are encouraged to connect face to face with referring physicians on a regular basis (lunch, dinner, etc.)	Effective Not Effective	
	Other:	Effective Not Effective	

TASK 04: DESIGN EFFICIENT PATIENT FLOW PATTERNS TO MAXIMIZE PHYSICIAN SCHEDULES

Providers are the resource in your practice, and part of your responsibility as a manager is to ensure that processes are in place to maximize their patient care time. Patient flow processes, such as registration, appointment scheduling, check-in, and check-out can enhance or disrupt that. Which do your processes do? An insufficient number of emergency slots results in an overextended schedule, excessive wait times, and overtime expense when the day is lengthened. Alternatively, excessive numbers of no-shows lead to underuse of physician time, decreased revenue, and overstaffing. Are you effectively handling these aspects of scheduling? There are numerous ways in which to structure physician schedules. Are you aware of them? Is your scheduling system the best approach for your physicians and practice? Staffing levels are also critical to physician efficiency. Do you have the right people scheduled at the right place and at the right time? On-call coverage encompasses emergency, night, weekend, holiday, hospital, nursing home, and other coverage responsibilities. Calls can be a point of contention in practices. What protocols do you have in place? Answer the following questions to learn how well you handle maximization of physician schedules.

04.A Patient Flow Process

Questions to consider	YES	NO If no, why not?	NOT APPLICABLE (note reason)
Are patient flow processes (registration, appointment scheduling, arrival, check-in, encounter management, check-out, etc.) efficient, effective, and accurate?			
Is a patient flow analysis completed periodically?			
Is the timing of processes conducted periodically?			
Is the flow analyzed for slow-downs and bottlenecks?			
Is corrective action taken as necessary?			
Are alternatives identified in the event of a computer failure?			

04.B Daily Practice Flow

Questions to consider	YES	NO If no, why not?	NOT APPLICABLE (note reason)
Are good scheduling practices (planning, communicating, appointment scheduling system, and so on) in place?			
Are effective procedures in place to handle daily flow issues (emergencies, calls from other physicians/hospitals/ nursing homes/labs, cancellations, no-shows, etc.)?			
Are staff members trained, committed, and empowered to handle daily flow issues?			

04.C Scheduling Methodologies and Physician Maximization

Questions to consider	YES	NO If no, why not?	NOT APPLICABLE (note reason)
Are you knowledgeable about different scheduling systems (single interval, multiple interval, block [or wave] interval, open access, etc.)?			
Is the practice open a sufficient number of hours to accommodate patient needs?			
Are a sufficient number of appointments available (for example, daily, weekly, monthly)?			
Are a sufficient number of appointments available by type (new, established, consultation, pre-op, post-op, emergency, etc.)?			
Does the staff follow checklists and written guidelines about scheduling practices and protocols?			
Does the staff schedule appropriately for appointment type, condition and diagnosis, and so on?			
Are holds maintained for emergencies?			
Is the schedule not overbooked?			

Questions to consider	YES	NO If no, why not?	NOT APPLICABLE (note reason)
Are provider schedules available for one year in advance?			
Do providers plan time out of the office with sufficient notice to close schedules without requiring a significant number of reschedules?			
Are last-minute cancellations of office hours by providers reviewed by a senior physician to ensure appropriateness of cancellation and reduce occurrences?			
Are follow-up appointments scheduled during the check-out process?			
Are checklists used to communicate reminders to patients prior to appointments (download and complete patient registration data, arrive a specified time in advance of an appointment for registration processing, bring current insurance card, obtain referral, copay is due at time of service, etc.)?			
Are exam rooms cleaned and stocked at the beginning and end of each day, as well as between patients, and in a timely manner?			

Questions to consider	YES	NO If no, why not?	NOT APPLICABLE (note reason)
Are medical records prepared, readily accessible, and reviewed prior to appointments to ensure readiness to provide care?			
Do appointment slots allow sufficient time to complete necessary tasks (history, exam, treatment plan, patient education, informed consent, referrals, chart documentation, coding, completion of encounter form, etc.)?			
Do providers start, stay, and finish on time?			
Are provider interruptions controlled throughout the day?			
Is provider time routinely maximized?			
Are all staff members aware of the daily schedules?			
Are schedules periodically analyzed for issues with inefficiency and corrective action taken?			

04.D Scheduling of Clinical and Nonclinical Staff

Questions to consider	YES	NO If no, why not?	NOT APPLICABLE (note reason)
Are staff schedules based on need, referencing historical information regarding volume?			
Do schedules provide sufficient coverage of clinical staff to support patient flow?			
Do schedules provide sufficient coverage of nonclinical staff to support patient flow?			
Are clinical and nonclinical staff schedules reviewed periodically and adjusted as necessary?			

04.E Emergency Calls

Questions to consider	YES	NO If no, why not?	NOT APPLICABLE (note reason)
Are protocols in place for emergency calls (weekend, weeknight, holiday, hospital, nursing home, etc.)?			
Do protocols address provider sign-out to the on-call provider?			
Do protocols define when a call begins and ends? (For example, a call begins at 5:00 p.m. and concludes at 7:00 a.m.)			
Do the protocols suit the needs of the practice?			
Is the call schedule communicated in advance to all parties needing it (clinical and nonclinical staff, administration, providers, answering service, etc.)?			
Are call schedule changes communicated to all parties needing them (clinical and nonclinical staff, administration, providers, answering service, etc.)?			
Is the call schedule equitable?			

TASK 05: MANAGE FRONT OFFICE OPERATIONS TO MAXIMIZE PATIENT SATISFACTION, COLLECTION OF PAYMENTS, AND CUSTOMER SERVICE EFFORTS

How do you manage front office operations to best satisfy customers and stay competitive? First, to maximize patient satisfaction you must select employees with a strong customer orientation, train them in ways to delight and dazzle the customers, and pay competitively. Then ask yourself if you have the kind of call center processes and procedures that fit your kind of patients. For example, an older patient with a chronic condition may not be able to cope with complex telephone options. Next, do you make your pre-visit registration process as simple as possible for the patient? Beware of designing the process to fit internal needs only – consider the patient as well.

When patients arrive for check-in, how does the front desk staff treat them? Patients get immediate positive – or negative – vibes about your group depending on how they are received when they arrive. How do you promote patient-focused customer service throughout the organization, and particularly with front office staff? Training specific to these staff members is well worth offering. And of course, there are HIPAA challenges related to protecting patient confidentiality in the front office. How do you ensure a high level of privacy at the front desk? You may need to modify procedures and reconfigure the area. Now let's get specific.

05.A Call-Center Processes and Procedures

Check the methods that are established in the practice's call center.

Check all that apply	Method	Circle one	Describe action needed
	The staff is selected with a customer orientation and compensated competitively.	Effective Not Effective	
	Specific orientation and ongoing training is provided to call-center staff.	Effective Not Effective	
	The staffing level is adjusted to call volume fluctuations and call capture needs.	Effective Not Effective	

Check all that apply	Method	Circle one	Describe action needed
	Calls are taken promptly for appropriate triage and scheduling appointments.	Effective Not Effective	
	The call center is designed so that staff members are in close proximity for information sharing.	Effective Not Effective	
	The telecommunications systems and equipment are designed to be staff- and patient-friendly.	Effective Not Effective	
	The call center staff performance is monitored and measured by observation, surveys, and processing volumes.	Effective Not Effective	
	The staff is dedicated and empowered to put the patient first via the call management system.	Effective Not Effective	
	Managed care referral requirements are met by staff following certain protocols.	Effective Not Effective	
	A system is in place to handle overflow calls	Effective Not Effective	
	Other:	Effective Not Effective	

05.B Pre-Visit Registration Process

Note ways that are used to develop pre-visit relationships with patients and note any challenges or actions needed.

Check all that apply	Method	Circle one	Describe action needed
	Patient demographic and insurance data are obtained prior to the appointment.	Effective Not Effective	
	Front desk operations are facilitated so that no-shows are reduced and payments are increased.	Effective Not Effective	
	Pre-registration is handled by phone or via the practice's website as appropriate.	Effective Not Effective	
	Insurance information is verified with the patient and the insurer by staff prior to the visit.	Effective Not Effective	
	The patient is informed if coverage is an issue so that it can be resolved before the visit.	Effective Not Effective	
	All information is verified with the patient at the time of check-in.	Effective Not Effective	
	Other:	Effective Not Effective	

05.C Patient Check-In

Check methods that are used to handle check-in.

Check all that apply	Method	Circle one	Describe action needed
	Patients are greeted warmly and, if not pre-registered, asked to provide information.	Effective Not Effective	
	Standardized forms are used to collect medical, demographic, and insurance data as well as HIPAA/privacy notification.	Effective Not Effective	
	Forms are designed to follow data input of practice management software.	Effective Not Effective	
	If available, self-service methods are used such as kiosk, personal computer, and so on.	Effective Not Effective	
	The physician referral process is coordinated to verify that physicians are in sync with patient needs.	Effective Not Effective	
	Follow-up appointments are booked at check-out.	Effective Not Effective	
	Patient flow is coordinated with clinical staff to ensure minimal waiting time.	Effective Not Effective	
	Other:	Effective Not Effective	

05.D Billing and Collections

Check methods used to oversee billing and collections at registration.

Check all that apply	Method	Circle one	Describe action needed
	The registration staff is included in billing and collection meetings and memos.	Effective Not Effective	
	A rotation in the billing office is included in new staff training.	Effective Not Effective	
	Techniques for collecting payments from patients are included in the training.	Effective Not Effective	
	A registration proficiency test is required after training and annually.	Effective Not Effective	
	Claims needing rework because of the front office missing data are counted monthly.	Effective Not Effective	
	The registration error rate is noted in performance measurements.	Effective Not Effective	
	To the extent that copay obligations can be identified prior to delivery of care, copays are collected at check-in.	Effective Not Effective	
	Other:	Effective Not Effective	

05.E Patient-Focused Customer Service

Note techniques that are used to promote customer service.

Check all that apply	Technique	Circle one	Describe action needed
	The waiting room is designed for comfort, education, and entertainment.	Effective Not Effective	
	Wait times are minimized, and when excessive, patients are informed and given options.	Effective Not Effective	
	Patients are greeted by name at the registration desk in a pleasant manner.	Effective Not Effective	
	The staff is trained in customer service principles, and performance is observed and critiqued.	Effective Not Effective	
	The use of basics such as "please" and "thank you" are emphasized.	Effective Not Effective	
	Dealing with difficult patients is included in the training along with the use of "I'm sorry."	Effective Not Effective	
	Exit matters are handled in a friendly manner so that patients leave with a positive image.	Effective Not Effective	
	Other:	Effective Not Effective	

05.F HIPAA Compliance

Check ways that are used to ensure HIPAA compliance in the front office.

Check all that apply	Method	Circle one	Describe action needed
	The front office staff is trained about confidentiality of PHI.	Effective Not Effective	
	Registration information is electronically retained and protected according to HIPAA protocols (for example, access control, shredding original documents).	Effective Not Effective	
	Patients are given a "Notice of Privacy Practices" in the prescribed format.	Effective Not Effective	
	Information on how and when PHI is disclosed is provided in the Notice.	Effective Not Effective	
	Patients are informed of their rights regarding complaints and access to medical records.	Effective Not Effective	
	Space and systems are designed to protect patient privacy.	Effective Not Effective	
	Other:	Effective Not Effective	

TASK 06: IMPLEMENT A PLAN TO CONTROL PHARMACEUTICAL SUPPLIES

Supplies used in the delivery of care including drugs – both narcotic and non-narcotic, from topicals to pills to injectibles – as well as medical supplies must be on hand when needed and in the required quantities. How complete is your knowledge about the types of supplies used in your practice? Do you have effective procedures in place to secure, store, and access the supplies? Inventory systems allow us to compare actual to book quantity on hand. Do you have an effective system to check your inventory? With drugs, a practice must be compliant with a variety of rules and regulations. Do you know what those requirements are, and do you meet them? Interactions with pharmaceutical representatives require management effort to ensure a variety of practice needs are met, from maximizing provider time and patient flow to managing gifts and incentives. How well are you doing in this area? Read on to find out.

06.A Pharmaceuticals

Questions to consider	YES	NO If no, why not?	NOT APPLICABLE (note reason)
Do you possess a working knowledge of the various types of pharmaceuticals (vaccines, injectibles, narcotics, samples, etc.)?			
If injectable medications are used, are they in single-dose vials to reduce the risk of contamination and infection?			
Is a written policy in place for dispensing and distributing sample medications?			

Check all topics included in the policy for dispensing and distributing sample medications.

Check all that apply	Topic	Circle one	Describe action needed
	Storage	Effective Not Effective	
	Security	Effective Not Effective	
	Dispensing	Effective Not Effective	
	Disposal	Effective Not Effective	
	Labeling	Effective Not Effective	
	Providing directions for use, warnings, and patient education	Effective Not Effective	
	Other:	Effective Not Effective	

Questions to consider	YES	NO If no, why not?	NOT APPLICABLE (note reason)
Do you maintain up-to-date knowledge about necessary changes in the policy?			

06.B Security, Storage, and Access of Pharmaceutical Supplies

Questions to consider	YES	NO If no, why not?	NOT APPLICABLE (note reason)
Are protocols in place for appropriate storage of pharmaceuticals including samples (for example, refrigerated if required)?			
Are pharmaceuticals kept in a secure location with limited access?			
Are medications stored in the original packaging or container?			
Are narcotics and controlled substances stored in a secure location with tightly controlled access?			

06.C Inventory System

Questions to consider	YES	NO If no, why not?	NOT APPLICABLE (note reason)
Is an automated pharmaceutical and medical supply (both billable and nonbillable items) inventory system in place?			
Does the system capture items in and items out?			
Is inventory counted and reconciled on a periodic and regular basis?			
Is a system in place to regularly monitor quantities on hand and place replenishment orders based on order points?			
Are purchases based on an individual product, brand, or style avoided? (In other words, do you attempt to adopt a policy of standardization?)			
Is a bidding process used periodically to ensure competitive pricing?			
For larger, more expensive items, is the total cost (item, supplies, maintenance, renovation, biohazardous and nonbiohazardous waste created, etc.) evaluated and the price negotiated?			

Questions to consider	YES	NO If no, why not?	NOT APPLICABLE (note reason)
Are appropriate quantities kept on hand at all times?			
If items are billable, is a process in place to capture CPT codes and charges?			
For items with an expiration date, is stock rotated based on expiration dates?			
Are items with an expiration date monitored on a regular and periodic basis for expiration?			
Are expired items appropriately disposed of (not discarded into regular waste, returned to the manufacturer, etc.)?			
Is a log kept of pharmaceuticals as well as their distribution to patients?			

Note all items that appear in the pharmaceutical log.

Check all that apply	Item	Circle one	Describe action needed
	Name of pharmaceutical	Effective Not Effective	
	If a wearable item, size	Effective Not Effective	
	If a drug, strength	Effective Not Effective	
	If a drug, size of container	Effective Not Effective	
	If a drug, lot number	Effective Not Effective	
	If a drug, expiration date	Effective Not Effective	
	Date received	Effective Not Effective	
	Date of distribution	Effective Not Effective	

Check all that apply	Item	Circle one	Describe action needed
	Patient name	Effective Not Effective	
	Patient identifier (date of birth, for example)	Effective Not Effective	
	Patient chart number	Effective Not Effective	
	Lot number distributed	Effective Not Effective	
	Other:	Effective Not Effective	

Questions to consider	YES	NO If no, why not?	NOT APPLICABLE (note reason)
Is the dispensing of pharmaceuticals documented, including samples, in the patient's medical record?			

06.D Regulatory Compliance of Pharmaceutical Supplies

Questions to consider	YES	NO If no, why not?	NOT APPLICABLE (note reason)
Are you knowledgeable about and compliant with state and federal laws as well as state board regulations regarding pharmaceuticals?			
Do you stay abreast of changes?			

06.E Relationships with Pharmaceutical Sales Representatives

Questions to consider	YES	NO If no, why not?	NOT APPLICABLE (note reason)
Is a program in place to govern relationships with pharmaceutical company representatives?			
Is there a program in place to control pharmaceutical representatives' access to providers?			
Are conflicts of interest in relationships and interactions avoided?			
Do you not accept "giveaways" or gifts?			
Do you accept only medication samples and educational information?			

BOTTOM LINE–PATIENT CARE SYSTEMS

Patient care systems are the backbone of the practice, enabling providers to maximize patient care visits and procedures and positively affect practice revenue. Effective operations including referral management, patient flow routines, pharmaceutical and medical supply control, and patient participation in care all enhance this process.

Patient Care Systems
Supplemental Notes
(copy as needed)

Task	Notes

Patient Care Systems
Action Items
(copy as needed)

Task	Action	Responsible Party	Due Date	Priority

CHAPTER 7

Quality Management

Quality control, quality assurance, and quality improvement have long been common in medical practices with the focus primarily on occasional looks at patient care. Recently this vital responsibility has evolved to become continuous quality improvement, now checked frequently across the organization with new tools and techniques. The impetus: research from the Institute of Medicine and others that called for the healthcare industry to substantially improve patient safety and medical quality and reduce costs. Well publicized, these studies have triggered increased public awareness and demand for quality report cards. As a medical practice administrator, you have a key role in meeting all these demands. What is your system for improving healthcare delivery and patient safety? Involving all departments facilitates this effort. What are your malpractice statistics? Protocols related to adverse events and improving peer review are critical. Do you have an adequate incident reporting system? In today's world the medical practice is dealing with well-educated consumers who not only know but understand more about their needs as well as the capabilities of your practice. What are you doing to ensure patient satisfaction? Techniques from the business world can help. Are benchmarks in place that serve as performance standards? Everyone needs a way to compare performance. Have you implemented pay for performance to meet the requirements of third parties? These programs offer incentives – and disincentives. How about credentialing? A database about reporting requirements, agencies, and dates is a significant help. Quality management requires everyone's attention – especially yours.

TASK 01: DESIGN AND IMPLEMENT A QUALITY MANAGEMENT SYSTEM THAT LEADS TO THE IMPROVEMENT OF HEALTHCARE DELIVERY AND ENSURES PATIENT SAFETY

A physician who practices medicine in a "status quo" manner in effect provides "old fashioned" care, both clinically and operationally. Today's standard is vastly different. Society demands that physicians continue to improve healthcare and the way in which it is delivered. From the latest tests to the newest drugs, top-notch service and quality matter. What is your approach to quality? Are you using techniques that will help instill quality, such as total quality management? There are a number of tools that help institute quality in the practice setting. Which ones do you use? Quality can cost; failure is one way this happens. Are you taking steps to minimize quality costs? Literally every process in a practice will benefit from quality management. Which do you periodically review? Answer the questions below to see how you are doing in the area of quality management in your practice.

01.A Application of Quality Management

Note the elements that are included in your quality management system.

Check all that apply	Element	Circle one	Describe action needed
	Challenges current processes	Effective Not Effective	
	Standards of care and the delivery of that care	Effective Not Effective	
	Identifying and monitoring of benchmarks related to quality of care	Effective Not Effective	
	Produces positive change for the practice	Effective Not Effective	

Check all that apply	Element	Circle one	Describe action needed
	Entails an element of risk for gain	Effective Not Effective	
	Encompasses asking why things are done the way they are	Effective Not Effective	
	Incorporates structure, process, and outcome	Effective Not Effective	
	Compares to prior data, processes, etc.	Effective Not Effective	
	Corrective action taken when appropriate	Effective Not Effective	
	Pilot programs for testing	Effective Not Effective	
	Use of outside compliance review and audit services (inside if the organization possesses the necessary resources)	Effective Not Effective	
	Review by clinical and administrative leadership	Effective Not Effective	

Check all that apply	Element	Circle one	Describe action needed
	Communication to appropriate parties (charts, reports, historical data, surveys, etc.)	Effective Not Effective	
	Teaching on a need-to-know basis	Effective Not Effective	
	Buy-in at all levels of the organization	Effective Not Effective	
	Reinforcement of quality message throughout the organization	Effective Not Effective	
	Knowledgeable about accrediting and review organizations and associated requirements	Effective Not Effective	
	Relationship with accrediting and review organizations	Effective Not Effective	
	Pay for performance and other external measures	Effective Not Effective	
	Other:	Effective Not Effective	

01.B Quality Management Approaches and Philosophies

What are the common and popular quality management approaches and philosophies that are used in the practice?

Check all that apply	Approach/Philosophy	Circle one	Describe action needed
	Statement by practice leadership committing to quality of care standards	Effective Not Effective	
	Total quality management	Effective Not Effective	
	Six Sigma	Effective Not Effective	
	Lean thinking	Effective Not Effective	
	Other:	Effective Not Effective	

01.C Quality Management Tools

Questions to consider	YES	NO If no, why not?	NOT APPLICABLE (note reason)
Is brainstorming used to begin to develop quality improvement ideas?			

Indicate the common and popular quality management tools that are used in your practice.

Check all that apply	Tool	Circle one	Describe action needed
	Process maps	Effective Not Effective	
	Run charts	Effective Not Effective	
	Pareto diagrams	Effective Not Effective	
	Flow charts	Effective Not Effective	
	Affinity diagrams	Effective Not Effective	
	Ishikawa diagrams (cause and effect)	Effective Not Effective	
	Decision matrices	Effective Not Effective	
	Grid analysis	Effective Not Effective	
	Checklists	Effective Not Effective	
	Other:	Effective Not Effective	

01.D Cost of Quality

Do you have processes in place to avoid these factors that affect the cost of quality in your practice?

Check all that apply	Factor	Circle one	Describe action needed
	Internal failure costs (for example, having to redo a task)	Effective Not Effective	
	External failure costs (for example, diminished referring physician satisfaction)	Effective Not Effective	
	Appraisal costs (for example, underinsuring assets)	Effective Not Effective	
	Prevention costs (for example, undertraining staff)	Effective Not Effective	
	Other:	Effective Not Effective	

01.E Continuous Process Improvement Review and Practice Assessment

Note the processes that are assessed.

Check all that apply	Process	Circle one	Describe action needed
	Patient safety	Effective Not Effective	
	Medical outcomes	Effective Not Effective	
	Malpractice claims	Effective Not Effective	
	Patient complaints	Effective Not Effective	
	OSHA requirements (biohazards, sharps, etc.)	Effective Not Effective	
	Coding documentation (codes vs. chart documentation)	Effective Not Effective	
	Chart audits	Effective Not Effective	
	Risk assessment	Effective Not Effective	

Check all that apply	Process	Circle one	Describe action needed
	Regulatory requirements	Effective Not Effective	
	Payer rules and regulations	Effective Not Effective	
	Patient waiting times	Effective Not Effective	
	Patient flow process, including processing times	Effective Not Effective	
	Patient satisfaction	Effective Not Effective	
	Staff satisfaction	Effective Not Effective	
	Physician satisfaction	Effective Not Effective	
	Referring physician satisfaction	Effective Not Effective	
	Patient phone calls (number of rings, wait times, busy signal, etc.)	Effective Not Effective	

Check all that apply	Process	Circle one	Describe action needed
	Patient no-show rate	Effective Not Effective	
	Employee orientation (OSHA, practice compliance plan, etc.)	Effective Not Effective	
	Employee training (annual and ongoing)	Effective Not Effective	
	Employee satisfaction	Effective Not Effective	
	Employee turnover rate	Effective Not Effective	
	Other:	Effective Not Effective	

TASK 02: MONITOR THE PEER REVIEW PROCESS FOR CLINICAL STAFF

Healthcare is provided by people, and people sometimes make mistakes. System errors also occur. Ideally, in your professional career as a practice manager you have had to deal with few situations involving errors. While all practices need systems in place to prevent errors, the focus of this section is on processes after an error occurs. Most physician practices choose to carry traditional malpractice insurance (either claims made or occurrence) and not "go bare" or self-insure. Payers have their own set of requirements about reporting claims. Do you have a relationship with your payer as well as a working knowledge of the payer's protocols? What about processes for managing unexpected events? Do your protocols identify what needs to be done when one of these difficult events occurs? Sometimes peer review is needed. Either the practice requires it or, based on the event, it is a necessary step. Answer the following questions to find out how you are doing in the area of peer review.

02.A Reporting Claims

Questions to consider	YES	NO If no, why not?	NOT APPLICABLE (note reason)
Do you have positive relationships with your malpractice carrier representatives?			
Are you familiar and compliant with the malpractice insurance carrier's protocols on reporting potential and actual malpractice claims as well as researching and defending claims?			

02.B Protocols and Processes for Managing Adverse Events

Note the ways in which adverse events are managed.

Check all that apply	Method	Circle one	Describe action needed
	Protocols are in place.	Effective Not Effective	
	Training in the management of adverse events is provided at all levels of the practice.	Effective Not Effective	
	The administrator works with and understands the malpractice carrier's approach, tools, and training programs.	Effective Not Effective	
	Disclosure is made to the patient of an unanticipated outcome (for example, the facts as known, explanation if the facts are known, next steps with regard to the patient, steps to avoid again in the future if the facts are known or commitment to an investigation to find out what happened, and accommodation; avoid laying blame on anyone).	Effective Not Effective	
	An immediate investigation is launched.	Effective Not Effective	
	After the facts are known, protocols are implemented to avoid similar events in the future.	Effective Not Effective	

Check all that apply	Method	Circle one	Describe action needed
	A full and sincere apology is made to the patient (for instance, with empathy, sensitivity, honesty, and remorse).	Effective Not Effective	
	Immediate clinical care and medical intervention (as required) are undertaken.	Effective Not Effective	
	A report is submitted to the risk manager, malpractice carrier, and legal counsel.	Effective Not Effective	
	Authorization to communicate disclosure is received from the risk manager, malpractice carrier, and/or legal counsel.	Effective Not Effective	
	The practice is in compliance with related state and federal laws and accrediting organization protocols.	Effective Not Effective	
	Direct discussions are held with the physician(s) and/or others involved in an event.	Effective Not Effective	
	Counseling is provided as needed.	Effective Not Effective	
	All interactions include transparency, honesty, accountability, and integrity.	Effective Not Effective	

Check all that apply	Method	Circle one	Describe action needed
	All adverse events (regardless of how minor) that occur in the practice are monitored and tracked.	Effective Not Effective	
	Ideally, "good catches" – incidents identified before a patient is involved – are also monitored and tracked.	Effective Not Effective	
	A root cause analysis and an internal informal review are conducted.	Effective Not Effective	
	Results of the review are kept confidential and access to the analysis is limited.	Effective Not Effective	
	A peer review is conducted and appropriate physician action is recommended.	Effective Not Effective	
	Appropriate informed consent protocols are in place and followed.	Effective Not Effective	
	Other:	Effective Not Effective	

02.C Peer Review Process

What incidents trigger the peer review process?

Check all that apply	Incident	Circle one	Describe action needed
	Medical record requests with medical record review and a physician-related problem	Effective Not Effective	
	Patient complaints leading to medical record review and a physician-related problem	Effective Not Effective	
	Physician issues affecting licensure, credentialing, and so on	Effective Not Effective	
	Other:	Effective Not Effective	

Questions to consider	YES	NO If no, why not?	NOT APPLICABLE (note reason)
Are issues documented as to action taken, physician response, and so on?			
For owner physicians, are buy-out parameters in place, as required?			
For smaller groups, is a reciprocal peer review arrangement in place?			
Is the peer review process promoted within the practice as a means toward improvement?			
Are risk management, the malpractice carrier, and legal counsel consulted, as required, in the peer review process?			
Is the practice in compliance with related state and federal laws and accrediting organization protocols regarding peer review?			
Are peer review activities protected from disclosure?			

TASK 03: DEVELOP AND OVERSEE PATIENT SATISFACTION AND CUSTOMER SERVICE PROGRAMS

In this consumer-directed world, how do you ensure your practice keeps patients satisfied? Once, physicians and their practices could just concentrate on providing patient care. Now that care must be "packaged" in ways that satisfy customers. They will form an impression of excellent, good, or poor service based on factors including how long they see the physician, how well he or she listens to them, how long they wait in the reception area, and even how old the magazines are. Do you and the leaders of the group foster a culture of customer service? Do you survey patients and gather specific measurement and trend information? What do you do with the results? Do you provide customer service training to everyone, including physicians? Patient satisfaction is a key element of quality management and must involve everyone in the organization.

03.A Survey Usage

Check the ways in which patient satisfaction is surveyed.

Check all that apply	Method	Circle one	Describe action needed
	Survey value is recognized and demonstrated by the use of several survey methods.	Effective Not Effective	
	Forms and calls, patient discussions, patient complaints, and focus groups are used.	Effective Not Effective	
	Some questions target clinical operations and physician communications.	Effective Not Effective	
	Other questions focus on scheduling, the facility, and whether patients recommend the practice.	Effective Not Effective	
	Results are used to identify pluses and minuses and improve business and clinical operations.	Effective Not Effective	
	Benchmark data are shared showing that groups using surveys perform better financially.	Effective Not Effective	
	Other:	Effective Not Effective	

03.B Survey Implementation

Check methods that are used to design and implement a survey. Consider alternative presented options to improve.

Check all that apply	Method	Circle one	Describe action needed
	A standard boilerplate survey design is used and vendor mailing is provided.	Effective Not Effective	
	A customized survey is developed with vendor and custom reports provided.	Effective Not Effective	
	A custom version focused on clinical aspects such as length of time with physician is developed.	Effective Not Effective	
	Amenities are surveyed such as parking, staff politeness, and waiting room environment.	Effective Not Effective	
	The survey is done in house using a standard form and distributed to a random sample.	Effective Not Effective	
	Mailing, calling, and exit surveys are used to try to get statistically significant results.	Effective Not Effective	
	Survey results are tallied internally and externally and reported to leadership.	Effective Not Effective	

Check all that apply	Method	Circle one	Describe action needed
	Perceptions of care appropriateness, thoroughness, and communication are measured.	Effective Not Effective	
	Changes are authorized by leaders and carried out by the administrator including training.	Effective Not Effective	
	Other:	Effective Not Effective	

03.C Staff Training

How is training implemented for the staff?

Check all that apply	Method	Circle one	Describe action needed
	Customer service training focuses on processes, knowledge, and behavior.	Effective Not Effective	
	Customer service training is provided to all clinical and nonclinical staff.	Effective Not Effective	
	Communication skills are targeted in physician training with emphasis on listening.	Effective Not Effective	
	Measurement results are used by senior managers to set and change goals and deadlines.	Effective Not Effective	
	Department managers are charged with improving service processes in their units.	Effective Not Effective	
	Customer service knowledge is conveyed by educational materials and workshops.	Effective Not Effective	
	Videos and role plays are used effectively to convey how to (and how not to) interact.	Effective Not Effective	
	Other:	Effective Not Effective	

03.D Customer Service Focus and Culture

Check ways in which you foster customer service in your culture.

Check all that apply	Method	Circle one	Describe action needed
	The importance of making a good impression on patients is emphasized to everyone.	Effective Not Effective	
	Statistics on referrals (from patient to patient, physician, other) are gathered and reported.	Effective Not Effective	
	Leaders are committed to a culture of customer service, demonstrated through their behaviors.	Effective Not Effective	
	Service delivery quality is designated as a priority and measured against goals.	Effective Not Effective	
	Service measurements and internal/external benchmarks are shared with everyone.	Effective Not Effective	
	Examples of customer service best practices are distributed and discussed.	Effective Not Effective	
	Achievement of service-delivery goals is rewarded and publicized.	Effective Not Effective	
	Employees are recognized and rewarded for successful events.	Effective Not Effective	
	Other:	Effective Not Effective	

TASK 04: IDENTIFY, DEVELOP, AND MAINTAIN BENCHMARKS FOR ESTABLISHING PRACTICE PERFORMANCE STANDARDS

Benchmarking provides a means by which to measure results and redirect processes as required. Think about this concept for a minute. If we don't compare results, how do we know our level of success? Benchmarking is a crucial part of analyzing how a practice is doing. A manager can compare financial and/or statistical results in a given year to the prior year as a way to determine practice performance. That comparison represents a simple means of benchmarking. Alternatively, as a more sophisticated way of benchmarking, the practice might obtain data that shows the summarized financial results of other similar practices to determine how it performed compared to the peer group. Before beginning a benchmarking program, it's necessary to determine what should be measured and how the task will be completed. What's your strategy? Some organizations develop more of a focus on benchmarking, and over time, implement more sophisticated tools such as dashboards and scorecards. Are you using these tools? There are many metrics to measure, from financial to quality to service, and more. What categories do you measure and how do you measure them? Using good, reliable benchmark data is paramount to success in the area of benchmarking. How good are your sources? Complete this section to find out.

04. A Data Collection Strategy and Plan

Questions to consider	YES	NO If no, why not?	NOT APPLICABLE (note reason)
Is internal and external benchmarking completed to evaluate performance both periodically and regularly?			
Does the process entail not just comparison of data and statistics but also analysis and comparison of what, when, where, why, how, and so on?			
Is best-practice action – as appropriate for the practice – taken when appropriate (for improvement, for example)?			
Are results evaluated on a post-implementation basis?			
Are areas that are important for organizational success benchmarked?			
Is current and reliable benchmarking data from well-respected sources used?			

Questions to consider	YES	NO If no, why not?	NOT APPLICABLE (note reason)
Are systematic methods (formulas, ratios, etc.), checklists (lists to make certain all steps are taken), scales (weak, good, better, etc.), and comparable measures (ways to compare to other organizations, for example) used in benchmarking?			
Is benchmarking done in a consistent (for example, the same metric is used each time) and defensible manner?			
Is baseline data developed when benchmarking is started?			

04.B Benchmarking Reports

Questions to consider	YES	NO If no, why not?	NOT APPLICABLE (note reason)
Are benchmarking reports (dashboards, scorecards, etc.) used to monitor performance and implement strategy?			
Do the reports represent strategic objectives?			
Are the reports used to react to issues and opportunities and then adjusted accordingly?			
Is the decision-making process data driven?			
Are key performance indicators used that are clearly defined, simple to measure and understand, and clear indicators of performance?			
Is the "owner" of each key performance indicator noted?			

List the activities you monitor. Use the Supplemental Notes worksheet for this domain section if additional space is needed.

_____

_____

_____

_____

_____

_____

_____

04.C Metrics for Financial Growth, Customer Service, Quality, and Innovation

Questions to consider	YES	NO If no, why not?	NOT APPLICABLE (note reason)
Are quality, service, and financial indicators benchmarked?			
Are these factors compared among peers?			

Note which of the following financial indicators are benchmarked.

Check all that apply	Indicator	Circle one	Describe action needed
	Gross revenue	Effective Not Effective	
	Collections	Effective Not Effective	
	Profit/net income	Effective Not Effective	
	Unit productivity	Effective Not Effective	
	RVU (total and/or work)	Effective Not Effective	
	Operating costs	Effective Not Effective	
	Provider compensation	Effective Not Effective	
	Staff compensation	Effective Not Effective	
	Other:	Effective Not Effective	

Indicate which of the following service indicators are benchmarked.

Check all that apply	Indicator	Circle one	Describe action needed
	Patient complaints	Effective Not Effective	
	Busy rings	Effective Not Effective	
	Hold times	Effective Not Effective	
	Patient processing times	Effective Not Effective	
	Patient satisfaction (new and established)	Effective Not Effective	
	Employee satisfaction	Effective Not Effective	
	Physician satisfaction	Effective Not Effective	
	Referring physician satisfaction	Effective Not Effective	
	Other:	Effective Not Effective	

Create a list of quality indicators that are benchmarked. Use the Supplemental Notes worksheet for this domain section if additional space is needed.

_____

_____

_____

_____

_____

_____

_____

Record how innovation is benchmarked. If additional space is needed, reference the Supplemental Notes worksheet for this section.

_____

_____

_____

_____

_____

_____

_____

04.D Internal and External Benchmark Data

List the sources of internal and external benchmarks and note how each helps guide strategy. Use the Supplemental Notes worksheet if additional space is needed.

_____

_____

_____

_____

_____

_____

_____

TASK 05: CREATE INTERNAL PROCESSES AND SYSTEMS TO PARTICIPATE IN PAY-FOR-PERFORMANCE PROGRAMS TO ENHANCE HEALTHCARE QUALITY

Pay for performance (P4P) has been around in business organizations for some time and recently has affected educational systems. This incentive program to improve quality medical care is now in use in the healthcare industry as well. The basic premise: If you achieve performance goals, you get rewarded monetarily. In the medical world it means one must have satisfactory report data on quality measures to get paid – or not. Beyond this is the concept of effectively using evidence-based medicine throughout the practice to meet or exceed current acceptable standards of patient care. How do you capture the clinical data needed for such reporting? Do you have internal ways of monitoring as well as knowledge as to who gets the information and what data is provided externally to achieve P4P and evidence-based standards? It's critical to gather information across the board on structures, processes, and outcomes. Are you involved in a P4P program and are your physicians willing participants? Designed to promote excellence in patient care at the lowest possible cost, P4P will likely be a goal for years to come. How about licensing and credentialing; does everyone understand their quality improvement (QI) value? Is it clear that there is business credentialing as well as medical? A credential means that you are qualified to provide something; the credentialing process means getting approval to provide care and do business.

05.A Clinical Data Capture

Check processes that have been developed for capturing clinical data.

Check all that apply	Process	Circle one	Describe action needed
	Data capture methods are set up for patient safety, effectiveness, patient centeredness, timeliness, efficiency, and equity are reliable and simple.	Effective Not Effective	
	Leaders are updated regularly on the P4P expectations of payers and others.	Effective Not Effective	
	The performance measures used cover structural, process, and outcomes aspects.	Effective Not Effective	
	The responsibility for the P4P program is clearly designated.	Effective Not Effective	
	Data is obtained from a variety of sources such as surveys, records, and tallies.	Effective Not Effective	
	Safety data is obtained from internal records on patient injuries at the practice; that is, injuries sustained by patients while they were visiting the practice.	Effective Not Effective	
	Effectiveness data on avoiding care underuse and overuse is obtained from records.	Effective Not Effective	

Check all that apply	Process	Circle one	Describe action needed
	Patient-centeredness data is obtained from satisfaction surveys.	Effective Not Effective	
	Timeliness data is gathered from reports showing reduced waits and harmful delays.	Effective Not Effective	
	Equity data is obtained from demographics showing the population balance.	Effective Not Effective	
	Processes are in place to change and improve the quality of care provided to patients.	Effective Not Effective	
	Other:	Effective Not Effective	

05.B Pay-for-Performance Program Effectiveness and Value

Note how you measure the value of participating in P4P programs.

Check all that apply	Method	Circle one	Describe action needed
	Conference attendance by leaders and administrator is used to evaluate programs.	Effective Not Effective	
	Reference publications are used to match the program against best-practice models.	Effective Not Effective	
	Public reporting of quality and cost information is used to compare the practice's program.	Effective Not Effective	
	Evidence-based research is used to get measurement ideas.	Effective Not Effective	
	Patient satisfaction and cultural changes are measured to test quality improvement.	Effective Not Effective	
	Cost savings from quality improvement and continuous process improvement programs are tracked and trended.	Effective Not Effective	
	Other:	Effective Not Effective	

05.C Physicians and Clinical Pathways and Protocols

Check ways you engage physicians in clinical pathways.

Check all that apply	Method	Circle one	Describe action needed
	The development of pathways and protocols is endorsed by executive and clinical leaders.	Effective Not Effective	
	Physicians are committed to pathway and protocol development.	Effective Not Effective	
	All disciplines are involved in the development including clinical and nonclinical staff.	Effective Not Effective	
	Pathways and protocols are implemented throughout the organization.	Effective Not Effective	
	The effectiveness of pathways and protocols is measured frequently over time.	Effective Not Effective	
	Other:	Effective Not Effective	

05.D Physician Participation

Note how you get physician involvement in P4P programs.

Check all that apply	Method	Circle one	Describe action needed
	Physicians are educated on all aspects of P4P including incentives and disincentives.	Effective Not Effective	
	Research is conducted to determine physician concerns and fears about change.	Effective Not Effective	
	Physician readiness and willingness for organizational change is measured.	Effective Not Effective	
	A plan is developed to move physicians along the change continuum to buy-in.	Effective Not Effective	
	Market-based benchmarks are used to help physicians maintain competitive pay.	Effective Not Effective	
	A financial bonus is designed with meaningful award timing and payment mechanisms.	Effective Not Effective	
	Disincentives are discussed such as reimbursement withheld by health plans.	Effective Not Effective	
	Other:	Effective Not Effective	

05.E Third-Party Requirements

Check ways that are used to increase an understanding of requirements.

Check all that apply	Method	Circle one	Describe action needed
	Leaders, physicians, and all staff are educated on National Committee for Quality Assurance (NCQA), Healthcare Effectiveness Data and Information Set (HEDIS), and other QI efforts.	Effective Not Effective	
	Information is given on the Physician Quality Reporting Initiative (PQRI) and incentives.	Effective Not Effective	
	Emphasis is on CMS's annual updating of measures required to participate.	Effective Not Effective	
	Value of participation is translated for staff into a percentage of Medicare charges.	Effective Not Effective	
	The importance to consumers of third-party quality measurement reports is stressed.	Effective Not Effective	
	The staff is aware of Internet grading and reporting systems.	Effective Not Effective	
	Other:	Effective Not Effective	

TASK 06: DEVELOP AND MONITOR A PROGRAM FOR STAFF, BUSINESS, AND EQUIPMENT CREDENTIALING AND LICENSURE

Do you have systems in place to help newly hired physicians and those on staff to complete the complex, lengthy paperwork demanded by licensure and credentialing agencies? This is an exhausting process well served by administrative systems. Are you in line with the requirements of the accrediting agencies such as the Joint Commission (formerly the Joint Commission on Accreditation of Healthcare Organizations), and the Accreditation Association for Ambulatory Healthcare, AAAHC? The emphasis of these agencies these days is on ongoing quality measurement. Do you make sure you comply with the Clinical Laboratory Improvement Act (CLIA) if you perform laboratory tests on site? Even one will put you in that ballgame.

06.A Physician Enrollment

Check methods you implement to help physicians obtain hospital privileges and health plan credentialing and to maintain medical licenses.

Check all that apply	Method	Circle one	Describe action needed
	Pre-employment verification of physician credentials is conducted.	Effective Not Effective	
	Form I-9 and other basic employee documents are completed and filed.	Effective Not Effective	
	Physicians are listed in the National Practitioner Data Bank.	Effective Not Effective	
	Credentials are reviewed annually to ensure information is accurate and current.	Effective Not Effective	
	The physician's month and year of training, work history, and practice start date are included on the curriculum vitae.	Effective Not Effective	

Check all that apply	Method	Circle one	Describe action needed
	The physician's National Provider Identifier letter, social security card, and licenses are received.	Effective Not Effective	
	Malpractice insurance information is available for credentialing purposes.	Effective Not Effective	
	Drug Enforcement Administration (DEA) certificates (federal; state if applicable) are applied for and received.	Effective Not Effective	
	The completion and assembly of paperwork is facilitated by administrative staff.	Effective Not Effective	
	Other:	Effective Not Effective	

06.B Compliance with Licensing and Credentialing Requirements

Check methods that are in place for tracking licensing and credentialing.

Check all that apply	Method	Circle one	Describe action needed
	A database is built to gather licensure and credentialing information.	Effective Not Effective	
	A credentialing manual is created and maintained.	Effective Not Effective	
	Agencies requiring information and reporting dates are included in the database.	Effective Not Effective	
	Spreadsheets are developed to show the state of credentialing and serve as a tickler file.	Effective Not Effective	
	A person is designated as responsible for maintaining the database and reporting.	Effective Not Effective	
	Reports are shared with leaders to identify conflict areas and outdated information.	Effective Not Effective	
	Other:	Effective Not Effective	

06.C Accreditation Organization Requirements

Note methods used to comply with the Joint Commission (JC) and other organizations and indicate challenges and actions.

Check all that apply	Method	Circle one	Describe action needed
	A person is designated to be the internal expert on the JC and other accreditors.	Effective Not Effective	
	Accreditors are contacted regularly to obtain current accreditation criteria.	Effective Not Effective	
	Current JC, AAAHC, and other accreditors' requirements are distributed to key staff.	Effective Not Effective	
	Leaders and department managers are expected to fulfill accreditation requirements.	Effective Not Effective	
	Emphasis is put on clinical quality, documentation, confidentially, patient safety, practice protocols, error prevention, and physician certification.	Effective Not Effective	
	The staff is informed of deadlines as well as what is required to pass accreditation requirements.	Effective Not Effective	
	Other:	Effective Not Effective	

06.D Clinical Laboratory Improvement Act (CLIA) Requirements

Check ways you deal with CLIA.

Check all that apply	Method	Circle one	Describe action needed
	Leaders are informed that an entity doing even one test is considered a laboratory.	Effective Not Effective	
	Registration with CLIA is handled administratively in the practice.	Effective Not Effective	
	CLIA information requirements are fulfilled regarding the laboratory's operation.	Effective Not Effective	
	The staff is educated that the certification type and fee amount are determined by CLIA.	Effective Not Effective	
	A pre-inspection review is conducted.	Effective Not Effective	
	A post-inspection follow-up and remediation are conducted.	Effective Not Effective	
	Other:	Effective Not Effective	

BOTTOM LINE—QUALITY MANAGEMENT

Quality is here to stay, and medical practice administrators have a distinct role in the effort to create and maintain a culture of quality in their practices. It requires a team approach, with the involvement of clinicians, management, and staff all working toward improving systems, service, and care. In some instances, quality is linked to reimbursement, making the incentive to create quality even stronger. If quality is not currently on your radar screen, make a commitment to add it.

Quality Management
Supplemental Notes
(copy as needed)

Task	Notes

Quality Management
Action Items
(copy as needed)

Task	Action	Responsible Party	Due Date	Priority

CHAPTER 8

Risk Management

We've all heard nightmarish reports of risk events – malpractice claim horror stories, the impact of claims on reputations, investigations by regulatory agencies, and employee reporting of alleged practice "wrongdoings" to authorities. Effective risk management enables a practice to avoid these scenarios. Protecting the assets of the organization – and avoiding fines, penalties, settlements, awards, and even jail time – is the goal of risk management. It requires a proactive approach and an ongoing, regular focus. Risk management starts with the development of a plan to ensure the safety of all – patients, staff, and visitors. Do you have one in your practice? It also involves managing adverse events when they occur. Is your practice able to function in a controlled manner when an event occurs, or does it become chaotic and lacking in direction? Disaster (contingency) response and recovery is a key part of risk management. Events such as Hurricane Katrina and 9/11 taught us that we all need to have a plan in place to address whatever happens as a result of natural and man-made disasters. Do you have a comprehensive plan in place? Yet another area of risk management involves compliance with a range of federal and state laws and requirements, from CMS to OSHA to the Office of Inspector General, and more. What's your knowledge about these types of laws and requirements? Are you compliant? Complete the next section to find out your effectiveness in the area of risk management.

TASK 01: DEVELOP AND IMPLEMENT A RISK MANAGEMENT PLAN TO ENSURE A SAFE ENVIRONMENT FOR PATIENTS, STAFF, AND VISITORS

A risk management plan has many components. The first is identification of risk. Have you ever taken the time to consider all of the potential clinical and environmental risks to your practice – from the simple (such as a minor cut from the exam table) to major (like an earthquake)? Even the smallest of risks deserves attention if it is to be avoided. So many events can and do occur – finger sticks from needles, fires, falls, chemical spills, and more. Is your plan all encompassing as to the types of events and situations that might occur, taking into consideration the natural disasters in your region, your patient population, and the complexity of patient care your practice provides? Bloodborne pathogens requirements first came into play in 1991 and were revised in 2001 in response to the Needlestick Safety and Prevention Act. In 1994, the Hazard Communication Final Rule was published. Laws, healthcare regulations and requirements, and industry-wide practices change over time. Monitoring changes and updating the risk management plan are required. How do you stay abreast of new risks?

On a day-to-day basis, events occur in practices that involve potential risk situations. Methods need to be in place to identify and address those situations. What are you doing to monitor them in your practice?

Record-keeping is a key component of risk management. The idea of documenting who, what, when, where, and why helps address some situations. In others, medical record documentation is critical. (Note: Medical record documentation is covered in the Information Management chapter of this workbook.) Different documents require different retention periods. Some can be destroyed at a given point in time. When an event occurs, does your documentation meet the grade?

Employee involvement – or lack of it – can help or hinder risk management. Think about a potential situation in which a patient informs the receptionist that she tripped over the doormat just inside your waiting room door and fell, hitting her head. The receptionist asks her if she is okay and the patient responds yes. The receptionist doesn't tell anyone in the practice about what occurred. Hours later the patient is rushed to the emergency room with a head injury. Think about how differently the situation might have turned out if the receptionist had reported the fall to you and the physician of record. Staff training and empowerment is a crucial part of a risk management program. How well is your staff equipped to respond to events? Find out the answers to these questions and more.

01.A Risk Management Process

Do you understand the following aspects of risk management? Mark those you are knowledgeable about.

Check all that apply	Aspect	Circle one	Describe action needed
	Identifying risk exposure (determining what can go wrong)	Effective Not Effective	
	Analyzing risk exposure (analyzing what can go wrong, and the potential frequency and the severity if it does go wrong)	Effective Not Effective	
	Identifying options to manage potential risk exposure and reducing the potential frequency	Effective Not Effective	
	Selecting methods to manage particular risks and reducing the potential severity	Effective Not Effective	
	Financing medical malpractice insurance (via commercial insurance, self-insurance vehicles, risk financing, etc.), including the need to finance risk even when it is controlled	Effective Not Effective	
	Periodic scheduled monitoring of methods to control risk to evaluate their effectiveness	Effective Not Effective	
	Eliminating risk when possible	Effective Not Effective	
	Other:	Effective Not Effective	

01.B Risk Management Plan

Questions to consider	YES	NO If no, why not?	NOT APPLICABLE (note reason)
Is a risk management plan in place?			

Does the plan include the following items? Note all that are included.

Check all that apply	Item	Circle one	Describe action needed
	Bloodborne pathogens	Effective Not Effective	
	Hazardous communications	Effective Not Effective	
	Material safety data sheets	Effective Not Effective	
	Hazardous waste	Effective Not Effective	
	Ergonomics	Effective Not Effective	
	Personal protective equipment	Effective Not Effective	
	Respiratory safety	Effective Not Effective	

Check all that apply	Item	Circle one	Describe action needed
	Fire protection and safety, including emergency exit planning	Effective Not Effective	
	Emergency response	Effective Not Effective	
	Radiation	Effective Not Effective	
	Disease-specific issues (HIV, AIDS, TB, etc.) Note them:	Effective Not Effective	
	Chemical- and drug-specific issues (chemotherapy, anticoagulants, etc.) Note them:	Effective Not Effective	

Check all that apply	Item	Circle one	Describe action needed
	Lab-specific issues (for example, on-site lab drawing station, specimen handling) Note them:	Effective Not Effective	
	Other toxic and hazardous substances (for example, ethylene oxide [EtO]) Note them:	Effective Not Effective	
	Compressed gasses, stored upright and secured	Effective Not Effective	
	Electrical	Effective Not Effective	
	Medical services/first aid and emergency drugs	Effective Not Effective	
	Safety and health	Effective Not Effective	

Check all that apply	Item	Circle one	Describe action needed
	Workplace violence	Effective Not Effective	
	Patient privacy and confidentiality	Effective Not Effective	
	Workplace safety	Effective Not Effective	
	Workplace security	Effective Not Effective	
	Drug testing	Effective Not Effective	
	Workplace harassment	Effective Not Effective	
	Grievances	Effective Not Effective	
	Other:	Effective Not Effective	

Is the practice compliant with all federal, state, and local laws and requirements regarding workplace safety? (Note: For more information see www.osha/gov, www.cdc.gov, and www.cdc.gov/niosh.)

Check all that apply	Law/Requirement	Circle one	Describe action needed
	Occupational Safety and Health Act of 1970	Effective Not Effective	
	OSHA guidelines for occupational exposure to tuberculosis	Effective Not Effective	
	NIOSH guidelines for respiratory protection of healthcare workers exposed to tuberculosis	Effective Not Effective	
	Centers for Disease Control and Prevention (CDC) guidelines for preventing TB transmission	Effective Not Effective	
	OSHA hazardous waste standard	Effective Not Effective	
	OSHA personal protective equipment standard	Effective Not Effective	
	OSHA bloodborne pathogens standard	Effective Not Effective	
	OSHA hazard communication standard	Effective Not Effective	
	OSHA recording and reporting occupational injuries and illnesses standard	Effective Not Effective	

Check all that apply	Law/Requirement	Circle one	Describe action needed
	OSHA access to employee exposure and medical records standard	Effective Not Effective	
	OSHA ionizing radiation standard	Effective Not Effective	
	OSHA exit routes standard	Effective Not Effective	
	OSHA electrical standard	Effective Not Effective	
	OSHA accident prevention and emergency preparedness standard	Effective Not Effective	
	OSHA laser safety and hazard assessment standard	Effective Not Effective	
	OSHA emergency action plan	Effective Not Effective	
	OSHA fire prevention plan	Effective Not Effective	
	OSHA ergonomics standard	Effective Not Effective	
	OSHA compressed gasses standard	Effective Not Effective	

Check all that apply	Law/Requirement	Circle one	Describe action needed
	OSHA poster (It's the Law...)	Effective Not Effective	
	Other federal regulations Note them:	Effective Not Effective	
	Violence in the workplace	Effective Not Effective	
	List state and local requirements:	Effective Not Effective	
	Other:	Effective Not Effective	

01.C New Issues Relating to Risk Management

Questions to consider	YES	NO If no, why not?	NOT APPLICABLE (note reason)
Do you stay abreast of information pertaining to risk management (via public media; news; federal, state, and local authorities; professional associations; medical malpractice insurance carriers, and so on)?			
Do you periodically review the risk management plan and make adjustments as required based on changes in law, industry standards, and modifications in practice protocols?			

01.D Risk Exposure Monitoring

Questions to consider	YES	NO If no, why not?	NOT APPLICABLE (note reason)
Do you monitor risk exposure on a regular and ongoing basis, particularly when changes are made in clinical practice?			
Is an incident report form available and actively used to report events?			
Is the report kept confidential and protected from discovery?			
Is incident reporting required immediately following an event?			
Is there a policy about objective documentation of the incident in the medical record without mention of the incident report?			
Is corrective action, if any, documented separately from the incident report?			

Which of the following elements does the risk exposure report contain?

Check all that apply	Element	Circle one	Describe action needed
	Name of individual reporting the event	Effective Not Effective	
	Date and time of the event	Effective Not Effective	
	Description of the event	Effective Not Effective	
	Location of the event	Effective Not Effective	
	If equipment is involved, type, brand, model, and serial number	Effective Not Effective	
	If equipment is involved, it is removed from use	Effective Not Effective	
	Names of others involved in the event	Effective Not Effective	
	Names of witnesses	Effective Not Effective	
	Other:	Effective Not Effective	

Is an incident report required for the following types of events?

Check all that apply	Event	Circle one	Describe action needed
	Workplace injuries and illnesses, including equipment-related injuries	Effective Not Effective	
	Patient and visitor injuries	Effective Not Effective	
	Wrong patient treated	Effective Not Effective	
	Wrong area treated	Effective Not Effective	
	Wrong procedure started or completed	Effective Not Effective	
	Misdiagnosis (Note: may be difficult to identify)	Effective Not Effective	
	Missed diagnosis (Note: may be difficult to identify)	Effective Not Effective	
	Unanticipated outcome	Effective Not Effective	
	Lost, stolen, or broken personal property	Effective Not Effective	

Check all that apply	Event	Circle one	Describe action needed
	Improper consent or absence of consent	Effective Not Effective	
	Allergic reaction	Effective Not Effective	
	Medication errors	Effective Not Effective	
	Other:	Effective Not Effective	

Questions to consider	YES	NO If no, why not?	NOT APPLICABLE (note reason)
Is a multidisciplinary risk team in place to analyze, minimize, and address all aspects of risk, including safety?			
Are events reported as required to federal and state authorities?			
Are events reported as required by the medical malpractice carrier?			

01.E Compliance with Legal Requirements of Record-Keeping

Questions to consider	YES	NO If no, why not?	NOT APPLICABLE (note reason)
Are you knowledgeable about federal, state, local, medical malpractice insurance carrier, and other requirements on retention of records relating to risk?			
If stored, are records readily accessible?			
If destroyed, are records shredded?			
If on CD, are records effectively destroyed?			

01.F Staff Training in Risk and Safety

Questions to consider	YES	NO If no, why not?	NOT APPLICABLE (note reason)
Is the risk management plan communicated at all levels of the organization?			
Is risk management training provided as part of orientation for all new employees?			
Is a philosophy of safety routinely practiced?			
Are new employees trained promptly in safety?			
Is retraining provided as changes in the environment or practice occur?			
Is annual training provided?			
Does training incorporate lecture, reading, and demonstration?			
Is there documentation of all training, including type, topics, trainer name and credentials, date of training, and attendee names with signatures?			

Does training cover the following topics?

Check all that apply	Topic	Circle one	Describe action needed
	Bloodborne pathogens	Effective Not Effective	
	Emergency response	Effective Not Effective	
	Respiratory safety	Effective Not Effective	
	Fire protection and safety	Effective Not Effective	
	Personal protective equipment	Effective Not Effective	
	Material safety data sheets	Effective Not Effective	
	Hazardous communications	Effective Not Effective	
	Ergonomics	Effective Not Effective	
	Hazardous waste	Effective Not Effective	

Check all that apply	Topic	Circle one	Describe action needed
	Radiation	Effective Not Effective	
	Workplace violence	Effective Not Effective	
	Workplace security	Effective Not Effective	
	Workplace harassment	Effective Not Effective	
	Infection control	Effective Not Effective	
	Medication errors	Effective Not Effective	
	Safe needle use	Effective Not Effective	
	Other:	Effective Not Effective	

Questions to consider	YES	NO If no, why not?	NOT APPLICABLE (note reason)
Is training a combination of general (applicable to all) and job specific (for example, bloodborne pathogens for those with exposure risk)?			
Is a periodic drill of emergency responsiveness (a medical emergency for all ages of the patient population, fire drill, telephone outage, etc.) conducted?			
Is a periodic drill of the emergency evacuation plan conducted on weekdays and weekends (if the practice is open)?			

TASK 02: DEVELOP AND IMPLEMENT POLICIES AND PROCEDURES TO MANAGE THE IMPACT OF ADVERSE LEGAL EVENTS

Medical malpractice insurance coverage is one way to manage the impact of adverse events. Most practices will have certain basic policies and coverages, but there are some, such as office life and employment practices liability, that are less commonly purchased. Have you completed a risk assessment and do you have the necessary policies in place to cover the practice in the event of a claim or loss? The list of potential risks for a practice is never-ending. Some common ones are listed in this section. They include everything from noncompliance matters to injuries to human resource matters. Have you thought of all of them, weighing the likelihood, impact, cost, and remedy?

What about the impact of an event on providers and the practice? A malpractice event can send a physician into a tailspin, affecting him or her personally and professionally. The effect can be devastating. How would you handle this situation or other risk events?

Practices need processes by which employees, patients, and visitors can report events. Standard protocols should be employed, and everyone needs to know what those are. Are these types of protocols in place in your practice?

When an event does occur, it's time to call the experts. Solid relationships with legal counsel, brokers, and the malpractice carrier – all of whom have regular and routine expertise in risk and adverse events – will help. The advice received will enable you and your practice to better handle a risk event. Complete this section to learn how well you are doing in the area of managing the impact of adverse legal events.

02.A Insurance Coverage

Do you have an array of applicable insurance policies in place to cover a range of risks? Check all that are in place.

Check all that apply	Policy	Circle one	Describe action needed
	Professional liability, physician	Effective Not Effective	
	Professional liability, corporate	Effective Not Effective	
	Professional liability, named, for mid-levels and other clinical staff	Effective Not Effective	
	General liability	Effective Not Effective	
	Building and contents	Effective Not Effective	
	Internet liability	Effective Not Effective	
	Umbrella coverage	Effective Not Effective	
	Employee Retirement Income Security Act	Effective Not Effective	
	Fiduciary liability	Effective Not Effective	

Check all that apply	Policy	Circle one	Describe action needed
	Employment practices liability	Effective Not Effective	
	Directors and officers liability	Effective Not Effective	
	Commercial auto	Effective Not Effective	
	Workers compensation	Effective Not Effective	
	Officer life	Effective Not Effective	
	Officer disability	Effective Not Effective	
	Other:	Effective Not Effective	

Questions to consider	YES	NO If no, why not?	NOT APPLICABLE (note reason)
Are there any gaps in coverage?			
Is there excess coverage?			
Are insurance bids obtained annually?			
Are all options evaluated, including self-insurance?			
Is pricing competitive for the coverage obtained?			
Are benefits and risks reviewed as part of the insurance review process?			

02.B Adverse Legal Events

Do you have a clear understanding of adverse legal events? Review the list below and check all for which you have a working knowledge. List others in the space provided.

Check all that apply	Event	Circle one	Describe action needed
	Medical malpractice claim or suit	Effective Not Effective	
	Billing and/or coding fraud	Effective Not Effective	
	Routine waiver of copays and deductibles	Effective Not Effective	
	Stark law	Effective Not Effective	
	Anti-kickback regulations	Effective Not Effective	
	HIPAA privacy	Effective Not Effective	
	HIPAA security	Effective Not Effective	
	Red Flags Rules (identity theft)	Effective Not Effective	
	Complaint to the Department of Health	Effective Not Effective	

Check all that apply	Event	Circle one	Describe action needed
	Complaint to the Board of Registration in Medicine	Effective Not Effective	
	CLIA	Effective Not Effective	
	Limited English proficiency	Effective Not Effective	
	Fire, water, or other property damage	Effective Not Effective	
	Hazcom	Effective Not Effective	
	Bloodborne pathogens	Effective Not Effective	
	Other OSHA regulation	Effective Not Effective	
	Workplace injury or illness	Effective Not Effective	
	Wrongful discharge	Effective Not Effective	

Check all that apply	Event	Circle one	Describe action needed
	Discrimination	Effective Not Effective	
	Hostile work environment	Effective Not Effective	
	Harassment	Effective Not Effective	
	Theft	Effective Not Effective	
	Errors and omissions	Effective Not Effective	
	FMLA (if ineligible, applicable state law)	Effective Not Effective	
	Americans with Disabilities Act	Effective Not Effective	
	COBRA	Effective Not Effective	
	Felony	Effective Not Effective	

Check all that apply	Event	Circle one	Describe action needed
	Auto liability	Effective Not Effective	
	Slip and fall	Effective Not Effective	
	Other:	Effective Not Effective	

Questions to consider	YES	NO If no, why not?	NOT APPLICABLE (note reason)
Is a periodic focused and ongoing analysis conducted to identify potential adverse legal events?			
Are risk reduction and remediation implemented as appropriate?			
Is documentation created and maintained on all analyzed adverse events?			

02.C Impact of Legal Events

Questions to consider	YES	NO If no, why not?	NOT APPLICABLE (note reason)
Does proactive risk assessment and discussion on prevention of legal events take place before adverse events occur?			

Are you aware of the potential effect of legal issues on physicians and the practice?

Check all that apply	Issue	Circle one	Describe action needed
	Events that affect a single physician also affect the practice as a whole.	Effective Not Effective	
	Events bring forth a range of emotions and physical symptoms, including anger, frustration, depression, insomnia, illness, and more.	Effective Not Effective	
	Providers may need to take extra time off to cope.	Effective Not Effective	
	Providers may become less productive.	Effective Not Effective	
	Malpractice claims are a part of practicing medicine.	Effective Not Effective	
	Many suits have no basis in fact but are simply "nuisance" based.	Effective Not Effective	
	Change is in store for providers and the practice.	Effective Not Effective	
	Other:	Effective Not Effective	

Have you identified who will fulfill the following needs and roles when a legal event occurs? (Note: The medical malpractice carrier may be able to fulfill several of the roles and meet the identified needs.)

Check all that apply	Role	Circle one	Describe action needed
	Leader	Effective Not Effective	
	Counselor	Effective Not Effective	
	Support	Effective Not Effective	
	Guidance	Effective Not Effective	
	Other:	Effective Not Effective	

Do you ensure that the persons selected to fill these roles possess the following attributes?

Check all that apply	Attribute	Circle one	Describe action needed
	Respectful	Effective Not Effective	
	Strong	Effective Not Effective	
	Caring and compassionate	Effective Not Effective	
	Other:	Effective Not Effective	

Do you ensure that the following tasks are completed when a legal event occurs?

Check all that apply	Task	Circle one	Describe action needed
	Determine and coordinate the resources needed by the providers and the group.	Effective Not Effective	
	Provide professional remediation (change in practice routine via new service, additional training, etc.) when warranted.	Effective Not Effective	
	Look out for the emotional and physical well-being of providers involved in the adverse event, including other staff.	Effective Not Effective	
	Make a referral for emotional support (through the state Physician Health Services or medical malpractice carrier).	Effective Not Effective	
	Other:	Effective Not Effective	

02.D Grievances, Claims, and Complaints

Questions to consider	YES	NO If no, why not?	NOT APPLICABLE (note reason)
Is a service-oriented culture in place?			
Are employees empowered to respond appropriately and in a timely manner?			
Is a formal process in place for patients to report issues or concerns?			
Do employees possess an understanding of what constitutes a claim, suit, or complaint, including the reporting process?			
Is a formal process in place for employees to report issues of all types?			
Is a grievance protocol in place?			

Does the grievance, claim, and complaint protocol detail the following items?

Check all that apply	Item	Circle one	Describe action needed
	Definition of grievance	Effective Not Effective	
	Procedure for reporting (to whom, initial complaint, escalation, etc.)	Effective Not Effective	
	Investigation	Effective Not Effective	
	Time frames for all steps involved in the process	Effective Not Effective	
	Communication	Effective Not Effective	
	Internal vs. external means to address (addressed within the practice or via outside means such as mediation or arbitration)	Effective Not Effective	
	Other:	Effective Not Effective	

Questions to consider	YES	NO If no, why not?	NOT APPLICABLE (note reason)
Is the protocol communicated to all employees?			
Are employees trained at hire and annually thereafter?			
Is the legal impact of all reported events assessed?			
Do you consult with counsel and/or the malpractice carrier as appropriate?			

02.E Relationships with Insurance Brokers and Legal Counsel

Questions to consider	YES	NO If no, why not?	NOT APPLICABLE (note reason)
Do you have effective relationships with insurance brokers and the malpractice carrier?			
Do you have effective relationships with the practice's attorneys (corporate, human resources, etc.)?			
Are these relationships evaluated on an annual basis in terms of effectiveness and cost?			
Is the team handpicked?			

TASK 03: ESTABLISH A PLAN FOR DISASTER RESPONSE AND RECOVERY

Risks that could occur because of disasters haunt all businesses, whether it is a natural disaster such as a flood or a man-made disaster such as someone placing a bomb inside your building. Disasters for medical practices are particularly horrific because of the patient factor. Patients expect a safe environment and experience. Do you have a disaster plan in place? Knowing you have a plan to implement if a disaster occurs, and the steps to take to recovery, will help you get through the event as safely as possible. Does everyone know your emergency and evacuation procedures? When the prearranged signal goes off, everyone should know how to respond – instantly. Does your team annually identify the organization's vulnerabilities? They may change during the year, so stay current. If disaster strikes, how will your practice continue its business? Your disaster plan must cover business continuation factors. A plan you hope you will never have to implement, except for drills, will reduce your stress because you know it's ready if you need it.

03.A Disaster Preparedness

Check the ways in which you coordinate disaster preparedness.

Check all that apply	Method	Circle one	Describe action needed
	Coordination is guaranteed via overall planning by senior managers and leaders.	Effective Not Effective	
	Specific planning, implementation, and recovery are managed by an identified disaster team.	Effective Not Effective	
	Step-by-step protocols are developed for each unit or practice site with designated back-up staff.	Effective Not Effective	
	All staff members are trained on their primary and back-up disaster responsibilities.	Effective Not Effective	
	A chain-of-command list of key personnel is developed to ensure leader availability.	Effective Not Effective	
	All staff members are trained on patient-related protocols to ensure patient safety.	Effective Not Effective	
	Other:	Effective Not Effective	

03.B Emergency and Evacuation Procedures

Note methods that are in place for emergencies and evacuation.

Check all that apply	Method	Circle one	Describe action needed
	Checklists are developed (or obtained) for patient safety, staff security, aftermath counseling, and financial viability of the practice.	Effective Not Effective	
	Everyone is educated on disaster – anything from a water pipe leak to the natural disasters appropriate for your geographic location.	Effective Not Effective	
	Participation in emergency and evacuation drills is mandatory for everyone.	Effective Not Effective	
	Back-up systems are in place such as a generator, computer server, and off-site telecommunications.	Effective Not Effective	
	A disaster manual is compiled including a staff telephone tree and emergency response list.	Effective Not Effective	
	A disaster team is designated, including a team leader, and policies are developed.	Effective Not Effective	
	An incident commander, liaison officer, public information officer, communications officer, safety and security officer, and recorder/transcriber are designated and their roles are defined (roles can be assumed by one or multiple individuals).	Effective Not Effective	

Check all that apply	Method	Circle one	Describe action needed
	Patient operation protocols are specified including isolation and quarantine, patient diversion issues, patient tracking and placement, reporting requirements, personnel issues, and statutory and regulatory considerations.	Effective Not Effective	
	If you have satellite facilities, their unique needs are identified and a plan is developed for how the offices work together.	Effective Not Effective	
	Lines of communication among staff, patients, vendors, and other key parties are planned and understood among all responsible parties.	Effective Not Effective	
	Flashlights are made available in every unit, and/or small ones are issued to everyone.	Effective Not Effective	
	Everyone is told to exit quickly, taking items such as key files and purses only when they are immediately available.	Effective Not Effective	
	Leaders are informed on their legal liability and duty related to employee safety.	Effective Not Effective	
	Certain employees are given tasks such as ensuring all employees evacuate.	Effective Not Effective	
	Clinical staff is made responsible for evacuating patients and not using an elevator.	Effective Not Effective	

Check all that apply	Method	Circle one	Describe action needed
	Designated staff is responsible for checking exam rooms to ensure all patients are evacuated.	Effective Not Effective	
	A designated person is responsible for closing the door and placing an item such as a pillow in front of the door to indicate the room is empty.	Effective Not Effective	
	Individuals are designated to take the day's receipts and current charts, as time permits.	Effective Not Effective	
	If time allows, designees shut down the servers, grab back-up tapes, and transfer phone lines.	Effective Not Effective	
	A final check is made by the disaster team leader to ensure everyone is out.	Effective Not Effective	
	Everyone checks in at a pre-arranged emergency meeting place to ensure all are safe.	Effective Not Effective	
	Instructions are given by the team leader such as when and where business will continue.	Effective Not Effective	
	Other:	Effective Not Effective	

03.C Risk Assessment

Check ways that are in place to identify disaster vulnerabilities.

Check all that apply	Method	Circle one	Describe action needed
	A benchmark risk assessment is developed by management and the disaster team.	Effective Not Effective	
	The likelihood of threat for disasters and catastrophic events is analyzed.	Effective Not Effective	
	Risks are ranked by probability and prioritized by the most likely to occur.	Effective Not Effective	
	Risks are identified as building-specific or affecting a specific area or region.	Effective Not Effective	
	Communication is conducted with local and regional emergency responders about the community plan.	Effective Not Effective	
	A disaster recovery overall plan is developed along with any needed specific miniplans.	Effective Not Effective	
	Miniplans are focused on the loss of electricity, loss of IT, loss of building, and so on.	Effective Not Effective	
	Outside consultants are used to assess specific elements such as the computer system.	Effective Not Effective	
	The fire department's and other inspectors' reports are gathered and analyzed.	Effective Not Effective	

Check all that apply	Method	Circle one	Describe action needed
	Deficits are corrected as quickly as possible and reinspected by outsiders.	Effective Not Effective	
	An annual review of vulnerabilities is conducted, or earlier if changes occur.	Effective Not Effective	
	Special attention is given to the building electrical, plumbing, and HVAC systems.	Effective Not Effective	
	Back-up systems are put in place at headquarters and satellite offices.	Effective Not Effective	
	Other:	Effective Not Effective	

03.D Business Continuation after Disaster

Indicate ways that are used to ensure the business recovers.

Check all that apply	Method	Circle one	Describe action needed
	Key business functions are specified by senior management and the disaster team.	Effective Not Effective	
	A business impact analysis is used to identify and prioritize vital continuity elements.	Effective Not Effective	
	The loss of personnel, facility, equipment, communication, and information is ranked.	Effective Not Effective	
	A business continuation plan is developed to target "first things first" steps.	Effective Not Effective	
	Tasks, time lines, responsible personnel, and alternative locations are identified in the plan.	Effective Not Effective	
	Critical processes are documented so substitute personnel can handle them if necessary.	Effective Not Effective	
	Process analysis is used to check procedures and get feedback from the person doing each recovery task.	Effective Not Effective	
	Aftermath counseling is provided to staff immediately after the event and ongoing.	Effective Not Effective	
	Business partners, legal counsel, and accounting advisers are consulted on the plan.	Effective Not Effective	
	Other:	Effective Not Effective	

TASK 04: DEVELOP AND IMPLEMENT A COMPLIANCE PROGRAM FOR FEDERAL AND STATE LAWS AND REGULATIONS

Medical practices are under the spotlight of many federal and state agencies that have responsibility for ensuring medical groups are in compliance with numerous laws and regulations. Your job as administrator is to ensure that systems, policies, procedures, and processes are in place to comply with these regulatory and legal mandates. Have you developed a compliance program, and what does it include? It is not enough to develop a policy and designate a compliance officer. Ongoing auditing and monitoring and consistent messages to staff about reporting issues are critical. How do you ensure your process is effective? Every aspect must be considered via auditing and monitoring, including having a process for finding and correcting uncovered issues and dealing with all issues carefully and quickly and reporting them to appropriate agencies. Are you aware of all the agencies, federal and state, whose laws and regulations you must comply with and how to report deviations? Dealing with regulatory agencies can be complex and confusing. It is strongly recommended to enlist your legal counsel for advice on your plan and on your reporting.

04.A Compliance Program Components

Check methods that are used to ensure legal compliance.

Check all that apply	Method	Circle one	Describe action needed
	A compliance program is developed to include policies and standards of conduct.	Effective Not Effective	
	A compliance officer is designated and the role defined.	Effective Not Effective	
	Lines of communication are defined and implemented, and their effectiveness is tested.	Effective Not Effective	
	Training and education is provided for new hires and ongoing, at least annually, for everyone.	Effective Not Effective	
	Systems are monitored regularly to detect breaches in policies and procedures.	Effective Not Effective	

Check all that apply	Method	Circle one	Describe action needed
	The plan is enforced via a disciplinary process covering the staff and physicians.	Effective Not Effective	
	A plan is in place for communicating issues that have been uncovered.	Effective Not Effective	
	A process is developed for reporting suspected issues without retaliation.	Effective Not Effective	
	A grievance procedure is available for employees who are involved in incidents.	Effective Not Effective	
	A process is developed for investigating uncovered issues and taking action, including measurement of the effectiveness of actions taken.	Effective Not Effective	
	A plan is in place for auditing and monitoring at least annually.	Effective Not Effective	
	Other:	Effective Not Effective	

04.B Compliance Audits

Note ways in which you audit your compliance program.

Check all that apply	Method	Circle one	Describe action needed
	An audit is conducted of the compliance system including the auditing and monitoring components.	Effective Not Effective	
	Standards and protocols are tailored to clinical and business needs and audited annually.	Effective Not Effective	
	The performance of the compliance officer and staff member(s) with related responsibilities is reviewed.	Effective Not Effective	
	Personnel who might take illegal actions are identified and barred from authority.	Effective Not Effective	
	The compliance education and information program is audited for effectiveness.	Effective Not Effective	
	Employees are reminded to report compliance issues without fear of retaliation.	Effective Not Effective	
	An audit is conducted of effectiveness of the enforcement and discipline process.	Effective Not Effective	
	Audit results are reported to leaders and agencies, and changes are made as necessary.	Effective Not Effective	
	Other:	Effective Not Effective	

04.C Regulatory Compliance

Check regulations, laws, and agencies you track for compliance.

Check all that apply	Regulation/ Law/Agency	Circle one	Describe action needed
	U.S. Department of Health and Human Services, Office of Inspector General	Effective Not Effective	
	Physician Self-Referral (Stark law), Anti-kickback law, and Antitrust	Effective Not Effective	
	Centers for Medicare and Medicaid Services (CMS)	Effective Not Effective	
	Health Insurance Portability and Accountability Act (HIPAA), including sections pertaining to waiving copays, deductibles, and so on.	Effective Not Effective	
	Occupational Safety and Health Administration (OSHA)	Effective Not Effective	
	Clinical Laboratory Improvement Act (CLIA)	Effective Not Effective	
	Centers for Disease Control and Prevention (CDC)	Effective Not Effective	
	Federal Drug Administration (FDA) as related to drugs, vaccines, and medical devices	Effective Not Effective	

Check all that apply	Regulation/ Law/Agency	Circle one	Describe action needed
	Employment laws	Effective Not Effective	
	State-specific regulations, laws, and agencies. Note all:	Effective Not Effective	
	Other:	Effective Not Effective	

BOTTOM LINE—RISK MANAGEMENT

Society has become more litigious. New legislation creates more types of risk, sometimes complex in nature. In the most extreme – likely a natural or man-made disaster previously unknown to you – your practice could be forced to shut the door. The need for attention to risk management is greater than ever. Lack of focus could be quite costly, financially as well as operationally. Make sure you are equipped to handle risk effectively, today and in the future, in your practice.

Risk Management
Supplemental Notes
(copy as needed)

Task	Notes

Risk Management
Action Items
(copy as needed)

Task	Action	Responsible Party	Due Date	Priority

Summary

Why an assessment workbook? Now that you have completed this evaluation of your medical practice and your performance as a practice administrator, we hope you agree with us about the value of a regular assessment, at least annually, for three reasons.

1. *You realize the importance of knowing how close your medical practice comes to best practices.* As you strive for excellence, it is vital that you understand how near the mark your medical practice is currently. That's why you regularly use benchmarks to measure performance. You also know that planning cannot be completed in an efficient and effective manner if you do not have assessment data and information to build your strategic plan, operational plan, annual plan, budget plan, and so on.

2. *You recognize how critical it is for you to know how you are doing as an administrator.* Have you put best-practice policies and procedures in place? Do you take action in a timely manner when you find an improvement opportunity? Have you acted on insights about your performance? You realize that keeping your job, advancing in your job, receiving increased compensation, or getting another position depends on your performance in your current job, how you measure up, and your credentials (such as certification, fellowship, and level of college education).

3. *You realize the power of this assessment workbook for team development in your practice.* For a subordinate who is aiming to climb the career ladder or needs help in understanding best practices, assigning some sections of the workbook is a great learning opportunity. Giving a copy of the assessment workbook to a person aiming for the top spot (remember, having a

management succession plan is one way the board evaluates you) provides a wonderful development opportunity for the individual and for you as the mentor/coach.

Ok, now what? ACTION! Take the workbook, along with the Supplemental Notes and Action Items pages, and with your team talk about whether this is the time to move to the best practice related to each item. Be sure to discuss resources such as time, funding, and people power, and to note which best practices will require completion of preliminary steps. Determine what actions you will take, then prioritize the action items. Next, designate a team leader for each action item you plan to undertake, as well as team members. Have the teams meet to determine steps to take, people to do them, time lines, deadlines, an outline for progress and final reports, and the budget, developing an overall plan. Remember to keep the board of directors informed and involved throughout the process. You need them to be ON BOARD!

STOP!

Before you begin to implement any best practices, return to the Practice Profile form at the front of the workbook. Note your best-guess estimate made prior to beginning the workbook as to how close you thought you would come to industry best practices. Next, note how you feel now that the assessment is complete. Were you on target, close, or off by a significant margin?

Also review what you wanted to learn. Did you? If yes, remember to continue to follow through on your own professional development and improvement in your medical practice. If no, seek opportunities via MGMA (see www.mgma.com for a multitude of resources) and ACMPE (see the link on the MGMA website for more resources and information on certification and fellowship). Remember, you are the master or mistress of your fate. We hope you gained insight and growth through this experience.

Carolyn Pickles, MBA, FACMPE
Alys Novak, MBA

Bibliography

Body of Knowledge Review Series. Englewood, CO: Medical Group Management Association, 2009.

Collins, Hobart. "Begone with You: Dismissing Problem Patients from Your Practice." *MGMA Connexion* 3, no. 5 (2003): 58–61.

Edwards, Kelly A. "Informed Consent." (1998). University of Washington School of Medicine. http://depts.washington.edu/bioethx/topics/consent.html. Accessed September 3, 2010.

Gans, David. Interview with Carolyn Pickles on emerging healthcare delivery systems, February 8, 2010.

Hertz, Kenneth T. "Meeting Management: Get the Most from Your Gatherings." *MGMA Connexion* 4, no. 5 (2004): 49–53.

Knapp, Donna. "Cover Up: Does Your Practice Have the Right Insurance Coverage?" *MGMA Connexion* 9, no. 10 (2009): 36–37.

McHugh, Heather. *ACMPE Examination Preparation Workbook*. Englewood, CO: Medical Group Management Association, 2010.

Mourar, Mary. *Experts Answer 101 Tough Practice Management Questions*. Englewood, CO: Medical Group Management Association, 2007.

Owens, David G. "Success by the Dashboard Light?" *MGMA e-Source*, April 22, 2008.

Pope, Christina. "Defining the Profession: Principles, Expertise, and Service That Bind Us Together: Shell Shocked." *MGMA Connexion* 4, no. 6 (2004).

Price, Courtney, and Alys Novak. *HR Policies & Procedures Manual for Medical Practices*, 4th ed. Englewood, CO: Medical Group Management Association, 2007.

"Risk Management Handbook." Yale–New Haven Hospital and Yale University School of Medicine. www.med.yale.edu/caim/risk/handbook/handbook.html. Accessed February 8, 2010.

Seymour, Patricia. "Quest for Knowledge: Is Clinical Research Right for Your Practice?" *MGMA Connexion* 2, no. 9 (2002): 70–74.

Snyder, Andrew T. "Identifying Best Practices in the Administration of Clinical Research." *APA Matrix* 20, no. 3 (2005).

Taft, L. "Disclosing Unanticipated Outcomes: A Challenge to Providers and Their Lawyers." *Health Lawyers News* 12 (May 2008): 11–16.

Trites, Patricia A. *Compliance Guide for the Medical Practice: How to Attain and Maintain a Compliant Medical Practice*. Chicago: American Medical Association, 2007.

Vuletich, Matthew. "Crunching Numbers: Physician–Patient Termination Policies Are Necessary, but Prevention Is the Best Medicine." *MGMA e-Connexion* 65 (November 2004).

Woodcock, Elizabeth. *Mastering Patient Flow: Using Lean Thinking to Improve Your Practice Operations.* Englewood, CO: Medical Group Management Association, 2007.

Wyrick, Russell. "Lease vs. Purchase Considerations." Missouri Small Business & Technology Development Centers. www.missouribusiness.net/sbtdc/docs/lease_vs_purchase.asp. Accessed March 1, 2010.

About the Authors

Carolyn Pickles, MBA, FACMPE, a consultant specializing in medical practice management, has more than 20 years of experience in the industry, both in private practice and hospital settings. Her experience includes operations, systems, billing and finance, risk management, governance, information management, and human resources. Her projects have included practice growth and expansion, implementing and integrating systems, developing an in-house billing system, implementing financial systems and controls, developing coding review processes, improving operational efficiency, minimizing risk, integrating information management systems, recruiting, and developing human resource protocols and systems.

In 2006 she started her own consulting firm to provide project-based consulting for single- and multispecialty physicians and physician groups as well as interim practice management services. Pickles earned both her MBA degree from the University of Massachusetts at Amherst and her Fellowship in the American College of Medical Practice Executives in the year 2000. She is a past president of Massachusetts/Rhode Island Medical Group Management Association and has served on both the Medical Group Management Association Eastern Section and American College of Medical Practice Executives boards of directors. She holds memberships in MA/RI MGMA, MGMA, and the ACMPE.

Alys Novak, MBA, has a private consulting and publishing practice. Her many assignments in the healthcare field have focused on medical practices, home health, and rural health. Her areas of expertise include human resource management, organizational governance, strategic planning, and marketing/ communication. For many years she served as adjunct faculty at the University of Colorado and Metropolitan State College of Denver, teaching a variety of business topics.

Novak has coauthored several books, including MGMA's *User-Friendly Psychology for Medical Practices* and *Financial Management for Nonprofits* (Discovery Communications, Inc., 2005). She is also the author of MGMA's *Governing Policies for Medical Practices*. Novak coauthored MGMA's *The Medical Practice Performance Management Manual, Job Description Manual for Medical Practices*, 3rd Edition, the *HR Policies and Procedures Manual for Medical Practices*, 4th Edition, and *Staff Handbook for Medical Practices*, with Courtney Price, PhD. For more than two decades she has edited publications for MGMA on the full range of Body of Knowledge topics.

Until recently she served as an administrator for the Visiting Nurse Corporation of Colorado, specializing in quality management, patient satisfaction, volunteer resources, marketing, healthcare ethics, and business planning.

About MGMA/About ACMPE

Medical Group Management Association
The Medical Group Management Association is the premier membership association for professional administrators and leaders of medical group practices. Since 1926, MGMA has delivered networking, professional education and resources, and political advocacy for medical practice management. Today, MGMA's 21,500 members lead 13,700 organizations nationwide, in which some 275,000 physicians provide more than 40 percent of the healthcare services delivered in the United States. MGMA's mission is to continually improve the performance of medical group practice professionals and the organizations they represent. MGMA promotes the group practice model as the optimal framework for healthcare delivery, assisting group practices in providing efficient, safe, patient-focused, and affordable care. MGMA is headquartered in Englewood, Colo., and maintains a government affairs office in Washington, D.C.

American College of Medical Practice Executives
Founded in 1956, the American College of Medical Practice Executives is the standard-setting and certification organization of MGMA. Through ACMPE, medical group managers can earn the Certified Medical Practice Executive designation and go on to earn the highest distinction of Fellow in the ACMPE (FACMPE). ACMPE members belong to a network of management professionals dedicated to becoming the best in medical practice management by combining experience, learning, and professional certification.

About the CD

Included with this book is a CD containing worksheets and other tools.

How to Use the Files on the CD

You must have Microsoft® Word installed on your hard drive to use the CD. To adapt the files to your own practice, simply follow the instructions below. The CD will work on Windows and Mac platforms. A list of links to all support files are in the document named "Contents.doc."

Microsoft® Word Instructions for Windows

1. Load the CD in your CD drive. The file "Contents.doc" will open in Microsoft® Word unless you have autorun disabled. If the file does not open automatically, go to My Computer and then the CD drive, and open the file.

2. Control-click a name on the list to open the linked Microsoft® Word file.

Microsoft® Word Instructions for Mac OS X

1. Insert the CD in your CD drive. A CD icon will appear on your desktop. Open the file "Contents.doc."

2. Click a name on the list to open the linked Microsoft® Word file.

   Use the "Save as..." command under the file menu or Microsoft Office Button to save the file to your hard drive and edit to suit your practice.